First published in the United States of America by
Quarry Books, a member of
Quayside Publishing Group
100 Cummings Center
Suite 406-L
Beverly, Massachusetts 01915-6101
Telephone: (978) 282-9590
Fax: (978) 283-2742
www.quarrybooks.com

Library of Congress Cataloging-in-Publication Data
Hampshire, Kristen.
  Cat lover's daily companion: 365 days of insight and guidance for living a joyful life with your cat / Kristen Hampshire, Iris Bass, and Lori Paximadis.
       p. cm.
  Includes index.
  ISBN-13: 978-1-59253-591-0
  ISBN-10: 1-59253-591-7
  1. Cats. 2. Cat lovers. 3. Human-animal relationships. I. Bass, Iris. II. Paximadis, Lori. III. Title.
  SF447.H29 2009
  636.8--dc22

                                                              2009018475
                                                              CIP

ISBN-13: 978-1-59253-591-0
ISBN-10: 1-59253-591-7

10 9 8 7 6 5 4 3 2 1

Design: everlution design
All illustrations by Colleen Hanlon except pages 156, 165, 181, 202, 253, 275 by Melanie Powell, Shybuck Studios; page 13 by Quayside Publishing Group

Printed in China

Cat Lover's
Daily Companion

Cat Lover's
Daily Companion

365 Days
of Insight and Guidance
for Living a Joyful
Life with Your Cat

Kristen Hampshire, Iris Bass,
and Lori Paximadis

BEVERLY MASSACHUSETTS

QUARRY BOOKS

contents

Introduction: For the Love of Cats

Cats are independent, yet endearingly affectionate. They walk their own path, but only if we are close by. They may sneak through the house, stealthlike, on a mysterious mission, but the promise of cozying up with us in a favorite chair will surely sidetrack their journey. Cats and their humans share a mutual respect for space, freedom, and each other's intelligence. They are our children, companions, and loyal guardians.

Cats have been associated with humans for some 9,500 years, perhaps explaining why we live so easily with our cats. They're a fixture in the household; the space feels empty without them. We seem to understand each other, and often that bond is reflected through silent communication, body language, and meows that only we understand. Cats listen. And they speak to us (they do!). In many ways, our dear felines are like humans who demand "more" from a relationship. They rub against our legs, insisting that we lavish them with attention. (If ignored, they'll invite themselves onto our laps. They don't take no for an answer.) Cats will go their own way sometimes, but they always return to us. They are deeply devoted creatures.

This book is for you, dear cat lovers. Its contents celebrate the spirit of cat companionship through stories, trivia, and practical information. The book is both a reference and a store of ideas. We cover food, wellness, toys, breeds, crafts, games, communication, and fun facts. We'll even show you how to grow your own catnip. And amidst the playful fun, we teach critical health information that all cat guardians need to know.

Although entries are presented in chronological calendar order, they are not organized by season, location, or time. This way, you can freely peruse the pages as you find time. We think you'll want to visit the book often. As you read, you'll bond with your cat and satisfy your own curiosity.

How to Use This Book

This book is organized as a day minder, a journal packed with a year's worth of ways to care for, understand, socialize, and honor your cat. Each unique entry will inspire, inform, and entertain. Every week contains six entries designed to feed your cat-loving soul.

There is more than one way to read this book. You can dive in and read from beginning to end, cozying up to it as you would a page-turner novel. (For cat lovers, there's no such thing as overdosing on cat information.) Or you can read an entry each day—it will last all year that way. You can crack the book open in the middle and read to the back, then backward to the front. Go ahead and read the last page first. That's not cheating. This book is yours to enjoy in your own way, at your own pace. Dog-ear the pages (no pun intended) so you can revisit your favorite entries time and again. Read out loud to your cats.

Each day is a surprise. You'll discover detailed cat health information, amusing trivia, and creative projects to make for your cat (and yourself). On every page, we explore the spirit and love between a cat and her human. This book is one more way to deepen the relationship.

The Cat Lover's Year

 MONDAYS provide practical information, from welcoming a cat home to understanding his basic needs.

 TUESDAYS contain engaging tales of cats in history and in literature.

 WEDNESDAYS explore feline health and wellness topics, from acupuncture to the zodiac.

 THURSDAYS deliver ideas for cat-friendly home decor, crafts, and household tips for cat lovers.

 FRIDAYS introduce a world of cat breeds, from from Abyssinian to York Chocolate.

 WEEKENDS are reserved for bonding, relationship building, and planning special occasions with your pet.

Gearing Up for a New Cat

WHEN ADOPTING A CAT (OR CATS), you'll need a few basic supplies immediately. Look for sturdy, well-made items that serve their purpose.

BOWLS AND FOOD

You'll need at least two per cat, for food and for water; add a third if you plan to serve your pet both dry and wet foods.

Thick china, food-safe ceramics (avoid artisan pottery), CorningWare, and Pyrex are best. Plastic attracts bacteria that can cause acne to erupt on your pet's chin. Some cats dislike the reflections and darkness of metal, so although stainless steel is safe, your pet may shun it. Never use vintage china or lead crystal, which could leach lead into a cat's food or water.

A water bowl shouldn't tip easily; some cats like to paddle a paw in the water. If you have multiple pets or your home has more than one story, provide multiple bowls in various locations. Note: Cats often prefer their water bowl to be at a distance from their food bowl(s); this also helps keep the water clean.

Dry food can be served in a curved or straight-sided cereal dish–size bowl. Resist using large bowls that could leave uneaten, drooled-on food mingling with the "fresh" food.

Wet food should be served in a deeply curved bowl about 4 inches (10.2 cm) in diameter. This will keep the food from being nosed out while Kitty chows down. In a multipet household, each cat should be given her own wet food bowl. Don't expect them to peaceably share a platter. Place on a washable mat or tray to catch spills.

LITTER BOX, LITTER, SCOOPER, AND CLEANING TOOL

Forget about fancy grids, flip-flop systems, and the like. A good-size litter box with high sides (start a kitten in a slightly lower one) is all you need. Note: Some cats balk at being enclosed by a lidded box; if you want to try this kind, get one whose separate lid could be left off if it doesn't agree with Kitty. See Day 106 for more about selecting litter. (Boxes made from plastics with a slightly metallic-looking sheen are formulated to keep wastes from sticking.)

Buy a scooper to remove solids and clumps of wet litter. Or just use a slotted spatula dedicated to that purpose.

Keep a stiff brush or nylon sponge on hand for litter-box/scooper cleanup. Do not use this to clean human toilets, because some waste-borne diseases can be shared by cats and humans (see Day 129).

CARRIER

Even if you don't plan to travel with your cat, a carrier will be useful for visits to the vet. You want to be equipped in an emergency. If you have multiple cats, consider buying more than one carrier, just in case. For more about choosing a carrier, see Day 36.

The Proverbial Cat

You may recognize these familiar cat proverbs: When the cat's away, the mouse shall play . . . curiosity killed the cat . . . there is more than one way to skin a cat . . . and so on. Other proverbs, however, seem unique to particular countries or regions.

- Books and cats and fair-haired little girls make the best furnishing for a room.
  —France

- A blind cat catches only a dead rat.
  —China

- A cat has nine lives. For three he plays, for three he strays, and for the last three he stays.
  —England

- A house without a dog or cat is the house of a scoundrel.
  —Portugal

- A peasant between two lawyers is like a fish between two cats.
  —Catalonia

- After dark all cats are leopards.
  —Native America

- An old cat will not learn how to dance.
  —Morocco

- Beware of people who dislike cats.
  —Ireland

- Cats don't catch mice to please God.
  —Afghanistan

- I gave an order to a cat, and the cat gave it to its tail.
  —China

- If stretching made money, all cats would be wealthy
  —Ghana

- In a cat's eye, all things belong to cats.
  —England

- In the eyes of a mouse, the cat is a lion.
  —Albania

- It is a bold mouse that nestles in the cat's ear.
  —England

- Nature breaks through the eyes of a cat.
  —Ireland

- The borrowed cat catches no mice.
  —Japan

- The cat was created when the lion sneezed.
  —Middle East

- The cat who frightens the mice away is as good as the cat who eats them.
  —Germany

- The man who loves cats will love his wife.
  —Russia

- To please himself only the cat purrs.
  —Ireland

- When the mouse laughs at a cat, there's a mouse hole nearby.
  —Nigeria

- Women and cats in the house, men and dogs in the street.
  —Catalonia

Find the Best Vet Possible

A VETERINARIAN IS AN ADVISER, a medical expert, and someone you can rely on for emergencies. You should feel comfortable expressing concerns to this person and asking questions—even the most basic ones, such as, "What if my kitty won't use the litter box?" You will turn to your vet when your cat experiences health issues, or when you have general questions about pet wellness. But also, your vet can serve as a valuable counselor as you raise your cat. You will share some of the most exciting (birth of kittens) and devastating (end of life) events with your vet. Do not make this decision without "interviewing" your vet and choosing a medical expert with whom you are compatible. (It helps if your cat warms up to the vet, too.)

Here are some pointers for finding a reputable vet:

- Ask your cat-lover friends and the breeder/kennel where you adopt your cat for referrals.

- Call each veterinarian on your list to schedule a consultation before you bring home your new kitten or cat. Your vet can provide valuable tips for selecting a kitten and supply you with questions to ask the breeder or other source.

- Find out whether there is a fee for your visit.

- How close is the vet's office to your home? Although the closest option might not be the best fit, consider the distance you will drive for routine appointments and in case of an emergency.

- What are the clinic's hours of operation? Find out how the office handles emergency calls after hours, too.

- Ask to be introduced to the staff so you can learn who is behind the scenes and how the clinic operates.

- Sit in the waiting room for a while to soak up the atmosphere and find out how the staff interacts with patients.

After your visit, consider your experience and fill out this worksheet, which will help you decide whether the vet you interviewed is the right match for you and your cat.

Veterinarian's Name:
Date of Consultation:

☐ Did you feel comfortable talking with the vet and staff?

☐ Are the vet's philosophies and communication style in line with your own?

☐ How do you rate the vet's bedside manner?

☐ Would you feel comfortable asking him or her any question, however silly it might seem?

☐ Is the staff friendly, efficient, and helpful?

☐ Is the office easy to reach and is the staff accessible in case of emergencies?

☐ Is the office inviting to adults and your pets, or is it either too sterile or too messy for you?

☐ Does the vet seem to know about the latest medical advances?

☐ Are there educational materials for you to take home?

☐ Do they offer boarding?

Making a Scratching Box

GIVE YOUR KITTY AN APPROVED PLACE to scratch with this simple box made of recycled cardboard. Choose a box that is longer and wider than your cat, so she will have room to stretch out when she scratches.

MATERIALS

Shallow corrugated cardboard box for the base (lids from office paper boxes work well)

Cardboard sheets

Tape measure

Cutting mat or scrap cardboard
(to protect work surface)

Long metal ruler or other straightedge

Fine, dark marking pen

Utility or craft knife

White household glue

Clamps or long, thick rubber bands

Catnip

1. Cut all sides of your box down to 3 to 4 inches (7.6 to 10.2 cm) in depth.

2. Measure the length, width, and depth of the interior of the box. Subtract ¼ inch (6 mm) from each measurement, and note those dimensions. Those will be the length, width, and height of your insert. Set the box aside.

3. Protect your work surface with a cutting mat or scrap cardboard.

4. Place a piece of cardboard on the work surface with the corrugation lines running vertically (away from you). If necessary, use a metal ruler and a utility knife to create straight edges. Repeat this for the remaining pieces of cardboard.

5. From the straight edge on the side of the cardboard, measure and mark the length of your box across the top and bottom of the cardboard. Connect these two marks with the metal ruler and cut along the metal ruler. Your cardboard should be square on at least three sides and as wide as the length of your box.

6. Using this first piece of cardboard as a template, mark matching cutting lines on the other pieces of cardboard. Use the metal ruler as a guide to cut along the lines.

7. Place one of the cut pieces of cardboard on the work surface with the corrugation lines running vertically. From the straight edge on the top or bottom, measure and mark off the cardboard in increments corresponding to the height of your insert. Using the metal ruler as a guide, connect the marks and cut along the metal ruler. You should now have several strips of cardboard that correspond to the length and height of your insert.

8. Repeat step 7 with the remaining pieces of cardboard, until you have enough strips that when stacked will fill the width of the box.

9. Apply a generous amount of glue to one side of a cardboard strip and glue it to another one. Glue a third strip to the first two. Continue this until you reach the correct width, aligning as you go. Once the glue gets tacky, align the strips once more and clamp or rubber band them together. Allow the glue to dry thoroughly.

10. When the glue is dry, remove the clamps or rubber bands and place the insert into the box. Put some catnip on the surface, and let your cat enjoy!

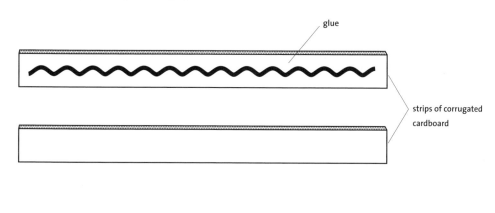

glue

strips of corrugated cardboard

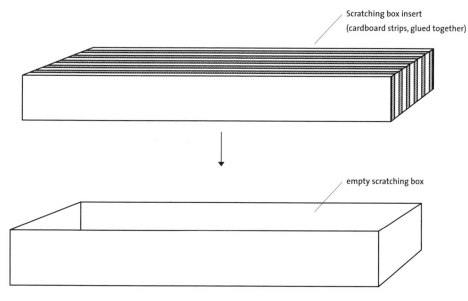

Scratching box insert
(cardboard strips, glued together)

empty scratching box

Cat Genetics

WE'VE ALL SEEN LITTERS OF KITTENS with a rainbow of colors and markings, or even different lengths of fur. How does this happen? In a word, genetics.

Cats have thirty-eight chromosomes (eight fewer than people). Every female cat has two X chromosomes, and every male has an X and a Y. Within each chromosome are genes that govern characteristics such as hair and eye color. Which genes link when parents "bond" determines a cat's looks, among other physical and behavioral traits.

Gender: A male kitten will inherit one or the other X chromosome from his mother and a Y from his father; a female kitten will inherit an X chromosome from each of her parents. There are four ways gender may be decided:

> Boy: Xa (mother) + Y (father)
> Boy: Xb (mother) + Y (father)
> Girl: Xa (mother) + X (father)
> Girl: Xb (mother) + X (father)

Fur length: Short fur is a dominant trait; long hair is recessive. This means that (a) if the kitten inherits both genes for short hair, the kitten will have short hair; (b) if one gene is for short hair and the other is for long hair, the kitten's fur will be short; (c) to have long hair, both of the kitten's fur genes must be long. There are exceptions to these rules, depending on the hair length of cats from previous generations.

Fur color: Cats' chromosomes carry genes for color and other genes that can prevent colors from emerging in their offspring.

The white gene is a special case: It is dominant and the cat equivalent of being albino, but with colored eyes. (Read more about eye color on Day 330.)

Bicolor cats such those with white bibs and feet have the white spotting gene, which cancels out color only in certain areas of the fur.

Silver cats have a dominant gene that prevents any yellow from appearing in their fur.

Red fur and black fur are carried by the X chromosomes. A female inheriting a red X chromosomes and a black X chromosomes may be a tortoiseshell or calico because both colors will show. But a male cat only has one X chromosomes, so he may be red or he may be black, but usually not both at the same time (if he does inherit both, that is a genetic glitch and he will be sterile).

The agouti gene produces ticking and stripes. Cats who inherit the agouti gene from both parents will have a tabby or ticked coat.

feline fun fact > X chromosomes dictate the red or black color of a cat, and because female cats have two X chromosomes, their coats can carry both colors. However, a male cat only has one X chromosome, so his coat can be red or black, but usually not both. If you see a male calico or tortie, you can be sure he has an extra X chromosome—a genetic mutation that renders him sterile.

Feline Body Language

CATS USE THEIR PAWS, LIPS, and entire body to show us what's on their mind.

Shaking a paw at her food: the universal cat gesture for disliking the offering. A cat may do this upon first encountering the offending item, or to subtly signal that she is finished eating.

Rubbing against an owner's legs: A sign of approval—and possession; your cat is marking you with her scent glands.

Bumping her head against you: A positive gesture you can interpret as a cat kiss, or approval for an action; the head bump signals, "Yes!" You can even offer your cat a gentle bump with your own. If you ask Kitty something and she responds with a head bump, there's your answer!

Smiling: Cats, like dogs, are capable of a smile. Stroke Kitty beneath her chin and watch her lips widen.

Kneading: A characteristic gesture tracing back to all those warm feelings associated with pressing their mother's teat area to express milk. Kittens and adult cats enthusiastically "make bread" on soft surfaces as they purr.

Pawing: Cats also make the connection that their front paws correspond to our hands, and may imitate human gestures. Some enjoy "holding hands" with yours, or wrapping their fingers around the tip of one of yours, squeezing it in a mini-knead. Your cat may use a hand to tug at you for attention, or even to tug or pat at the corresponding area of your head where she'd like to be rubbed or scratched on hers. An adept kitty will use her forepaws to open doors and cabinets, press on the buttons of electronic devices, or "claim" food from your dish with a tap. (She isn't stupid; she knows once she has touched it that you probably won't want to eat that piece!)

If you notice your cat holding a paw tightly across her face while she sleeps, do not intervene. This is her way of reducing oxygen flow to induce a deeper level of sleep. When she is refreshed, she'll wake up fine on her own.

feline fun fact **>** A cat's paws contain sweat glands; when your cat is feeling overheated, she will leave damp prints as she walks.

Introducing a Kitten to Her New Home

COMING HOME FOR THE FIRST TIME is a big change for a kitten. Here are some tips for making the transition less stressful for both of you.

Clear time: Schedule your cat's homecoming for a time when you'll have a few days at home without other obligations, such as the beginning of a weekend, so you'll have plenty of time to spend with her. Prepare a safe room for her (see Day 302) ahead of time.

Set boundaries: Confine Kitty to the safe room and keep a close eye on her for a few days. If you have children or other pets, keep them away from her until she becomes acclimated (see Day 309 and Day 351).

Take it slow: Let her come to you when she is ready. Leave her carrier in the safe room so she will have a somewhat familiar place to retreat to if she feels overwhelmed. Try not to hover, but do check on her every half hour or so and offer her a treat or a toy once she starts to get comfortable exploring on her own. Let her set the pace for your interactions, and recognize that it may take anywhere from a few hours to a few days for her to feel comfortable enough to approach you. Once she does, give her plenty of attention to help her bond with you.

Give her space: Once your new kitten is familiar with her new litter box and feels comfortable with you, you can introduce her to other parts of the house. Close off any rooms you don't want her to explore, then open the door to her safe room.

 # A Brief History of Commercial Food and Litter

ALTHOUGH CATS HAVE BEEN household pets for thousands of years, the notion of specially marketed food and litter for them is very modern.

For most of their time on Earth, cats have been expected to earn their keep by dispatching—and devouring—mice and other vermin, supplemented by scraps of butcher's meat and bowls of milk. For the most part, cats were expected to work for their supper until the 1950s, when canned cat food hit the market. Dry and semi-moist food followed, and in the 1980s, "scientific" diets were developed and brands rolled out specialty foods for older cats, overweight cats, and indoor cats. Today, some manufacturers add vegetables or herbs such as parsley to cat foods, to appeal to owners who are themselves turning away from a meat diet.

Meanwhile, the relatively recent exclusively indoor lifestyle of many cats sparked a need for cat litter. Its first major manufacturer was U.S. inventor Ed Lowe, who figured that fuller's earth, a superabsorbent clay, would be an ideal throwaway product for soaking up cat wastes. Lowe coined the term *kitty litter*, his brand name for his product. In 1964, he began to sell the clay nationwide under the Tidy Cat label.

Nowadays, various kinds of clay are used for litter, as well as products made from recycled newspaper pellets, grains, silica gel, and wood shavings. See Day 106 for how to choose the best litter for your cat.

Safe Toys for the Thrifty Owner

YOU INVEST IN A CACHE OF fancy cat toys, but your cat is more interested in batting at your newspaper or running off with the luxury yarn you purchased to make a sweater.

House cats need to stay busy with play, and we must make sure that the toys we offer are a safe and tempting alternative to household hazards. Avoid small balls, tassels, bells, yarn, ribbon, and rubber bands.

- Look for nontoxic labels on toys so you can make sure the materials, if ingested, will not harm your fair feline.

- Make sure trim and decorations are se-curely fastened to toys. Your cat will easily tear off glued-on "flair" and may swallow small pieces of fabric or plastic googly eyes, whatever the embellishment.

- Steer clear of toys with small pieces or parts that can become dislodged during play.

Introduce these safe toys to your kitty's play stash (some of them are household items, sav-ing you dollars at the pet store): plastic shower curtain rings, stuffed animals that are small enough to carry around or large enough to wrestle, plastic balls with noisemakers (squeak-ers), Ping-Pong balls, plastic practice golf balls, and catnip-filled soft toys. Allow your cat to play in a cardboard box (with the top removed). Buy your cat infant toys made for humans, which by law (in many countries) must be made of non-toxic, nonswallowable materials. Additionally, check Thursday entries in this book for safe cat toys you can make.

String is especially dangerous because a cat's tongue contains tiny hooklike barbs called papillae, which are helpful for grooming. Once a piece of string catches on these prickly barbs, the cat has difficulty spitting it out.

Taking Great Cat Photos

WITH TODAY'S DIGITAL CAMERAS, it's cheap and easy to take a few dozen shots and end up with one that looks okay for your holiday card. But taking great photos of your cat doesn't have to be left to chance.

- **Watch the background.** Simple, uncluttered backgrounds are generally best. Move your vantage point to put the focus on Kitty, not what's behind her.

- **Mind the contrast.** If your cat is dark, choose a light-colored background; if she's light, choose a dark-colored background.

- **Avoid using the flash when possible.** Using a flash often distorts colors, creates red-eye (or green-eye!), and causes harsh shadows, in addition to startling and temporarily blinding your cat—they have sensitive eyes. Plan your photo session for a time and place where you will have plenty of natural light, such as a sunny afternoon windowsill. You will need a flash for many action shots, though; just remember to back away to avoid startling her and prevent flash burnout.

- **Enlist help.** If you want a photo of your cat leaping, have a friend hold a tempting toy or treat above the cat's head. Or if you're having trouble getting your cat to look at you, have your friend stand behind you with the toy and attract her attention.

Showing Off Our Cats

THE CAT SHOWS WE ENJOY AS fanciers today started with less pomp and circumstance. The earliest cat shows were part of farmers' or country fairs.

The 1851 Great Exhibition at the Crystal Palace, in London, was the first world's fair, housed in an enormous, glassed building. Other world's fairs followed, and in 1871 cat fancier Harrison Weir organized the first cat competition at the Crystal Palace, with points for particular breeds, markings, and so on (see Day 303 for more about Weir). Inspired by this show, others began to crop up around the UK. The first successful U.S. cat show with a significant turnout of 150 cats was held at Madison Square Garden in New York City, in 1895. This led to other American cat shows, as well as the proliferation of shows in other countries. Today, many events are available for cat lovers and breeders to show their cats.

Concurrent with the rise of cat shows came the development of cat clubs, either those specializing in one breed or generalist organizations. These associations set the rules about what is and is not acceptable as feline traits at cat shows being held in their respective nation, as well as record pedigrees (see Day 19). Standards differ from country to country and even group to group.

Whether or not you want to raise and show a winning cat, cat shows are a valuable resource for learning about and seeing prime examples of particular breeds. There, you can network with other cat lovers and browse commercial and artisan merchandise. The best way to get the schedule of a cat show near you is to contact national cat fancier organizations and regional cat clubs on the Web or look in the resource section of your country's cat magazine(s).

Don't Worry, They're Only Playing!

YOUR CAT POUNCES ON HIS feline sibling, who counters with a paw in the face. More pouncing, stalking, chasing, and sometimes roughhousing ensues. Should you intervene? Determine whether your cats are on guard or only playing by tuning into these behavioral clues.

Healthy play: Stalking, chasing, and pouncing are normal play—and it can get rough. To make sure activity stays within safe boundaries, introduce toys, scratching posts, and other stimulators. By diverting attention away from the feline playmate and toward a toy, you can refocus the playtime and prevent any accidental scratches or nips. Play is generally quiet, though cats may hiss or make meowing sounds.

Foul play: You'll know that cats are fighting by the sound and look of their interaction. You'll hear wailing and howling, and one cat will act as a dominant force, intimidating the other. They won't "trade" pounces or take turns chasing one another. Unlike play, which is mutual, fighting is characterized by each cat's offensive or defensive roles. After play, cats will act as friends, even curling up together for a nap. Fighting cats walk separate ways, one scared of the other.

If you must break up a cat fight, keep your hands away from the action. Try directing a hose on the aggressive cat to drive it away. Splash a glass of water directly on the aggressor's face. Push a broom between the two cats to separate them. If cats are not yet making contact and are in the frozen position, hold a newspaper in front of them to block their view of each other. Ideally, the frightened cat will slink away and the aggressor will become calm enough for you to pick up and secure. (Never try to pick up a cat who is still in attack mode!)

Make sure your cat receives regular booster shots to protect against feline immunodeficiency virus (FIV). An unvaccinated cat can get the disease if an infected cat bites him. (Read more about vaccinations on Day 17.)

Litter Training Your Kitten

UNLIKE HOUSEBREAKING A DOG, litter training a kitten is a quick and relatively simple process. Litter boxes mimic the kinds of places cats in the wild select to eliminate wastes, so it's usually easy to direct their natural instincts toward the litter box.

1. Select a litter box that is kitten-size. Full-size litter boxes can be intimidating. Make sure the sides are low enough that your kitten can easily climb in and out of it.

2. Place the litter box in a quiet, low-traffic, cat-proofed area, well away from your cat's food and water but easily accessible.

3. Fill the litter box with 2 inches (5.1 cm) of unscented, nonclumping clay litter. Clumping litter is not recommended for kittens under six months, and scented litter can confuse them.

4. Place the kitten in the litter box and gently hold her front paws and scratch them in the litter. This is an instinctual action, so she should catch on quickly. Let her jump out of the box when she's ready, whether or not she has eliminated.

5. Watch Kitty closely. When she starts sniffing or scratching, especially after eating or playing, pick her up and take her to the litter box. Take a few steps away to give her some privacy. Praise her for sniffing and scratching there, even if she doesn't eliminate right then. Keep this up until she is regularly finding and using the litter box on her own.

Cats naturally prefer a clean litter box to other surfaces in your home, although some may be tempted by the soil in potted plants. Keep the litter box clean, and consider covering the soil in your potted plants with stones or netting. (See Day 172)

Most kittens arrive at their new home already litter trained if they've come from a breeder, shelter, or other third party. Even so, follow the litter training steps until your kitten is accustomed to her new home and litter box.

Black Cats: Good or Bad Luck?

IF A BLACK CAT CROSSES YOUR PATH, are you superstitious that this incident will bring you bad luck? That depends on which stories about the infamous *chat noir* you believe.

Black cats have been blamed throughout history for all sorts of turbulence and turmoil, and they have been widely associated with witchcraft. Some believed black cats could be manipulated by witches, transformed by spells to carry out evil doings. Black cats were thought to be a form of their witch owners. Even today, we hear of sick-minded humans who hurt cats on Halloween—a good reason to keep Kitty in the house on this holiday.

In the Middle Ages, before witchcraft was dinner conversation (if it ever was), some believed the devil took the form of a black cat, so these felines were regularly hunted down on holy days such as Easter.

But black cats don't have a bad reputation everywhere. In Scotland, it is believed that an unfamiliar black cat on a house porch is a sign of upcoming prosperity for those who live there. Black cats were protectors in England. Fishermen's wives were said to keep black cats in the house while their husbands were gone to keep the family safe. In America, aside from the belief that a black cat crossing one's path is a bad omen, some believe that the bones of black cats are magical.

Incidentally, black cats are less likely to be adopted from shelters than cats with different colored coats. Sadly, a superstition can result in an unfortunate fate for these cats—and for no sound reason. Talk to your animal shelter about how you can promote adoption of black cats and felines in general.

Essential Vaccinations

Vaccinations can minimize the impact of a future disease or prevent it completely. Indoor and outdoor cats have different vaccination needs; vaccines are especially important for young kittens, who are highly susceptible to infectious disease because their immune systems are not fully mature. Adult cats should receive regular booster shots to maintain disease protection.

So how much protection does your kitten or cat truly need? Your veterinarian will help you decide an appropriate regimen depending on your cat's lifestyle, but the FVRCP combination is a must. Kittens may begin a vaccination program immediately at four weeks of age.

- **FVRCP** shot is a core vaccine that protects against feline rhinotracheitis, calici, and panleukopenia viruses, which affect the upper respiratory, digestive, and nervous systems; bone marrow; and lymph tissue.

- **Feline leukemia** is the most common cause of cancer, and it can lead to immune deficiency that limits a cat's ability to ward off infection. The FeLV shot will protect cats who wander outside unsupervised from being exposed to an infected cat's saliva, excrement, or contact (bite). If your cat is not contained to the indoors, the FeLV vaccine is a must.

- **Chlamydophila** can cause pneumonia in kittens.

- **Feline infectious peritonitis** (FIP) is a viral immune-mediated disease.

- **Feline immunodeficiency virus** (FIV) is feline AIDS and is transmitted through bite wounds. Like other "optional" vaccines, house cats who have no exposure to the outdoors or are carefully supervised may not require this protection. However, some cat owners would argue that immunization is always a good idea—just in case.

- **Giardia** is a gastrointestinal disease that can spread by infected litter boxes in multicat households or impure drinking water.

VACCINATION PLANNER

4 weeks	FIP (intranasal; boosters every 6 months)
6 weeks	FVRCP series (administered every 2 to 3 weeks until 12 weeks of age)
8 weeks	FVRCP series; FeLV; chlamydophilia; giardia; FIV
10 weeks	FVRCP series; giardia (second in series; annual booster); FIV (second in series)
11 weeks	FeLV (second in series; boosters every 1 to 3 years); chlamydophilia (annual booster)
12 weeks	FVRCP series; FIV (third in series; annual booster)
4 months	Rabies; every 1 to 3 years depending on vaccine and location
1 year	Annual checkup; begin schedule of booster shots

Stimulation for the Indoor Cat

INDOOR CATS GENERALLY DO NOT receive as much stimulation from their environment as outdoor cats do, especially with their owners' busy lifestyles. Many feline family members stay at home while the "parents" go off to work. It is important to make cats' everyday environment interesting and engaging to prevent the boredom that can lead to weight gain or destructive behavior. Here are a few ways to provide much-needed stimulation for your indoor cats:

- **Provide plenty of toy options.** Offer catnip toys, rolling balls and toys, noisemaker toys, foraging toys in which you can place treats (see Day 67), and dangling toys that encourage jumping and stretching.

- **Rotate toys.** Change up the toy selection every other week or so by "hiding" some in the cupboard for later so toys feel new to your cat all the time.

- **Set aside playtime.** Laser pointers and "birdie"-on-a-string toys are great for encouraging vigorous play. (When playing with laser pointers, be careful not to shine the laser in your cat's eyes.)

- **Provide a perch.** A window to the world is easy entertainment for cats, who naturally like to keep an eye on birds and squirrels. Place a cushion on wide windowsills or attach perches to the windowsills. Another solution is to place a chair or low bookcase in front of a window that can become "his" spot.

- **Turn on the tube.** Many cats don't respond to what's happening on the television, but if yours does, consider occasionally tuning in a channel dedicated to animals or nature or playing a DVD made specifically for entertaining cats. Just make sure your television is out of reach or sturdy enough to take an occasional swat with a paw. You don't want Kitty to knock over your new flatscreen.

The Difference Between Registered and Pedigreed

NATIONAL CAT ORGANIZATIONS have complex rules for which qualities constitute a breed and which characteristics of those established breeds are acceptable for shows. Here are some important facts that cat fanciers planning to show their felines should know:

Classification: Cat classification is based on genetics (see Day 5). Some breeds have been distinct and plentiful for a long time. Others are not registered for decades, sometimes simply because the cats were not considered fashionable (Maine Coons suffered this fate), or perhaps because the characteristics are a new mutation.

Recognition: Registration begins with a voting process and is the first step in the pedigree process. Breed recognition is not global; countries often adopt different standards. Registration can take up to five years as cats pass through a *preliminary* and *provisional* stage. Standards are established to determine breed characteristics, including fur color and markings, body type, color of eyes, and other details such as tail length and ear shape. Full recognition is called championship status.

Pedigreed: To be *pedigreed,* a kitten must have fully registered parentage dating back at least four generations. Registration documents detail breed, ancestry, owners, cat name, and breeder name. Every time a pedigreed cat obtains a new owner, he must be reregistered, to track his lineage.

feline fun fact > A *natural* breed is one that developed without breeder intervention, such as the Turkish Van; an *established* breed developed from crossing two natural breeds to create a new breed, such as the Burmese; and a *hybrid* involves repeated crossbreedings to perpetuate the breed's standard, such as the Exotic Shorthair.

What's Your Cat's Zodiac Sign?

YOU DON'T NEED A HOROSCOPE to confirm you're compatibility with Kitty. But for fun, decide whether your cat displays behaviors that are characteristic with her sign.

Aries *(March 21 to April 19)*: Lively, energetic, daring, adventure seeking, and more independent than most. These cats know what they want and are confident they will get it. They can be impatient, impulsive, and fearless.

Taurus *(April 20 to May 20)*: Practical, cautious, purposeful, persistent, patient, and exceptionally sensitive. These cats have sharp intuition and an active mind.

Gemini *(May 21 to June 21)*: Physically active, athletic, stimulated, fast-paced, adaptable, and thirsty for new experiences. Your Gemini cat acts like a dog, loving attention from people.

Cancer *(June 22 to July 22)*: Emotional, generous, intuitive, adaptable, and nurturing. These cats are receptive to people and their surroundings. They have a maternal nature and an expressive face, and they love to play creative games.

Leo *(July 23 to August 23)*: Warm, bright, motivated, and eager to make an impression. Leos are dynamic balls of energy, generous in nature, and very loyal. Your Leo cat has a pioneering spirit and isn't afraid to blaze the trail.

Virgo *(August 24 to September 22)*: Analytical, investigative, cautious, studious, intelligent, and sometimes demanding. Virgo cats are quick, logical thinkers. They will outsmart you—watch out.

Libra *(September 23 to October 22)*: Social, caring, youthful, and even wacky. These cats will always be young at heart. They won't hide from houseguests and will look for every opportunity to entertain.

Scorpio *(October 23 to November 21)*: Strong but silent, determined, loyal, complex, and emotional. Scorpio cats give 100 percent to those they love—there are no half measures when they are attached to someone. Their amazing eyes are windows to their emotions. They can be manipulative, but they will never let down their owners. They work and play tirelessly.

Sagittarius *(November 22 to December 21)*: Confident, jolly, enthusiastic, light-hearted, and optimistic. These cats love adventure and freedom. They are easily bored without mental stimulation.

Capricorn *(December 22 to January 19)*: Practical, down-to-earth, shy, cautious, and suspicious of strangers, but committed to completing any task. Capricorn cats are known for their courage, concentration, and keen focus.

Aquarius *(January 20 to February 18)*: Revolutionary, self-sufficient, zesty, determined, and headstrong. No one will tell an Aquarius cat how to live. These cats occasionally have an attitude, but they make their mark as individuals who are deeply sensitive and caring underneath.

Pisces *(February 19 to March 20)*: Compassionate, sensitive, intuitive, deeply emotional, and a daydreamer. Pisces cats always lend a helping hand, and they sense their owners' feelings and respond by nurturing.

Introducing an Adult Cat to His New Home

BRINGING HOME AN ADULT CAT is much like introducing a new kitten to your home (see Day 8): You'll need to set up a safe room and allow him to acclimate at his own pace. But there are a few special considerations to be aware of when introducing an adult cat to your home.

Adult cats tend to take longer than kittens to adjust to new people and surroundings, so be prepared to give him more time to explore his environment and get used to his new family and home. Especially if he came from a shelter or a bad situation, he may need a week or longer to feel secure. Be patient and continue to let him set the pace for your interaction. Give him affection and praise whenever he will let you so he knows you're a caring person who can be trusted.

Consider using a spray or plug-in dispenser with synthetic feline facial pheromones in his safe room. These mimic the natural facial pheromones cats use to mark their territory and have a calming effect on most cats.

Follow the instructions that come with the product. You can also use these in other areas of the house once your new cat is free to roam.

Adult cats have established their personality, so take time to get to know his. If he doesn't enjoy sitting in your lap, don't try to turn him into a lap cat. If he doesn't prefer the company of other cats, make sure he has a space to call his own rather than forcing him to share bedding or bowls with others. If he doesn't like to be picked up, resist the urge to carry him like a child. Your cat will adjust to your home on his terms.

Adopting an adult cat can be a very rewarding experience for both of you. A bit of preparation and extra patience on your part can make his transition as stress-free as it can be.

The Owl and the Pussy-Cat

VICTORIAN WRITER EDWARD LEAR (1812–1888) was very much a cat lover. He adored his own cat, Foss, whose truncated tail resulted from an unfortunate run-in with a servant. Foss is immortalized in various sketches Lear made of his pet, and his owner purportedly cared so much for Foss's comfort that when he moved, he made sure the interior of his new dwelling exactly matched that of the last, so Foss wouldn't be disoriented! (Now, that's devotion!) Foss lived to the respectable age of fourteen, and a tombstone honoring him is in the Italian garden of Lear's estate.

Lear is probably best known today for his nonsense poem "The Owl and the Pussy-Cat," written in 1871 during the heyday of Lewis Carroll's Alice books (see Day 338) in which nonsense poetry also features cats.

Lear's owl flatteringly serenades and proposes to a plump tabby cat (bearing a distinct resemblance to Foss, in Lear's original illustrations of the poem, but granted a full-length tail—artistic license) as they sail in a green boat. For lack of a wedding ring, they postpone the wedding for a year and a day, until they reach a land where they meet a pig with a ring through its nose. The pig willingly gives up the ring so that the service can be performed by an obliging turkey, and the animals celebrate along the sandy beach by dancing by the light of the moon.

Lear also wrote a little-known unfinished poem about the couple's offspring, which charmingly begins, "Our mother was the Pussy-Cat, our father was the Owl, / And so we're partly little beasts and partly little fowl."

Know Your Cat's Vital Signs

UNDERSTANDING HOW TO MEASURE and evaluate your cat's vital signs will help you determine whether your pet is sick and needs veterinarian care. Determine your cat's "baseline" temperature, pulse, and respiration by measuring these stats on any given day. Take your cat's pulse following activity and naps to note the normal increase in beats per minute your cat experiences. Same goes for breathing. Feline body temperature also varies by a few degrees.

Record this information in your health documents (see Day 81). Your vet will record this information during health checkups, but it's handy to learn how to measure vital stats yourself and keep a record so you do not delay medical care in case of an emergency. We provide benchmarks here, but every animal is different.

TEMPERATURE

Use a digital rectal pediatric thermometer lubricated with petroleum jelly to take your cat's temperature. To prevent your cat from squirming, stand her on a counter or sit at her level on the ground. Hold her securely with one arm, her face resting in the crook of your elbow. Using your free hand, lift the cat's tail as you insert the thermometer ½ inch (1.3 cm) into your cat's rectum. You'll feel the muscle tighten and relax. Hold the thermometer there for two minutes to get an accurate reading. During this time, talk sweetly to your cat and assure her so she stays calm.

Normal temperature: 100°F to 103.1°F (37.8°C to 39.5°C)

HEART RATE

Shhh—listen carefully. What does your cat's heartbeat sound like? It should resemble a beating drum: lub-dub, lub-dub. Check heart rate by locating your cat's pulse along the femoral artery (inner thigh) or under the arm. Be sure to use your second and third fingers, not your thumb, which has a radial artery running through it that "beats" and can cause an inaccurate reading. Count heartbeats for one minute. (Set a timer or watch a clock as you count.)

Normal resting heart rate: 100 to 120 beats per minute (adult cats); 130 to 140 beats per minute (kittens)

RESPIRATION

When a cat breathes, her chest expands and deflates. The best time to measure respiration is while your cat is asleep. Count inhale-exhale breaths for one minute. Watch her breathing pattern. Are breaths even and calm? (They should be.) If you notice her abdomen expanding instead of the chest, panting, gasping, or shallow breaths, call your vet immediately.

Normal respiratory rate: 15 to 30 breaths per minute

Project: Start Your Cat Journal

A CAT JOURNAL IS A GREAT PLACE to collect memories and photographs of your cat. Amusing stories and silly pictures will remind you why you love your cat when your pet is trying your patience, and it can be a comfort when you're feeling low.

Your memory book can contain written passages, photo collages, or quick recollections. If you can draw, sketch with colored pencils. Paste in mementos of your travels together, even if your big "vacation" was an afternoon at a friend's home or a car trip to the pet store to splurge on a new cat toy. Use your imagination to record not just the special times, but the everyday, too.

Journals come in a wide variety of styles and forms. Craft stores have fancy scrapbooks with large, removable pages. Bookstores, art supply stores, and office supply stores have dozens of blank books to choose from in a range of sizes, some with lined paper and others with plain paper. If you want to make entries every day, you might even consider a daybook calendar, which has a dated page or spread devoted to each day. Even a simple spiral notebook will do.

Creatively decorate the pages if you wish. Craft and scrapbooking stores have a huge selection of decorations, including decorative papers, stickers, rub-on transfers, stamps, and three-dimensional embellishments. Use colored pencils, markers, paints—whatever strikes your fancy. There are no rules. (For inspiration, check out art journaling books in the craft section of your local bookstore.)

Abyssinian

CONSIDERED A REVERED BREED in ancient Egypt, the Abyssinian, or Aby, has an angular body and curved wedge-shaped head. The Aby resembles cat mummies found in that region, as well as paintings and statues of the goddess Bastet. Abyssinia is modern-day Ethiopia.

Characteristics: The Abyssinian has a royal appearance—tall and muscular, with a shiny short coat that typically comes in one of three colors: a warm, orangey tone called "ruddy," which can be as light as apricot; a deeper warm brown called "sorrel"; or a pinkish taupe called "fawn." Whatever the color, it is ticked with one or more bands of shading—an early name for the breed in Great Britain was British Ticked—with the color at its deepest along the spine and at the tip of the tail. Occasionally, recessive tabby markings emerge.

Instead of the tabby *M*, most Abyssinians have a vertical stripe of deep color above each eye. (Was this perhaps the inspiration for ancient Egyptians to shave off their own eyebrows when mourning the loss of a cat?) Unusually, Aby kittens are sometimes born with a dark coat that lightens as the cats mature.

Abys are generally playful but, perhaps yearning for their great sandbox of yore, do not always take to being confined as purely indoor cats. Some Abys carry a gene for PK deficiency, which causes anemia.

History: The first Abyssinian to come to the West was brought to Great Britain in 1868 by a soldier returning from the war in Abyssinia. He named the cat Zula. In 1909, British-born Abys were shown for the first time in an American cat show, in Boston, and were named Aluminium II and Salt, for their blue-ticked fur. It was not until 1935 that an Abyssinian was actually born in the United States; this landmark Aby was named Addis Ababa.

feline fun fact > When the Abyssinian was first brought to the West, its ticked markings led the breed to be called the Hare, Bunny, or Rabbit Cat.

Abyssinian

Kitty Talk:
Your Cat's First Ten Words

EVEN YOUR FIRST DAY TOGETHER is not too soon to speak with your cat. After all, if a foreigner joined your household, you would use simple words to find common ground. Although Kitty lacks the muscle coordination to speak your language, she can learn to understand your words, just as you can learn her body signals for what she is trying to express. Once she realizes there is a word for everything, she will pick up additional vocabulary more quickly.

Begin with these essentials:

1. Her name—Say it often; coo it, whisper it, and singsong it. Watch her perk up when she hears it. Test her by calling from a distance—see if she comes.

2. A name for you—Use your actual name, a nickname, Mama, even Me. Point to her and say her name; point to yourself and say yours. Introduce other humans and animals this way, too.

3. No—The concept of *no* as meaning "stop" or "don't," and actually *obeying* it are different. You will need a lot of patience to get both aspects across. When your cat misbehaves, say, "[Name], no!" sharply while immediately interrupting or removing her from her wrongdoing. She will probably want to go back to what she did. Stop her as necessary, repeating, "No!" In time, she will catch on.

4. Good—Tell your cat she's good if she licks you or initiates other positive things, and when she purrs. She will associate *good* with her pleasing you or feeling pleased herself.

5. Bad—Only when your cat has begun to master *good* should *bad* be introduced: "No! Bad [name]," saying *bad* as witheringly as you can. Continue to use *good* in positive situations. She will begin to realize it's her choice whether to be bad or good.

6. Sit—When your cat sits, say, "Good sit." Also, try gently pressing her rump down into a sitting position, saying, "Sit." If she sits and holds the position, say, "Good sit!" Ask her to sit while she is standing. Praise her when she obeys: "*Good* sit."

7. Food—When you feed your cat, hold up the can/package and say, "Food!" As she eats, say, "Good food." Say, "Food!" to call her to eat. (You may wish to specify kinds of food, such as *can* versus *crunchies*.)

8. Bedtime—When you go to bed, announce, "[Your name] bedtime." Eventually, hearing "Bedtime!" may bring your pet running ahead of you to bed!

9. Please and **10. Thank you**—Don't laugh! These serve a purpose: Use *please* to signal a request. When she obeys, say *thank you*, indicating she has accomplished your desire.

Choosing the Right Litter Box

LITTER BOXES COME IN VARIOUS SHAPES and configurations, and your cat will surely let you know whether he is unimpressed with his "facilities." (He may opt to take care of business elsewhere—one sign that the box is not his "type.")

Put simply, the right box is the one that your cat will use. Before committing to a fancy box, make sure your cat will use it regularly. Place the new box near the old one, and let your cat take his time to make the transition (or not).

Plastic pan: As the most popular, this pan-style litter box comes in different sizes and depths. Shallow litter boxes are useful for older cats who may have trouble climbing into and out of standard litter boxes, as well as for disabled cats. These simple litter boxes are the easiest to clean because there is nothing to take apart, and you can use any type of litter with them.

Sifting litter box: This variation consists of two stacking litter boxes and a sifting insert. You place one litter box inside the other, put the sifting insert in the top box, and then add clumping litter. To "scoop" the box, you lift out the sifting insert and, with it, the waste.

Covered litter box: This box features a rigid cover that attaches securely to the base litter box, with an opening for your cat to enter and exit. Many of these boxes also have top or side vents to allow air circulation, and replaceable air filters to control odors. Covered litter boxes provide privacy for your cat, but some cats don't like them, perhaps because they don't like being enclosed or because they don't like the concentrated odor.

Decorative litter box: These litter boxes are disguised as furniture, such as an end table, cabinet, or chest. Usually, these function like a covered litter box but use a standard plastic litter box inside the chamber.

Self-scooping litter box: This litter box is electrically powered, and most use scoopable litter. The mechanical details of these systems vary, but the basic theory is the same. When your cat leaves the box, sensors activate a raking device that sifts litter and deposits wastes into a separate receptacle. There are even systems that use nonporous "litter," water, and cleaning solutions and deposit wastes into your waste-water system.

Litter Box Dos and Don'ts

- **Do** place the litter box in an area without heavy foot traffic or commotion.
- **Do** experiment with various types of litter (see Day 106).
- **Do** purchase the correct size and height litter box.
- **Do not** scold your cat for missing the box. He will associate the box with your scolding and may avoid it.
- **Do not** move the litter box to a different location; your cat will eliminate in the spot he knows regardless of whether the box exists.

Cloned Cats

CATS CAN HAVE MORE THAN nine lives now, thanks to science. The first cloned cat, aptly named CC for Carbon Copy, was born out of a Texas A&M University research lab. While the university is responsible for a number of other cloned species, primarily farm animals such as pigs and goats, CC was the world's first cloned companion animal. Even so, CC is not identical to her donor.

Here are some facts to help you understand how cat cloning works:

- CC's clone material was produced using a nuclear transfer of Rainbow's cells into Allie, a "surrogate mother." CC's fetus developed normally and was delivered by cesarean section.

- Cloning does not create an absolutely identical copy, and CC is certainly the proof of that. Her "mother," Rainbow, a shorthaired calico, looks different from CC, who did not inherit the X chromosome that would give her the orange component of a calico's coat. Therefore, CC is white with black tabby markings.

- Even if CC were a calico, she would not have had the exact same markings as her molecular parent. Consider identical human twins born of a single cell that split. Their personalities are not the same, and they may look slightly different.

- Cloning by no means guarantees that the new animal will have the personality of the original source.

Some criticize that playing with genetics is unethical. And some find the notion of scientifically reproducing pets self-indulgent, especially when viewed in the light of the continuing problem of cat overpopulation. As the process refines, it promises to remain controversial.

> Given the available information about cloning, would you ever consider perpetuating your own kitty in this manner?

Oops! Missing the Litter Box

YOUR CAT IS TAKING CARE OF BUSINESS in all the wrong places—that is, everyplace except his litter box. Is he doing it on purpose? That depends on the type of bad aim he is displaying. (We'll give Kitty the benefit of the doubt.)

Spraying and marking are usually territorial responses, and the offending cat often is not neutered or spayed. (Altering a cat before these behaviors begin, usually before six months of age, may head off spraying and marking entirely.) If your male cat is intact, he will spray. Spraying also occurs in multicat households, or when there is a change in routine or environment that upsets the cat.

How do you solve the spraying dilemma? Reduce competition in a multicat household by providing multitiered cat trees so every cat has his own perch. If your cat sprays in response to other cats he sees outdoors, block his view. If he habitually sprays or "marks" in a few spots in the house, treat those areas with a commercial cat repellent or mothballs wrapped in cheesecloth.

Failing to use the litter box, and instead urinating right next to it or in another designated area, could point to a logistics issue. Where is the litter box located? If you place it in a high-traffic zone, Kitty may revert to a more private spot—box or not. What size and shape is the box? You may discover that the box requires kitty gymnastics to get in and out.

Other reasons for missing the box, not associated with stress, include:

- The cat may prefer a different surface (litter).
- A "bully" cat in the household may prevent the cat from stepping near the litter.
- Scolding her accidents or pain during urination may convince your cat that the litter box has bad karma.
- Logistics: Cats need easy access to the box.
- Older cats and kittens may forget where the litter box is located.

If Kitty keeps missing the box, a urinary infection may be the culprit. Talk to your vet about the behavior. A cat that experiences pain while urinating may associate that bad experience with the litter box and choose to "go" elsewhere.

A DIY Designer Collar

You can upgrade your pet's plain, nylon collar into a flattering neck piece with ribbon and a sewing machine. An abundance of inexpensive ribbon is available at fabric outlets and craft stores. Upgrading your kitty's collar is so easy you'll want to create collars for every holiday. These also make great kitty gifts for owners welcoming a new "baby" home. (Note: Always choose a cat collar with a breakaway feature; see Day 99 for more on safe collars.)

MATERIALS

Ribbon of choice

Scissors

Nylon collar, sized appropriately for your cat

Matching thread and sewing machine or fabric glue

1. *Select the ribbon for the collar.* Take the collar with you to the craft store to make sure you select ribbon of the appropriate width. Do not cut the ribbon horizontally; avoid ribbon thicknesses that exceed the width of your collar.

2. *Cut the ribbon to fit.* Unbuckle/unsnap the collar and lay it flat. Measure the ribbon against the collar and cut to the appropriate length.

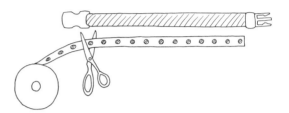

3. *Fasten the ribbon to the collar.* Choose thread to match the ribbon colors, then sew along the edges of the ribbon. For thicker collars, you may sew a center stitch for reinforcement. Create a small stitch on both ends to polish the look. (Glueing the ribbon to the collar will not be as secure.)

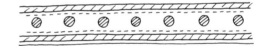

American Bobtail

THE AMERICAN BOBTAIL HAS A SHORT, upright poof of a stubby tail. This fairly new, longhaired breed emerged in the 1960s as a spontaneous mutation, like Cymric (see Day 131).

Characteristics: Because the American Bobtail's ancestry is so mixed, all manner of colors are acceptable at cat shows. The important qualification for competing cats is the tail length. Like the "stumpy"-tailed Cymric, the cobby-bodied American Bobtail typically has a tail from 1 to 4 inches (2.5 to 10.2 cm) long. Occasionally, kittens may be born with either a full-length tail or none at all.

History: A family named Sanders adopted a feral short-tailed cat wandering in Arizona and named him Yodie. He sired variously tailed kittens with the family's Siamese cat, and when one of those cats mated it produced kittens with very short tails. The fur was on the short side, too, but a crossbreeding with Himalayans (see Day 173) and other breeds caused semi-longhaired kittens to become the standard for this mongrel breed, which became recognized by U.S. cat associations in 1990.

feline fun fact > The American Bobtail often grows an extra-thick double winter coat with lynxlike markings.

American Bobtail

How to Name Your Cat

They say that the test of literary power is whether a man can write an inscription. I say, "Can he name a kitten?"

—Samuel Butler (1835–1902)

WHAT'S IN A NAME? Cats are often named for their physical attributes: coloring (Midnight, Snowball) and coat patterns (Boots, Patches). Some owners borrow names from favorite book or movie characters. There are a slew of cat-naming websites and pet name books to help you add more options to the name game.

Still stumped over what to call Kitty? Allow us to spark your imagination . . .

Animal metaphors: Go for more unusual ones, such as Raven for an all-black cat.

Unique characteristics: A calico, for example, might be called Harlequin or Columbine; or use Swash for a cat with a great plume of a tail.

Human names: Troll through baby-naming guides for ideas (e.g., you might call her Alva or Jennifer, if she is white, or Russell or Rupert if he is red), or honor a public figure or celebrity you admire. Commonsense tip: Avoid naming Kitty after friends or relatives who may not appreciate this tribute.

Themes: If you own more than one cat, consider giving them names that inherently go together. For example, a card-playing cat lover may name his pets Ace, Jack, and Queen.

Whatever you do, make sure you **select a name you wish to continue saying** throughout the nine lives your cat will be there to answer to it. It should be distinctive, neither too close to another term you might use regularly in conversation nor so similar to another pet or family member's name as to confuse your cat about whether he is being summoned. The latter is especially important if you have several cats. If you name one Aby Rudy and another Ruddy, they may both answer you when you call either name.

Cat Carriers

A STURDY CAT CARRIER IS AN essential piece of equipment for the cat owner. You'll need it to take Kitty to the vet, when you travel, and when you move. Cats should never be allowed to roam free in a car; they tend to like to curl up on the dashboard or under your feet, making for dangerous driving conditions.

Several types of carriers are on the market, including ones made of cardboard, wire, cloth, and wicker. Your best bet is a carrier constructed of high-impact plastic. Plastic carriers feature a hinged door and are very easy to clean, unlike the other types. The small openings along the sides allow for air circulation while providing enough shelter and privacy that your cat will feel secure while you move him. Place a washable blanket, towel, or carrier pad in the bottom of the carrier for your cat's comfort.

Train your cat to get used to the carrier (see Day 337) so that having to go in it won't be a traumatic experience. But accept that even the best-trained cat will be reluctant to enter the new carrier at first, so be prepared to put him in yourself. To do this, set the carrier on one end in another room, with the opening facing up.

Pick up the cat by the scruff of his neck with one hand and support his bottom and hind legs with the other. Quickly but gently lower him into the carrier and close and latch the door, being careful not to close it on a paw, tail, or ear. Cats can move like lightning, so you'll have to be quick about this. Slowly turn the carrier so the handle is on top.

If you have multiple cats, each cat should have his own carrier. You wouldn't want to find yourself caught in a situation, such as an evacuation, where you need to move all of your cats simultaneously and not be able to do so.

Feline Flicks—Animated

I tawt I taw a puddy tat. —Sylvester

EVERYONE HAS HEARD OF Tom and Jerry, the dynamic cat-mouse duo that evolved into a Saturday morning cartoon staple. Then, there was the infamous Tweety Bird, always at war with archenemy Sylvester the cat. Tweety and Sylvester were Loony Toon stars, and Sylvester even had a brief career as a spokescat for 9Lives cat food.

But what about other animated cats that have graced the silver screen and boob tube over the years? Next time you're in the mood for a cartoon cat flick, tune into one of these feline-lover classics:

- **Disney's *Pinocchio*:** The main character in this 1940 movie, Geppetto, has a pet cat named Figaro (voiced by Mel Blanc) that, unlike the cat in the original Collodi tale, is a friendly creature.

- ***Alice in Wonderland:*** There are many animated film versions of *Alice in Wonderland* (see Day 338); Sterling Holloway voiced the Cheshire cat in Disney's 1951 classic; in a 1999 movie produced for television, Whoopi Goldberg had that honor.

- ***Lady and the Tramp:*** The 1955 movie is about two dogs, but it also includes the unforgettable characters of Si and Am, voiced by singer Peggy Lee. Their "Siamese Cat Song," as well as other musical numbers, was cowritten by Lee and songwriter Sonny Burke.

- ***Gay Purr-ee:*** The 1962 musical cartoon paired singer-actors Judy Garland and Robert Goulet (in his film debut) as the voices of the cats Mewsette and Jaune Tom, whose on-again, off-again romance is set against the backdrop of Paris. Hermione Gingold played Madame Rubens-Chatte. There are many delicious puns on an adult level, such as that legendary café, the Mewlon Rouge.

- ***Aristocats:*** This 1970 film concerns a pampered white cat named Duchess (voiced by Eva Gabor) whose wealthy owner dies, whereupon the butler desires to steal the inheritance left to her and her three kittens. An enterprising tawny tomcat named Thomas O'Malley (voiced by Phil Harris) comes to their aid. The cast includes many other feline characters. Scat Cat (voiced by Scatman Crothers) was modeled on Louis Armstrong.

- **Don Bluth's *The Secret of NIMH* (1982), *An American Tail* (1986), and *An American Tail: Fievel Goes West* (1991),** and two additional American Tail sequels all include feline characters. Fievel is a mouse.

- ***Cats Don't Dance:*** In this 1997 film, a small-town cat named Jimmy (Scott Bakula) goes to Hollywood dreaming to act and sing on the silver screen, only to be rivaled by a malicious child star who wants the spotlight for herself.

- ***Puss in Boots*:** Lets not forget his appearance in the Shrek films, beginning with *Shrek 2* (voiced by Antonio Banderas, 2004).

The No-Fuss Guide to Administering Medication

FEELING SQUEAMISH ABOUT giving medication to Kitty? (My, what sharp teeth she has . . .) Ease the process with proper technique and the right tools for the job.

USING FOOD

When serving with food, crush the pill and mix with a meaty moist canned food. Do not mix a crushed pill with an entire meal. If your cat doesn't lick the bowl clean, she could miss out on a portion of the dosage. When administering whole pills, tuck the capsule into a semimoist food, soft cheese, or meat chunk. Feed your cat a tasty treat prior to giving her the masked pill to prime her taste buds for the second (medicated) helping.

PILLS

Ask your vet to show you how to administer pills by hand. You can use a pill pusher, or pill gun, to assist with the process.

1. Stabilize your cat by wrapping her in a towel so just her head peeks out. Otherwise, place her back against a surface, or squat on the ground and place her between your knees, so she cannot wriggle away as you feed her the pill.

2. Using one hand, cup your hand over your cat's head. Press your thumb on one side of the jaw (hinge) and your fingers on the other side.

3. Tilt back Kitty's head so she faces the ceiling. Her lower jaw will drop.

4. Place the pill between the lower canine teeth and push down, but not too far—just over the hump of the tongue. Close and hold your cat's mouth shut. She will naturally swallow. You may rub or blow on your cat's nose to stimulate a lick, which results in a swallow. Finally, reward her with a tasty treat and plenty of praise.

LIQUIDS

Feed your cat a tasty treat and praise her as you prepare the oral syringe or eyedropper. Withdraw the prescribed amount of medication. Stabilize your cat if she is fussy.

1. Place the syringe or dropper tip into the mouth behind the canine teeth.

2. Slowly administer the liquid.

3. Hold your cat's mouth closed and keep her head in a normal position to prevent gagging. If your cat spits out some of the medication, do not readminister a dose unless she spits out the entire portion.

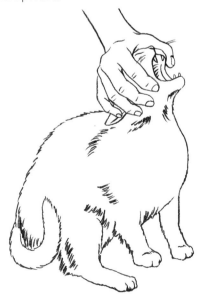

How to hold your cat's head when administering pills

"Green" Your Cat's Play with Eco-Toys

DON'T FORGET TO INCLUDE KITTY'S interests as you "go green" at home. These objects can be recycled into terrific cat toys.

- Full-size plastic drinking straws, especially the flexible kind. They make a neat popping sound when batted about, and can be carried in your pet's mouth.

- Rinsed and crumpled paper cups (don't use plastic or Styrofoam, which could crack or chip).

- Large empty thread spools. Remove the paper labels before giving to your cat. (Don't give your cat small spools or bobbins that can be swallowed.)

- The protective paper strip removed from a large self-stick envelope. Tie into a knot or two to add more dimension.

- Empty paper grocery or shopping bags, standing open on one side. Be sure to cut off and discard any handles.

- Cat-size or larger empty cardboard cartons. Remove any tape, foam pellets, Bubble Wrap, or sticky labels.

- A colorful blow-in card from a magazine, folded and twisted into a thin strip. Some cats go wild over batting these around.

- An empty childproof medicine bottle, well rinsed and dried, into which you have place a few pieces of dried cat food before recapping—instant, safe rattle toy!

- An empty toilet paper roll. Amuse your cat by peeking through it at each other as if it were a telescope, as well as letting Kitty roll it around.

- Not quite recycling but certainly green: See if your cat will accept a fresh string bean, celery stick, or carrot stick as a carry-and-bat toy.

- An old sweater, towel, or blanket past all hope for human use makes a cozy snoozing place that will remind Kitty of you.

American Curl

THIS UNUSUAL BREED IS A newbie in the cat world—it's less than thirty years old. Its story is equally modern: Two strays meet, fall in love (cat love, anyway), and start a family.

Characteristics: Because just one parent needs to have curled ears for the gene to pass along, several varieties of American Curl already exist— longhaired and shorthaired. Both kinds have silky fur without any undercoat, and a thick tail. The roundness of the ears varies from cat to cat; an ear that doesn't simply curve but folds all the way back is considered a fault at cat shows.

History: The American Curl originated when two stray kittens were taken in by a California couple named Ruga, in 1981. One, a black female they named Shulasmith, had backward-curling ears, and when she gave birth to four kittens, two had inherited their mama's curled ears.

Shulasmith and some of her offspring were shown at a California cat show in 1983. Descendants continued to display this characteristic, and in 1985 the American Curl became an official breed.

feline fun fact > The ears of an American Curl furl backward tightly a few days after birth, not taking on their full, softer curl until the kitten is about four months old.

American Curl

Spoil Your Cat

WHO DESERVES IT MORE? Kitty is your baby, the best listener, and she just loves people (really)— and especially you, of course. So why not spoil her? You don't need a special occasion to treat your cat right. Besides, you will follow a long line of cat worshippers. Consider the highly regarded ancient Egypt cat goddess, Bastet, associated with fertility, motherhood, grace, and beauty. (If your cat could read, she'd be giving you a feline dose of "Told you so.")

- *Dedicate a piece of furniture.* That's right. Make sure her lounger has a view of the outdoors, and it's okay to adorn that chair with a monogrammed kitty pillow.

- *Give her a plant.* Just make sure it's catnip or cat grass. If catnip were a vice, cats would be addicts. (Moderation is the key.)

- *Treat her to a massage.* You know her love-me spots. (Sometimes, they're strange, like between the toes.)

- *Break out the china.* It's mealtime, but you can make it special by serving her food in special bowls. Garnish her ordinary dinner with some smelly canned tuna. (Smell = good.)

- *Provide a window seat.* Window benches give cats a comfortable perch with a view.

The ultimate: *Create a cat room.* Call it the nursery, or the cat den, but whatever you call it the room is equipped with every kitty pleasure possible. Fountain? Check. Multiple scratching posts? Got it. Kitty hideout and built-in cat stairs so the pets can perch at leisure? Of course. Toys are a given. If you have the luxury of an extra bedroom or space in the basement, this is your opportunity to deck the space just for Kitty.

Purring

THE ABILITY TO PURR IS ONE OF your cat's most distinctive features, but also one of the most puzzling. Why do cats purr, anyway? There are several theories, and the question has been contemplated for centuries. Some say the lulling noise is caused by blood vessels; others point to bone vibration, or even a special purring organ (there is no such thing).

Researchers now believe purring is caused when a cat's brain sends signals to muscles in the larynx, which cause the glottis to vibrate. Passing air causes vibrations that result in the purring sound. The purr sounds continuous because it happens when cats are inhaling and exhaling.

The purrs of some cats can be heard across the room; others are so quiet that you know your cat is purring only by feeling the vibration. Cats purr when they are contented, much like humans smile or dogs wag their tails. But many people don't realize that cats also might purr when nervous, frightened, or injured. Just because a cat is purring, don't assume he's happy.

> There is speculation that the vibration frequency of a cat's purr stimulates muscles and bones and may promote healing in both cats and humans.

The Idiomatic Cat

CAT GOT YOUR TONGUE? Cats have been the source for many a metaphoric expression and idiomatic phrase. Here are some of them:

- "It's the cat's pajamas" and "It's the cat's whiskers" essentially mean the same thing: just right or superlative.
- When Australians have eaten a large meal, they say they are full "up to pussy's bow."
- Whereas Americans say they are "sick as a dog," when ill, in England they would be "sick as a cat."
- To "play cat and mouse" describes two individuals who deliberately pursue and evade each other.

- To "let the cat out of the bag" is to accidentally disclose a secret.
- To be "in the catbird seat" is to be in a position of prominence, such as to obtain a plum promotion at work.
- To "have kittens" is to be upset; a cousin of this expression is to "have a cow."
- To "put a cat among the pigeons" is to introduce an inflammatory comment or person into a situation.
- To look like "the cat that just ate the canary" is to behave smugly, whereas to "behave kittenishly" is to be coy.
- In French, to "disappear like a cat" is to leave without paying.

Does Kitty Need Pet Health Insurance?

YOUR CAT'S MEDICAL BILLS can really add up, and most owners are not prepared to cover the high cost of veterinary care, especially when emergency procedures are necessary. Because pet insurance is a topic usually discussed when your cat is a kitten, it's easy to discount the importance of coverage and justify that "Our cat is perfectly healthy!" But even routine costs, from spaying to deworming and vaccinations, can tax your wallet.

Also, accidents happen. Kittens are more susceptible to disease and nutritional issues than adults; aging cats may need cancer treatment or expensive medication. Pet health insurance works similar to insurance for people. There are various insurance packages and levels of coverage to accommodate cats' needs and owners' budgets.

Monthly premiums are relatively low, but they can vary widely depending on the plan you choose as well as your cat's age, medical history, and living situation.

Indoor cats are less likely to get hurt, so rates may be lower. Also, you can purchase pet insurance for a lower premium if you invest in coverage right away. If your cat develops pre-existing conditions before you purchase pet insurance, you'll pay more.

Plans range from accident-only to premium plans that include everything from vaccines and wellness exams to chemotherapy and complex surgeries. A few things that are not usually covered are congenital, hereditary, or pre-existing conditions. Deductibles and monthly plans will vary.

Before you buy pet health insurance, find out exactly which conditions are covered, review pricing schedules and limits, and discuss the plan with your veterinarian to make sure insurance will cover most common problems. He or she can also refer you to reputable providers and weigh in on the integrity of insurers.

Gifts for Cat Lovers

MANY CAT LOVERS ARE PASSIONATE about collecting images of their own pet's breed . . . or cat-themed anything. Here are some ideas to make any feline fancier purr with pleasure:

- Cat-print fabric or ribbon, or cat-shaped buttons, for someone who sews

- An embroidery or latch-hook kit depicting a cat who resembles the recipient's pet, if the person likes to work from kits

- Cat-shaped cookie-cutters or cake molds, for bakers

- Decorative home items, such as kitchenware or cat-print linens

- A photograph of the person's cat, enlarged and decoratively framed (or a series of photos of the cat in various poses, in a grouped arrangement). This is quite a touching gift for cat owners who haven't taken the time themselves to photograph Kitty.

- Cat-motif clothing or accessories, such as pajamas, socks, or jewelry

- Cat-motif playing cards or board games

- Cat-motif stationery, address books, mousepads, or posters

- A book about cats. Look for antique editions.

- Videos/DVDs of live-action or cartoon films for a cat's viewing pleasure, such as a nature film featuring birds

- Holiday tree ornaments depicting cats, strings of cat-shaped lights, or Halloween-theme black cats

- A subscription to a cat fancier's magazine would be enjoyed all year by someone who does not already subscribe.

American Shorthair

THE PILGRIMS' CATS WERE American Shorthairs, and they are hardy house cats that spent 350 years in the United States before being named an official breed.

Characteristics: Not as round of face or as husky as its British cousin but still broad cheeked and sturdy, the American Shorthair comes in every color as well as the several tabby varieties and calico. The most famous coloring is the deeply striped classic tabby, with a clear M on the forehead. Its fur is indeed short and quite dense, and it tends to grow more thickly in cooler months, perhaps thanks to this breed's origins as a pioneer cat that spent its days outdoors.

History: Also known as Domestic Shorthair, this breed was brought over from England by settlers who date back to the original Pilgrims, in 1620. Journeys of the British Shorthair to America continued for centuries, resulting in the first American Shorthair show cat's actually being a British-born cat named Belle of Bradford, back in 1900, brought by Jane Cathcart. In 1904, she submitted to a show an American-born nonpedigreed shorthair by the name of Buster Brown. But even in the twentieth century, such cats were not respected as more than an everyday house pet, condescendingly allowed to compete in an anything-goes pet category but not as their own breed. Today, they are an official breed.

feline fun fact > The American Shorthair is reputed to be an especially good hunter, perhaps dating from its hard-scrabble survival skills learned while living among the nation's early European settlers.

American Shorthair

Story: Toilet Training Lessons from the Dog

I GOT MY FIRST CAT when I was thirty-two years old. The cat antics staged at my home provide a lifetime of entertainment. The best is when my dog, Emma, and cat, Ernie, teach each other shenanigans. You can practically detect their scheming, the way they flee off together. Then the next thing you know, well … it can't be good.

Emma has always preferred drinking from the toilet bowl rather than the dog-appropriate dish I place in her eating spot. I refresh the water regularly. Emma doesn't care. She heads straight to the bathroom, and proceeds to what she believes is her personal drinking fountain.

My cat Ernie had only been with me for a week when Emma became his teacher. Her orientation started in the bathroom. I caught Emma lapping up toilet water and Ernie perched on the tank, peering over into the bowl. He was studying. I left, somewhat amused.

A few minutes later, the two were still "busy," so I checked in on them. Emma had retreated to the bedroom for a nap, but Ernie was circling the toilet bowl, walking the seat like a balance beam. He was trying to figure out how to get a sip of the cold water without getting his feet wet.

Ernie was completely oblivious to my watching. He straddled the seat, craning his neck to reach for the cool water. No luck. He slipped, his body like a hammock with front and back paws clinging to either side of the bowl. He leaped away, recovering from the awkward position, but didn't give up.

He tried to copy Emma's move, reaching in from the floor to the bowl, but Ernie's tongue just wasn't long enough. Frustrated, I could tell, Ernie made his final attempt. He stood on the bowl and eased his front paws inside, resting them just above the water line. Success! Ernie got the drink he'd been waiting for.

 # Cat Calls and Other Sounds

MEOWING IS THE SOUND most commonly associated with cats. Ask any kindergartener what sound a cat makes, and her answer will be "meow!" Meows usually mean "pay attention to me" and are employed when your cat wants something (such as a taste of your tuna sandwich) or just to say "hello."

What about all those other sounds cats make?

Hissing is a defensive sound, usually accompanied by laid-back ears and sometimes by hair standing on end.

Growling sometimes accompanies hissing, and is a sign of displeasure.

Chattering is a rapid clacking of the teeth sometimes heard when a cat is ready to pounce on prey.

Low-pitched yowling or crying is a sign of discomfort or frustration, not necessarily pain, as when a cat who doesn't like to travel is put in her crate.

Caterwauling is loud yowling exchanged between two cats that are preparing to fight, and is heard more often in outdoor tomcats in the mating season.

Screaming is a sign of pain and sometimes associated with sex.

When Is a Cat Not a Cat?

SOME WORDS SOUND AS IF THEY have something to do with cats, when actually they have nothing to do with Kitty.

cat burglar—a robber who enters through an upper story

catacomb—an underground cemetery

catalepsy—a trancelike state

catamaran—a sailboat with twin hulls

cataphoric—a word or phrase that refers to another word or phrase that follows it

cataract—a waterfall over a precipice; an eye condition

catbird—a "meowing" American songbird related to the mockingbird

catfish—a freshwater fish with long barbells resembling whiskers

catgut—the strings of a musical instrument or bow, actually made from the innards of farm animals such as sheep

cathead—a projection on a ship to which an anchor is attached

cathouse—a bordello

cat-lap—British slang for unappetizing food or drink

cat's eye (also *katzenauge* [German])—British for a light-reflective stud along a roadway

catwalk—a narrow path

kitty—a pool of collected money, as in poker

kitty-cornered—located on the diagonal (also called *catty-cornered*)

langues-de-chats—delicate cookies piped or molded into spatulate strips (literally, "cats' tongues")

tabby—a kind of cement

Treat and Prevent Hairballs

ALL CATS—EXCEPT, PERHAPS, THE SPHYNX—experience hairballs. The culprit: their prickly tongue, which forces any ingested hair down a one-way street into their stomach, where the cat's body finally recognizes that it is not food and wants to get rid of it. *Ccchhhhhwwwwuuuh!*

The typical cat regurgitation of a hairball involves two spurts—one a little drab of liquid, and the other, a wad of hair in a larger puddle of liquid. As long as the wad has come out, your cat is fine. She will not have lost her appetite, and you do not have to give her any medicine or take her to the vet. Stepping up your grooming of her should prevent most future problems (see Day 218).

But if hairballs seem to be a regular occurrence in your home, despite regular grooming, and especially if your cat tends to be constipated (look for hard, small stools), she may need a touch more lubricant and/or roughage added to her diet. This can take the form of:

- A little bit of vegetable oil (such as olive oil) or butter, mixed into her food or as a separate supplement

- A commercially prepared hairball preventive that often comes as a gel in a tube or as crystals that you can sprinkle on food (check pet supply stores). If the product contains mineral oil, be sure to give Kitty a vitamin supplement, because mineral oil can deplete her body of vitamin A.

- Hairball–remedy food (check cat food labels)

- A small amount (such as a half spoonful) of finely grated or cooked, pureed raw carrot or cooked, pureed sweet potato, pumpkin, or winter squash. For convenience, look for a jarred baby food version of this that is pure vegetable without any added salt or garlic; you only need a little bit at a time, so freeze it in spoonful-size dabs on a sheet of waxed paper and then store in an airtight container in the freezer (thaw before giving to Kitty).

- Cat grass (wheatgrass or other grass; avoid giving Kitty alfalfa or other sprouts, however)

- A pinch of ground psyllium mixed into the cat's food (check natural food stores for brands that do not contain citrus flavoring)

If your cat has stopped eating and is severely constipated, she may have developed a hairball that has gotten too stuck to vomit out. This is an urgent situation and requires a vet's attention. In extreme cases, such hairballs may even require surgical removal. Obviously, prevention is key to keeping Kitty in tip-top form, particularly if she has long fur.

Chocolate-Point Cat Cookies

THESE CHOCOLATE-POINT, orange-flavored Siamese cookies really do have chocolate points! Impress all your cat-loving friends with this easily decorated sugar cookie. If possible, use a cutter of a slim cat shown in profile, so you have clearly definable areas for the tail, paws, ears, and muzzle.

Makes about 6 dozen 3-inch (7.6 cm) cookies; count will vary, depending on the size and shape of your cookie cutter.

INGREDIENTS
Cookies

1¾ cups (397 g) unsalted butter, at room temperature

6 tablespoons (75 g) granulated sugar

½ cup (60 g) confectioners' sugar, sifted

1 large egg

2 teaspoons (10 ml) orange extract or orange-flavored liqueur, such as Grand Marnier

2 cups + 2 tablespoons (266 g) sifted all-purpose flour, divided

½ teaspoon (2.3 g) baking soda

½ teaspoon (1.5 g) cream of tartar

1 tablespoon (6 g) (pat dry) freshly grated orange zest or dried ground orange peel

Chocolate Glaze

1 (1-ounce [28 g]) square semisweet baking chocolate

1 teaspoon (4 g) vegetable shortening

1. *To make the cookies:* In a large mixing bowl, using an electric mixer on medium speed, cream the butter with both sugars, then beat in the egg and orange extract.

2. Add 1 cup (125 g) of the flour, the baking soda, and the cream of tartar; beat on low speed just until blended.

3. Beat in the remaining 1 cup and 2 tablespoons (141 g) flour and the orange zest.

4. Knead with just a few squeezes, and then press the dough into three disks, using your hands. Wrap each disk in waxed or parchment paper and place in the refrigerator for 3 hours or overnight.

5. Preheat the oven to 375°F (190°C, or gas mark 5). Have ready two ungreased baking sheets.

6. Dust two sheets of waxed paper well with flour. Remove one disk from the refrigerator and roll out the dough ⅛ inch (3 mm) thick between the prepared papers. Use a cat-shaped cookie cutter to cut as many cats as you can without re-rolling the dough. (Dipping the cutter into flour helps it release the dough.) Carefully transfer the cookies to a cookie sheet, leaving about ½ inch (1.3 cm) between the cats.

7. Between sheets of freshly floured waxed paper, reroll the scraps and start another disk of dough if necessary, to fill the two baking sheets with cats. (While the cookies bake, continue to cut out more dough, lightly placing the cutouts on the waxed paper in which you had chilled the dough, until the pans are ready for them.)

8. Bake the cut cookies for about 7 minutes, or until lightly browned. Let cool for a few minutes before removing from the pan with a sharp-edged spatula. Place on a cooling rack and transfer to fresh waxed paper sheets once completely cooled.

9. *To make the glaze:* In the top of a double boiler or small stainless-steel pan set over but not touching simmering water, melt the chocolate and shortening.

10. Using a clean pointed-tip brush, the tip of a small spoon, or the end of a chopstick, paint the chocolate glaze onto only the cookies' ears, muzzle, tail, and paws, keeping the glaze on the top surface of the cookies. Reheat the chocolate if necessary to keep it smooth and flowing.

11. Let the cookies dry completely in a single layer in a cool place before stacking in an airtight container. They keep for about a week at cool room temperature or in the fridge, or can be frozen for up to two months.

American Wirehair

TAKE AN AMERICAN SHORTHAIR (see Day 47) and cross it with another American Shorthair, and . . . surprise! The result is a male cat with a coarse, crimped coat.

Characteristics: The first few generations of American Wirehair were bicolor, with red and white fur, but now any color shared by the American Shorthair (see Day 47) can be found in this breed. Breeders have worked to produce evenly crimped fur, which should form ringlets right to its tips, as well as a more compact body than the first long-legged ancestors. Wirehair kittens are born with fur that is already tightly curled.

Because the wirehair characteristic is carried by a recessive gene, matings of cats even of this same breed can produce kittens with normal fur and, on the flip side, excessive inbreeding can cause respiratory problems in offspring; as a result, healthy, genuine Wirehairs are still relatively rare.

History: The first American Wirehair was bred, by accident, on a New York farm in 1966. The standard shorthaired breed spontaneously mutated to produce a unique coat. This rough-furred male, named Adam, was mated with one of his soft-haired littermates, named Tip-Top, and she produced two wirehaired kittens. Descendants of one, Amy, bore the numerous litters that have formed the basis of this new breed. Virtually every American Wirehair can be traced back to this special family. The breed was recognized in the United States in 1977.

feline fun fact > Even the whiskers of the American Wirehair are crimped!

American Wirehair

Welcome Home, Kitty!
Prepare a Shower Basket

YOUR FRIEND IS EXPECTING—a cat, that is—and you want to surprise her with a cache of cute kitty gear. First, purchase a basket or plastic storage container you can convert into a bed. Line the container with a cuddly towel or fleece blanket. This will double as a gift basket to hold the booty, and a cozy bed where the new kitten can snooze.

Now for the fun part: filling the basket with delightful and useful cat goods. Here are some items that new cat owners (and their kitties) will appreciate:

- A catnip-stuffed toy

- A laser pen (for the human); kittens get a kick out of chasing after the darting red light

- A small grooming comb designed for kittens

- Containers of tasty canned kitten food; you may inquire, ever so stealthily, what the kitten is eating so you purchase the correct brand

- A decorative collar and matching leash

- A box of litter (it runs out quickly)

- A special book about cat care that you found helpful while raising your own kitten

Cleaning Up "Accidents"

SOMETIMES A CAT MAY SPRAY or "mark" an area to send a message: "My litter box needs cleaning!" Other times, kneading a squishy surface, such as a blanket or a favorite object of yours, may trigger a little too much excitement: "This feels soooo good . . . oops!" Or your cat may be signaling you that she has a urinary tract infection or other condition that doesn't feel quite right down there: "Get me to a vet, please!"

As you get to know your pet, you will recognize which behavioral pattern is occurring. But what should you do about removing the evidence?

If the affected surface is washable, your best bet is white distilled vinegar. Pluck or scrape off any solids first, using a dry paper towel. If the soiled item is a fabric that can be machine washed, use about a cup of vinegar to start in an entire washing cycle and let it run all the way to spin dry, then use another cupful of vinegar for a second cycle, following up with a complete wash and rinse using your usual detergent.

If hand washing, do the same on a smaller scale, using either detergent or castile-based soap after the second vinegar wash, and rinsing well. Hard surfaces, such as tile or wooden flooring, can be washed with an appropriate product for the surface material once some vinegar has removed and neutralized your pet's waste.

Upholstery or carpets or dry-clean-only clothing can be dabbed carefully with vinegar and then rinsed with water, using damp rags or paper towels. Never rub in solid wastes. It is often easier to remove solids by letting them dry and then snapping or even vacuuming them off. A thin putty knife can also be dedicated to this purpose. When in doubt, test the effect of vinegar on an unobtrusive section of the soiled item, using just a few drops on a cotton swab. An alternative to vinegar is to sprinkle the affected area heavily with baking soda, let it rest for thirty minutes to absorb the odor, then vacuum up the powder.

If any trace of a scent remains, your cat may return to the spot as a repeat offender. Add a drop of peppermint or lavender oil to the last rinse to mask any faint odor that remains and provide a pleasant, catnip-family fragrance that he may be loath to ruin with his own stinky contributions. Resist using any commercial cleansers that will leave behind an undesirable presence of their own (and which could be toxic to Kitty).

The best prevention of future accidents is to remove the temptation to repeat them, be it by covering a targeted soft chair with a firmer slipcover or by placing visitors' personal things in a closed cupboard . . . or making sure your uncomfortable little one has her elimination issue checked by a medical professional as soon as possible. (See Days 122 and 311 to learn more about urinary disorders, and Day 353 for the lowdown on intestinal diseases.)

Cat Games for Humans

CATS AREN'T THE ONLY ONES who play cat games! These games keep animal lovers of all ages occupied, indoors and out.

- **Cat's cradle**—In this game string is woven upon the hands of one player and then deftly passed back and forth when a second (or more) enters the game.

- **Cat tarot**—Not a game to some, but serious divination, Tarot is done with a deck of cards featuring symbolic figures and numbers. These decks date back to the early fifteenth century.

- **Cat parlor games**—Parlor games involve spoken-aloud challenges, acted-out charades, or pen-and-paper puzzlers. One of the speaking games is "The Minister's Cat," which works through the alphabet. The first player says something like, "The minister's cat is an attractive cat." The next person repeats this, adding another *a* adjective, such as, "The minister's cat is an adventurous, attractive cat," and so it goes around the room until someone stumbles and has to drop out. Then the letter *b* begins, and as long as there are sufficient players the game could advance all the way to the letter *z*! Another popular game in Victorian times was "Poor Pussy": A player had to stroke another's head and say mournfully, "Poor Pussy"—and anyone who laughed was out of the game.

Why Is My Cat Eating Dirt?

CATS EXPLORE WITH THEIR PAWS and mouths—they taste and see the world for themselves. It's normal for your cat to chew on bits of cloth, eat paper, or take in a mouthful of dirt from time to time. But there are cases when a cat's nibbling habits are cause for concern. A cat that eats dirt or litter may be seeking trace minerals such as iron, a sign of anemia. (If your cat chews on cloth, stop the habit by keeping her busy with other toys. If swallowed, it will obstruct the cat's bowel.)

Anemia is most prevalent in cats that roam in the spring and summer, increasing their risk for flea infestation. Proper flea prevention (see Day 80) is important for preventing parasites (fleas, ticks, lice) from spreading harmful organisms to your cat, which can cause feline infectious anemia.

Other symptoms of anemia are weakness and jaundice. If you suspect anemia, see your vet immediately.

Your cat's oral fixation may just signal the urge to "explore." Here are some tips to modify the behavior:

- Secure targeted items, such as blankets, houseplants, and electric cords.

- Entertain your cat with interactive toys. Plant catnip indoors to lure your cat to this "houseplant" instead. Cats chew when they are bored, so keep them busy.

- Consult with your vet to determine whether dietary changes are necessary to fulfill your cat's nutrition needs.

Catnip Blanket

THIS EASY-CARE FLEECE sitting surface has a little something extra—not only is it comfy but it's also laced with catnip, to give Kitty extra-sweet dreams and perhaps help calm an anxious traveler. Launder with a gentle detergent and tumble dry on low; once your pet remembers the blanket contained catnip, she will continue to enjoy it even after the scent has faded or washed away.

Seek out paw- or cat-print fleece at your craft store or at online quilter's fabric sites.

MATERIALS

2 pieces polyester quilt batting, 18 inches x 22 inches (45.7 x 55.9 cm) for blanket, or 1 inch (2.5 cm) shorter and narrower than your cat carrier's base

2 pieces fleece, the same dimensions as the batting

2 tablespoons (4 g) dried catnip

Straight pins

Scissors

Coordinating or contrasting acrylic yarn and tapestry needle

1. Place a piece of batting atop the wrong side of one piece of fleece, sprinkle the batting side with the catnip, then cover with the other piece of batting and finally with the second piece of fleece, wrong side against the batting. Pin all around and trim away any uneven edges.

2. Using the yarn and needle, blanket-stitch around the entire perimeter of the blanket, concealing any ends of the yarn inside the blanket.

Balinese (Javanese)

BREED NAMES CAN BE DECEIVING. Although it's true that the Siamese cat originated in Siam, the Balinese cat's roots are in the United States.

Characteristics: Unlike most other longhairs, these supersleek cats have no ruff. Their fur is called "erminelike" for its softness. Like their Asian ancestors, they are born white before they develop colorpoint coloring. They have blue eyes and an exotic bone structure. But, in contrast to their shorthaired cousins, they are generally far less vocal!

History: In 1955, in two separate instances, one on the West Coast and the other on the East, two longhaired Siamese (genetic mutations of the normally shorthaired breed) were brought together by breeders to produce kittens that shared the longhaired characteristic. At first, the fuzzy exotics were simply called Longhaired Siamese, and were presented by that name at a U.S. cat show in 1961, but breeder Helen Smith decided to call such fluidly graceful creatures Balinese, after the dancers of Bali.

The name stuck, and British recognition of the breed followed two decades later. Interestingly, cat shows in Great Britain accept more color varieties for this breed than do shows in the United States.

This is where the term *Javanese* enters the picture. The name simply means a Balinese with a solid-color coat.

feline fun fact **>** If a Balinese is mated with a Siamese, the result will be shorthaired kittens. But if these kittens are mated with a Balinese, voilà—that third generation will again have long hair!

Balinese

Warming Up Miss Independent

SHE DOESN'T MEAN TO GIVE YOU the cold shoulder, but she really prefers not to sit on your lap and rarely does Kitty brush up against your leg, or give you that swooning gaze. Don't mistake her meow for, "Mommy me! Mommy me!" Nope. Not happening at your house. Although you understand your cat needs personal space (don't we all?), you sometimes wish she would check that aloof attitude in her kitty condo and curl up with you once in a while.

You can't change your cat's personality. And it's important to note that not all cats are underattached or dismissive; some are lovers—Velcro cats, we'll call them. So the excuse that Kitty's disinterest in you is a "cat thing" just doesn't hold water. There are some techniques you can employ to encourage your cat to warm up to you. This is by no means a directive to force Miss Independent into cuddling with you. (As you know, she'll do exactly what she pleases.) However, these tips will help her associate you with a reward, so she'll come around and aim to please you more often.

- Offer your cat small meals throughout the day so she associates your presence with food.

- While feeding your cat, speak to her in a soothing tone. Praise her. Tell her she's the diva of the house, that she's beautiful. (Cats understand this language—or at least it seems they do.)

- Find your cat's favorite spot. Sit there, on the floor, and encourage her to come to you.

- Don't wait for her to jump into your lap. Instead, invite her to play a game: get out the laser pen and have some fun! She'll connect playtime and friendship with you. She may even brush up against your leg if she wants to play another round.

- Resist the urge to pick up your cat if she is not cooperative.

- Do not try to chase her down or force quality time. This will only make her stray from you.

- Be patient. Building relationships takes time, and your cat will eventually trust you for more than just a square meal.

There may be deeper reasons why your cat is not interested in human contact. Adopted pets might have a hurtful past; they associate humans with unpleasant experiences from previous owners or time on the streets, if the cat was a stray. Give her time to trust you. Use food to encourage her to come to you so she will associate you with good things. Over time, she will recognize you as her caring owner.

Contending with Clawing

YOUR CAT'S CLAWS CAN TAKE a toll on furniture, carpet, family heirlooms, hand-knitted throws, and just about any other object that your cat envisions as a handy scratching post. No cat owner's home goes scratch-free, though some cats claw more than others do. Even declawed cats sometimes go through the motions.

Clawing is a natural action for cats. Their claws grow in layers, and clawing is how they shed the old claw sheaths and expose the new claws underneath. Cats also claw to mark their territory and to get a good stretch. You can no more stop a cat from clawing than you can stop her from grooming herself.

However, you can control clawing by providing alternative clawing surfaces and doing some basic training. A good scratching post and scratching box (see Day 4) are essential. Make the post or box attractive to your cat by spraying them with pheromones (see Day 88) and/or rubbing them with catnip. Praise her when she uses her scratching post or box.

Commercial sprays may help keep your cat from clawing unapproved surfaces. These usually contain clove oil, citrus oils, or other strong-smelling substances that make the area unappealing to your cat. Different cats have different reactions to these formulas. You may have to try several until you find the one that works best, and always test these products in an inconspicuous area before spraying the entire surface.

Some owners have luck with vinyl claw covers that adhere to the cat's claws. They last until your cat sheds that layer of claw and must be reapplied when they fall off. Altering your cat may lessen the clawing instincts of course. (For information on the controversial procedure of declawing, see Day 316.)

Say "Cat" in Many Languages

CATS HAVE BEEN OUR COMPANIONS since ancient history. The root of each word for *cat* often describes how cats look or act, or what they do. For instance, terms used for cats in the Middle Ages translate to "mouser."

Here are some modern words for our feline friends in several languages:

Albanian: mace
Arabic: biss/hirrah/qitah/quttah/qatt
Armenian: gatz
Basque: catua
Berber: kadiska
Bulgarian: kotka
Catalan: gat
Cherokee (Tsalagi): wesa
Chinese: mao
Cree: bushi
Czech: kocka
Danish: kat
Dutch: poes
Egyptian: kut
English: cat
Esperanto: kato
Estonian: kiisu
Farsi: gorbe
Filipino: pusa
Finnish: kissa
French: chat
Fula (New Guinea): gnari
Gaelic: cait
German: Katze

Greek: ga'ta
Gujarati: biladi
Hawaiian: popoki
Hebrew: chatul (with a guttural, *k*-like *ch*)
Hindi: billy
Hungarian: cica/macska
Icelandic: köttur
Italian: gatto/a
Japanese: neko
Korean: ko-yang-i
Lithuanian: katinas
Malay/Indonesian: kucing
Maltese: qattus
Mayan: miss
Norwegian: katt
Polish: kot
Romanian: pisica
Russian: kot/koshka/olena
Saudi Arabian: biss
Slovak: macka
Spanish/Portuguese: gato/a
Swahili: paka
Swedish: katt
Syrian: qati
Thai: meo
Turkish: kedi
Ugandan: paka
Ukrainian: kotuk
Vietnamese: meo
Welsh: cath
Zulu: ikati

Changing Cat Food

IF YOU DECIDE TO TRANSITION your cat to different food, do so gradually. Say you decide to dump a dry-food regimen for wet food, which contains the protein that cats desire without carbohydrates that can become problematic for overweight cats. Maybe you want to switch food brands because the one you're currently feeding your cat is no longer available. Plan several days, and ideally one week, to introduce this dietary change to your cat. Otherwise, she will have no interest in dining (see Day 171).

Every cat will respond differently to dietary changes. Some can stomach a quick change, but most need time to adjust.

Spend time mixing old and new food, and the mealtime switch will be minimally disruptive. (Your cat's litter box will let you know otherwise.)

Day 1: 90 percent original food, 10 percent new food

Day 2: 80 percent original food, 20 percent new food

Day 3: 70 percent original food, 30 percent new food

Days 4–10: continue pattern of decreasing original food and adding more of the new variety

Make a Foraging Box

THIS EASY-TO-MAKE BOX will keep your cat occupied and develop his foraging abilities. The kibble you add to the box should be a share of his normal portion, not an additional amount.

MATERIALS

4 flat stones, 2 to 3 inches (5.1 to 7.6 cm) across (to weight the box down)

Pencil

Cardboard shoe box with lid

X-acto knife or razor knife

4 to 6 small plastic balls, such as Ping-Pong balls

4 to 6 smooth, plain plastic napkin rings

8 to 10 pieces dry cat kibble

Masking tape

DIRECTIONS

1. Rinse the stones to remove any dirt and dry them thoroughly.

2. With a pencil, mark six small circles or squares around the box, two on each of the long sides and one on each short side. The circles or squares should be smaller than the balls you are using, but big enough for your cat to get her paw through, and about ½ inch to 1 inch (1.3 to 2.5 cm) from the bottom of the box.

3. Using the knife, carefully cut out the openings you marked.

4. Set the box right side up. Put a stone in each corner of the box, then add the balls and napkin rings. Distribute the kibble in the box. Replace the lid and tape down with the masking tape.

5. Place the box on the floor and let your cat enjoy figuring out how to get to the kibble.

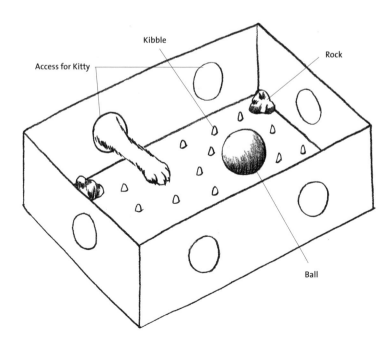

Kibble

Access for Kitty

Rock

Ball

Bengal

THE BENGAL COMES FROM A family of exotic relatives; it's the descendant of an Egyptian Mau and an Asian Leopard.

Characteristics: Bengals' coats have expanded to several colors—silver and various tones of brown, from buff to sepia—with a high-contrast marbled or spotted coat. The marbled variety is deeply swirled along the horizontal, unlike striped tabbies. One particularly interesting color is known as "hot rufus" for its intense orange hue; another variation, the seal lynx point, is spotted all over but with darker point markings. The preferred style of spotting for show cats features rosettes rather than the ordinary polka-dot sort of spots. Whatever their color or pattern, Bengals have complex stripes on their faces, and their spots continue all the way down their tail and along their belly.

Perhaps the most striking characteristic of the Bengal is its size; males can reach 20 pounds (9 k) or more without being chubby. They have a strong and muscular build. Although Bengals can be real pussycats if raised with affection, they do tend to exhibit innate feral behavior when playing, such as attacking their toys as if genuine prey.

This rare breed's availability is hampered by the fact that, because its genetic mix crosses species barriers, the males are often born sterile. On the upside, further experiments with crossbreeding have resulted in even some longhaired Bengals.

History: Most of today's Bengals have descended from experiments by California breeder Jean Mills, who mated several early Bengals with several different domestic cats to see what would happen. The result was tawny, spotted litters of remarkable size and strength. They began to enter cat shows in 1991.

Bengal

feline fun fact > Bengals take well to being leash trained.

What Your Cat's Tail Is Telling You

THE TYPICAL CAT'S TAIL HAS twenty to twenty-four bones. Although the flexible tail helps a cat balance, it is also an important communication tool. We all know that a cat who walks with a drooped tail between his legs is feeling very sorry for himself. An upright tail signals a secure cat that feels so full of himself that he's raised his proud "flag." Here are some other interesting "tell-tail" signs:

A quiver in an upright tail: This can indicate anticipation, generally of a positive kind; many cats use this gesture when they expect to be fed imminently.

A full, erect tail: Often coupled with hair standing on end all over the cat's body, this tail position signals aggression. He is making himself as large and threatening as possible. An angry cat will also wave the enlarged tail to make it seem even more enormous to an enemy.

A horizontally, sharply twitching or whipping tail: Kitty is annoyed—by another cat, or even by you—or he feels frustrated. If you admonish your cat, for example, he may not talk back vocally, but a twitching tail will give away his displeasure. A submissive cat, threatened by an aggressor, will thump his tail.

A wagging tail: This is a softer gesture, and is done such as while listening to music or to indulgently provide an object of play for a kitten; the entire tail may move, or just the tip.

An extended tail, or a tail wrapped closely around the body: This is performed while sitting or sleeping, or when the cat feels threatened by another animal, or even the vacuum cleaner.

A tail held to the side: Called the lordosis position, a female cat in heat, crouching low, may position her tail this way.

Tail sniffing: Cats sniff and even taste the base of each other's tails, where scent glands are located, to confirm each others' identity. This can be an aggressive gesture, an invitation to play, or a simple "hello" greeting. Kitty may even present his rear end to you, expecting you to appreciate his presence. Greeting him pleasantly by name will usually satisfy his urge to check that you know who he is!

feline fun fact > You may be able to defuse your cat's aggression simply with a sharp command, "Put that tail down!" if you have taught him the words *tail* and *down*. He may automatically obey—and once his tail goes down, slimming toward looking normal, it's difficult for him to remain angry! Chances are, he'll do an embarrassed lick and walk away nonchalantly, as if he had never issued a threat.

Choosing a Shelter Cat

ANIMAL SHELTERS ARE USUALLY full of cats of all different types and personalities, all looking for a safe and loving home. As an animal lover, you will want to fill your home with these sweet pets—how can you choose just one? There are limits. Ask yourself these questions to narrow down your decision and choose the kitten or cat that is right for you.

- Before you go to the shelter, think about what kind of cat you want to adopt. Male or female? Independent or a clingy personality? Short hair or long hair?

- How much time do you have to devote to training? A cat with behavioral problems will require plenty of attention to overcome them.

- How much time can you devote to grooming? A longhaired cat requires frequent brushing and sometimes bathing.

- Can you handle a cat with medical problems, one that might require daily pilling or frequent vet visits?

- Are you looking for a kitten, or would you consider an older cat? Kittens are adorable, but older cats can be just as loving once they get to know you.

When you get to the shelter, ask to see cats that fit your criteria. The staff at most animal shelters are usually familiar with the cats in their care; find out about the personalities of the different cats. Keep in mind, though, that shelters can be stressful places for cats, and they might not be displaying their best manners or be as friendly as they normally are out of that environment.

Once you narrow down your selection to a few cats, spend some quality time with each cat, away from the other cats, if possible. Give them time to warm up to you and show you a little of their personalities. Usually, there's one cat that tugs a little harder at your heartstrings than the others.

Before you fall completely in love, though, ask the shelter staff about that cat in particular. What do they know about the situation she came from? How does she behave around other cats? Is she generally friendly to people? Are there any behavioral or medical problems they know of? Ask them about their return policy, too, in case the match doesn't work out—it does occasionally happen. If the answers satisfy you, congratulations! You've found your special kitty.

Cats Under the Big Top

IN THEATER, A CAT THAT CROSSES the stage will bring bad luck to the performance, but a well-known troupe of Russian felines has bucked this superstition. In 1971, Yuri Kuklachev, then studying to be a clown, came upon a cat that earned its food by performing acrobatics for passersby. The clown study envisioned a partnership. He adopted the cat, figuring they could work together. He named her Strelka, and the duo performed together with the Moscow State Circus.

When Kuklachev left the circus to create his own, he promoted cats to the main act, and the circus became known as the Moscow Cat Theatre. The troupe is still going strong, led by Kuklachev's son, Dmitri. The four-footed company roster comprises about 150 cats, some shelter cats and others given to the company. An occasional dog (meow!) also takes the stage.

The troupe's tricks include tightrope walking, riding skateboards and bicycles, standing on their forepaws, rolling hoops and balls, jumping incredible distances, and other awe-inspiring feats. Some cats even accept being dressed in Russian folk costumes, which they wear while walking erect on their hind legs. Themed performances include *Prince Nutcracker and the Mouse King* and even a feline take on *Swan Lake*.

Trainers work with the cats for eight months to two years. Cats that display particular gifts for, say, jumping or rolling, are encouraged to do them on command.

Protect Against Rabies

RABIES IS A SERIOUS DISEASE that affects animals and can be transmitted to humans. It is critical to keep your cat safe from rabies for your own protection and for the safety of other people and animals that come in contact with your cat.

The most common carriers of rabies are raccoons, bats, and to a lesser extent skunks. These animals are nocturnal and usually come out at dusk. If a raccoon or skunk is in daylight, it can be a sign of sickness. Stay away, bring your cat inside, and call your local animal control officer.

To keep your cat safe:

- Keep rabies vaccinations up-to-date for all cats (and dogs and ferrets), especially if they could possibly encounter wildlife.

- Spay or neuter your cat to reduce his impulse to wander.

- Do not allow your cat to roam without supervision.

- Call your local animal control officer to remove stray animals from your neighborhood.

- Train and socialize your cat to reduce the risk of his biting a person or another cat.

- If you plan to travel internationally with your pet, contact the Department of State in your destination country to find out about health documentation requirements and quarantine laws.

Rabies is responsible for 55,000 deaths per year in the world, per the Global Alliance for Rabies Control. Preventive measures such as vaccination have greatly reduced the risk to pets and humans of contracting rabies, but it is still a serious concern.

Growing Catnip Indoors

CATS LOVE CATNIP, and growing your own is easy. Here is a brief tutorial to get you started.

Catnip (*Nepeta cataria*) is a member of the mint family and related to basil and oregano. It grows to about 2 to 3 feet (61 to 91 cm) high and has clusters of white or purple flowers. Catnip has a pleasant lemon-mint scent. The leaves, stems, and seedpods contain an essential oil that most cats can't resist. If you plant catnip in your garden, expect to see a stray rolling around in the garden once in a while.

The plants are available at many nurseries and garden centers, or they can be grown from seed after the threat of frost has passed. Catnip thrives in well-drained soil in a sunny location, but will also do well in partial shade. If your soil has a lot of clay, add a few trowelsful of sand to the soil as you're preparing it for planting to improve drainage.

Catnip is a perennial, so it will come back year after year once it is established. Like other mints, it can easily spread out of control and crowd out other plants because it reproduces by seed and by sending up new shoots from existing roots. You can help prevent rampant spreading by planting it in a container, then planting the container in the ground (this will confine the roots to the diameter of the pot), and by keeping the plant trimmed back and not allowing it to flower, thus preventing seeds from forming.

Trimming will also prevent the plant from getting "leggy" and encourage full, dense growth. When the plant has grown to 3 to 4 inches (7.6 to 10.2 cm) high, trim the stems just above the last set of leaves. This will cause the plant to start two new stems just above those leaves. Repeat this procedure through the growing season, allowing the plant to grow 3 to 4 inches (7.6 to 10.2 cm) between trimmings.

Harvest catnip when the flowers are just starting to bloom. Cut the stems a few inches (7.6 cm) below the flowers. Your cat can enjoy some of the bounty fresh, and you can dry the rest for later use. To dry, spread out the leaves and flowers on trays or hang them in a cool, well-ventilated area. Once they are completely dry, seal them in airtight bags or containers out of Kitty's reach. Dried catnip will maintain its potency for about a year, longer if you keep it in the freezer.

Humans use catnip, too, for herbal teas and in cooking. Practitioners of herbal medicine say it is good for treating cold symptoms and general aches and pains.

Birman

THE BIRMAN IS THE SACRED CAT of Burma, now called Myanmar.

Characteristics: The Birman has a silky, long coat that has a unique twist with regard to color. Although its ears, mask, legs, and tail are color-pointed, and its body may be creamy or silvery in tone, its feet are pure white. Birmans don't have exotic characteristics, such as a long nose or an angular body. They are broad-faced, with a Roman nose, and have a powerfully built, cobby body under all that fur. Except for their white feet, they share point colors with the Siamese.

A shorthaired cousin of the Birman that has developed in the United States is called the Snowshoe (see Day 299).

History: Burmese legend has it that in olden times, a temple renowned for its resident white longhaired cats was attacked by bandits, and one of the cats, named Sinh, jumped onto the head of the most venerated of the priests, Mun-Ha, to protect him. Although Mun-Ha died, the holy act produced colorpointing on the cat—except on its feet, which clung to Mun-Ha, and Sinh's amber eyes turned vivid blue. The cat stayed by the priest's corpse for an entire week. Then, Sinh died, and all the other cats of the temple instantly turned the same colors. They collectively selected Mun-Ha's successor among the priests by solemnly walking in a circle around him.

Fast-forward to 1919, when a British major named Russell Gordon and French explorer Auguste Pavie, who helped priests and their cats flee that very same temple to Tibet when it was again under attack, were given a pair of Birmans in thanks. The female cat was already pregnant, and that litter, reproducing in France, developed the breed in the West. Skeptics say, however, that the cats originated in France from crossbreeding a Siamese with black and white longhaired cats. Whatever the truth of the matter may be, cat associations in Great Britain recognized Birmans in 1966; in the United States, in 1967.

feline fun fact > The Birman is an entirely different breed from the short-haired Burmese, which also comes from Myanmar.

Birman

Cat Tricks: Roll Over, Stretch, Wiggle, and Squish

CATS OFTEN ROLL OVER AND STRETCH all by themselves. To turn this into delightful tricks, catch your cat in the moment and use verbal cues to identify the action.

Roll Over—Your cat may roll around on her back in sheer pleasure, or to wash a hard-to-reach spot. When she does a full roll, immediately call out enthusiastically, "[Name] roll over!" while making a small circle in the air with your hand. Do this whenever you can, as appropriate to each incident being a full roll.

Phase two: When she is already comfortably lying on the floor, begin to introduce the phrase as a command, complete with the gesture. Praise your cat any time she does the rollover for you: "Good [name] roll over!"

Phase three: When she has mastered phase two, ask her to roll over if she is not lying down, but sitting, standing, or walking, and praise her if she complies. Remember to praise her any time she rolls over spontaneously.

Continue to use the terms in context to reinforce the behavior, and work your cat to the point of doing it with either just the verbal command or the hand gesture.

Stretch—This is very much the same as rolling over, but entails catching your cat in a full-body stretch and identifying it verbally: "[Name] stretch," while stretching your own body, arms in the air, or using just a hand signal of opening a fist into wide-apart fingers. Repeat the phases as above, with these substitutions.

Wiggle—This is a cousin of the rollover command, only here you are watching to see your cat squirm happily on the floor. Identify it verbally, in the moment: "[Name] wiggle," while flopping a hand in the air, then reinforce as above.

Squish—You can command your cat to knead a soft surface. Use the above method, while she is already doing it, stating, "[Name] squish," while opening and closing your fingers from a fist shape. Once your cat masters this, she may even be willing to open and close her own fists in the air when she is lying down, in response to your verbal or hand command.

In all cases, be sure to praise your cat with a repetition of the correct command term when she obeys your order, to reinforce her having done the action correctly.

Choosing a Purebred Cat

IF YOU HAVE YOUR HEART SET ON a purebred cat, chances are you will need to go through a breeder. Common breeds such as Persians and Siamese do occasionally end up in shelters, but not often. To begin your search, first you need to decide which breed of cat you want. Friday breed descriptions in this book provide information that can help guide the decision.

Once you narrow down the vast cat kingdom and isolate a few breeds that interest you, talk to breeders and other owners who have experience with these cats. Many breeds have a tendency toward certain medical problems; what are they in the breeds you are considering? What are the personalities of those breeds like? What kind of grooming or other special care is required? How do these answers mesh with your lifestyle and budget?

After you decide on a breed, find a reputable breeder. Good breeders should be very knowledgeable about the breed and happy to answer any questions you might have. They should allow you to inspect their facilities and should be just as interested in evaluating you as a prospective owner as you are in evaluating them.

Above all, remember that an impressive legacy and prize-winning parents do not necessarily mean a good, healthy cat. Check out your new kitten to be sure she is healthy, friendly, and well adjusted before taking her home.

This Little Piggy …

MOST CATS HAVE FOUR TOES on each back paw, arranged in a line, and five toes on each forepaw, with four arranged in a line and the fifth offset, somewhat like a human thumb. This offset toe is called a *dewclaw*. Although the dewclaw is positioned like a thumb is on a human hand, it is normally not opposable and can't be used to grasp an object.

A common genetic mutation in cats sometimes results in cats with six, seven, or more toes. This condition is called polydactyly, and it is considered in most cases to be merely an anomaly, not a deformity. When it occurs, it almost always affects the forepaws and sometimes also the back paws, but rarely only the back paws.

Polydactyly is observed in cat populations all over the world, but is more common in some areas than in others, including the east coat of North America and southwestern Britain. Because it is a dominant genetic trait, it is easily passed on to a polydactyl cat's offspring. The offspring of Ernest Hemingway's cat colony in Key West, Florida, are famous for having an abundance of polydactyly.

Polydactyly generally doesn't cause any health problems, unless the toes or claws are malformed. Your vet will be able to tell you whether there is any cause for concern and will recommend treatment if it is warranted.

Shoo Away Fleas

A FLEA IS A SMALL, JUMPING, parasitic insect that lives by consuming an animal or a human host's blood. Fleas used to be considered merely a nuisance, but today we know they can carry diseases harmful to both humans and animals. These include plague, bubonic plague, pneumonic plague, and flea-borne typhus. When the flea bites its host, it can transmit whatever disease it may be carrying.

Cats aren't the only carrier of fleas, either. Other house pets, including dogs, as well as outdoor creatures such as squirrels, rabbits, mice, horse, chickens, raccoons, possums, and foxes—and even humans—are all possible hosts for fleas.

Fleas are similar to cockroaches in that they outlive and outlast most other insects. They are difficult to kill because of their four-stage life cycle and because they don't spend most of their time on their host, which makes the problem of locating them and wiping them out even harder.

Fleas have four stages of life, and at every stage they can lay dormant for several months. Female fleas lay about twenty eggs per day and up to six hundred in a lifetime. Eggs can be laid in animals' fur, carpeting, bedding, and even the family couch. Even your car and vacuum bag are attractive breeding grounds for them. Flea eggs typically hatch within two days to two weeks. In the first stage, the larva, the flea is blind.

Its food source is digested blood from adult fleas' feces, dead skin, hair, feathers, and organic debris. Fleas mature within a cocoon-type sac built with pet hair and carpet fibers. In anywhere from five days to two weeks, an adult flea emerges. Now the hunt for a host begins, so it can find its first meal and begin growing.

When trying to eliminate fleas, it's not just about the animal; it's also about your living environment, your mode of transportation, and your outdoor facilities. In addition to treating your cat, you will have to pay close attention to these areas, to keep the flea situation under control. For your car and couch at home, try sprinkling some borax powder into your carpet and on your furniture. It is most important to keep your cat's sleeping area clean and free from fleas at all times.

Be careful using do-it-yourself flea treatments. Read and understand the directions before starting. Many of these products can be harmful to you and your cat if not used correctly. If you have a severe flea infestation, hire a professional exterminator, who will be able to recommend the safest and most effective course of treatment for your particular situation, inside and out.

Compile Vital Stats in a Cat Binder

COLLECTING ALL OF YOUR CAT'S important health and contact information into a sturdy three-ring binder makes it easy to keep track of all her paperwork and notes. You can tote this binder with you to the vet, or leave it as a manual for the cat sitter.

Binders with clear plastic pockets on the outside allow you to personalize it with your cat's name and photo, or you can choose a beautiful leather version or a fun and colorful design. Use plastic page protectors to preserve important original papers and tab dividers to organize the sections. Loose-leaf paper is handy for keeping notes.

Here is what you should keep in your binder:

- A current photo of your cat (handy if she gets lost)

- Your cat's name

- Your name, address, telephone number, and other contact information

- Your vet's name, address, telephone number, and other contact information

- Your animal hospital's name, address, telephone number, and other contact information

- Written directions to the animal hospital (you don't want to get lost if there is an emergency)

- The name, address, telephone number, and other contact information for an emergency contact, should you be unavailable

- City or county registration numbers, paper licenses, and other government paperwork

- Breed information and registry papers, if your cat is a purebred

- Type and amount of cat food she eats

- Feeding schedule

- Vaccination records

- Type and amount of any medications she takes regularly

- Records of illnesses and vet visits

- Microchip type and registration number and contact information for the registrar (in case you need to change your contact information)

- Names and contact information for cat sitters

- Notes on any special things a stranger caring for your cat should know; for example, "doesn't like catnip," "doesn't like her belly to be touched," "prone to escape through the side door," or "likes to hide under the sofa"

Bombay

THE JET-BLACK, SATINY APPEARANCE of the Bombay sets it apart from all other domestic cats.

Characteristics: Bombays have a round face, with amber to copper eyes, the latter being the most prized color. Their fur is very short and they shed very little. Whatever skin leather can be seen, on nose and paws, is pure black.

History: The Bombay was developed in the United States in 1958, when a brown Burmese was mated to a black American Shorthair. The all-black kittens had Burmese-type super-short fur, and a new breed was born. The name was chosen because of the cats' resemblance to the panthers of India; had they been born a few decades later, they might have been known as Mumbais!

For a while, confusion reigned in the show world over how pure this breed was, because Bombays continued to be mated with American Shorthairs rather than among their own separate breed.

Genetics sometimes skew the classification of offspring in another way: Some Bombay kittens are born deep brown rather than black. To this day, some cat registries balk at allowing the brown ones to be shown as Bombays. The breed was accepted into American cat associations in the 1970s, but Great Britain has dragged its feet in this regard.

feline fun fact > The Bombay's coat color is so striking that in some U.S. cat shows, fully half the award points concern the pure blackness of the fur.

Bombay

Story: On Being a Foster Mom

MY HOUSE FELT COMPLETELY EMPTY. After having two cats for more than a decade, hearing the pitter-patter of eight paws and the banter between the longtime sibs, a house without cats was simply not home.

I began volunteering at Public Animal Welfare Society (PAWS) shortly after I solved my empty-house problem and adopted two cats. They were bottle-fed, extremely sociable, and thank goodness, accepting of other "visitor" cats. I've hosted plenty of them since their homecoming.

I was a foster mother to fifteen cats during a high point, though usually I care for an average of four (not including my two cats and dog, also adopted from foster homes). I never would have imagined setting up cat condos in my home to cater to homeless cats. But that's exactly what I do. I have fostered kittens, feral cats, a pregnant mother, and other homeless felines I simply can't turn down when the agency asks me to give them shelter. They must have pegged me for a sucker. They were right!

PAWS is a grassroots organization that finds foster homes for homeless cats, then carefully screens adoptive parents, matching families with appropriate pets. Our return rate is low, and the community's need for our service is tremendous. We cannot save every cat, and we certainly will not find a warm home for every stray on the street. But we can make a big difference for the cats we do foster, and for the families who welcome a new pet into their homes.

Fostering is not for the faint of heart. I wasn't sure how I would handle taking in cats, caring for them, and then giving them away to another family. I had never experienced that sort of temporary love, though I realized pretty fast that my heart would just keep getting bigger and bigger—more room for more cats. I decided right off the bat to dedicate a room in my house to fostering. For the most part, I keep my house cats separate from foster cats. By not integrating foster cats into my pet family, I have been able to tend to them like a nurse, giving them medicine and food and love.

Only a couple of times did I wane from my self-imposed duties. I kept the mother cat I found in my backyard. Her social behavior improved dramatically, and I integrated her into my home. I worried about her fate as a potentially undesirable adoptee for families, so she's mine now. There have been extended-stay incidences, times when foster cats live here so long I wonder what will happen. But eventually, they get what they've deserved all along: a loving, permanent home.

In a way, I feel like I'm still mother to the cats who live here, even if only for a week . . . I care for them, raise them up, then proudly say goodbye when it is time for them to move on. Fostering cats is tremendously fulfilling. And between my volunteer work at PAWS and my own pet family—now three cats and a loyal dog—I never experience a quiet house. And that's a good thing.

Cat-Proof Your Home

WE'VE ALL HEARD THAT SAYING, "Curiosity killed the cat." Even the best-maintained household contains dangerous items that could hurt or poison your cat. Here is how to keep Kitty safe:

GENERAL TIPS

- Protect electric cords and unplug small electronics when not in use. Cords and plugs can be blocked by objects or encased in dedicated materials available in hardware stores. Use childproof covers for unused outlets, if necessary.

- Discourage Kitty from sitting atop electronic devices such as stereo or video equipment, heaters, and so on, which could overheat if vents are blocked.

- Use candles only with human supervision.

- Store plastic bags and bags with handles out of Kitty's reach, as well as rubber bands, twist ties, thumbtacks, paper clips, staples, erasers, and all other items small enough to be ingested.

- Put away scissors, knives, razors, craft blades, and other sharp objects that your cat might chew on or bat around.

- Store all drugstore items, potpourri and essential oils, cleaning materials, toiletries, and cosmetics out of reach of your cat, preferably in a latched cabinet.

- Keep cat-friendly plants only (see Day 269). Be careful about using cut, dried, or artificial plants, which Kitty may chew.

- Take extra care when selecting holiday decor (see Day 242).

- Put away batteries and small electronics that contain them (such as hearing aids). Batteries contain chemicals that are very dangerous to a cat's insides!

- Secure windows so that your cat cannot squeeze through even a small opening. Use screening, screwed into place if necessary, to keep Kitty inside. See Day 130 for more about preventing "high-rise syndrome."

- Block off unsafe areas, such as rooms where painting, repairs, or construction is occurring.

- Create at least one cat-free zone if you can, either if the room is too hard to cat-proof or you would like a place where you can work undisturbed on crafts or other activities.

KITCHEN

- Store foods and beverages in closed containers, cabinets, or the fridge, especially those that could make your cat ill (see Day 178).

- Keep your trash in a bin your pet cannot open, and empty it often. Carefully dispose of used food wrappers and Styrofoam containers; your cat may try to chew on them.

- Clean up spills. Do not leave soapy water or cat-unfriendly food/drink in dishes or pans sitting in the sink.

- Feed your cat from dishes, not opened cans, whose sharp rims could cut Kitty's tongue.

- If your cat raids cupboards or has learned to open the fridge, install childproof latches or hooks to keep the doors closed.

- Turn pot handles toward the inside of your stove top, and use protective covers for your stove's control dials if your cat can easily reach them. Teach your cat not to sit immediately next to the burners.

- Consider shutting your cat out of the kitchen (if possible) if you are doing any high-heat procedures, such as deep-frying.

BATHROOM

- Put away ribbons, hair elastics, and other such items that your cat may attempt to ingest.

- Don't share hot or herbal/toiletry-scented baths with your cat.

- Keep your toilet's lid shut!

- If you use the bathroom to launder your clothing, shut your cat outside the room if anything has been left to soak.

OTHER LIVING SPACES

- Avoid using electric blankets and pads with inner wires that can shock a cat's claws.

- Be particularly careful with craft items, such as needles and pins, sewing thread, yarn, beads, glue, paints, and chalks. If your cat is nearby while you work on a craft project, know where such materials are at all times and put them away immediately or bring them with you, if you are called away.

- Do not let Kitty play with yarn, thread, or cut fabric that can ravel easily—a swallowed length of thread is sharp and can kill a cat! (If your cat has swallowed thread or yarn, bring him to the vet immediately without attempting to pull it out by its end!)

- Avoid decor that includes cords, fringes, beading, or other edible decorative elements. Remove them or tie them well out of reach of Kitty.

- If your cat likes to chew on wool, vinyl, rubber, or other materials, be mindful of what substances rugs, furniture, and soft furnishings are made of, and take measures to protect or replace them.

- Absolutely do not use naphtha or other chemical insect repellents, or traps/poisons to kill vermin. Use natural, cat-safe herbal mixtures only.

THE GARAGE, BASEMENT, AND OUTDOORS

- Carefully store such materials as antifreeze, petroleum products, paint, cleansers, and so on, as well as sharp tools, nails, and screws. Clean up spills of such substances or objects.

- Use all-natural insect/vermin preventives and lawn-care products.

- Always check that your cat is not inside a washer or dryer before turning it on. Shut washer and dryer doors when not in use.

- Protect any dangerous areas your cat could climb into/under/behind, such as openings in walls or ceilings, behind large electronics, and so on. Be especially careful with any heated units your cat might want to snuggle against or into, such as a furnace.

- Check that Kitty is not trapped in the garage before you shut its door.

- Check that fencing or open drains do not have openings of a size a cat could wedge into and get stuck.

Guardian Angel

SOME PEOPLE BELIEVE CATS HAVE special psychic powers or extra senses. In 2007, a gray and white cat named Oscar rocketed to fame worldwide for a special ability that is a mixed blessing: He knows when someone is about to die.

From kittenhood, he has lived in Rhode Island's Steere House Nursing and Rehabilitation Center for people with Alzheimer's and other forms of dementia. The staff began to notice something very odd about Oscar's relationship with hospice patients. Just like the human staff, he would circulate among the rooms, checking up closely on everyone—but when he would curl up to a particular patient, that person would die within the day.

Oscar has correctly predicted patients' last hours at least twenty-five times, outstripping the nurses and doctors' abilities in that capacity. And he is not a lap cat, either; ordinarily, he is not a cuddler. Yet, if he is shut out of the room of a dying patient, he is distressed, wishing to be let in to lie beside the person.

His behavior is so accurate that the nurses know to call an individual's family if he appoints himself to that man or woman's bed.

So, what draws Oscar to the terminally ill? Staffers guess that something changes about a dying person's body chemistry—and therefore, his or her scent—which only Oscar is able to detect. Whatever the case, the patients Oscar consoles in their final hours are grateful for the companionship. Only one family demanded his removal from their loved one's room.

In geriatrician David Dosa's article about the cat's special gifts in the *New England Journal of Medicine*, the daughter of a woman being tended by Oscar explained it thusly to her young grandson: "He is here to help Grandma get to heaven." To have a concerned cat snuggling close, keeping vigil by your side, must surely be a comforting, rather than grim, way to go.

The Importance of Playtime

PLAY IS ESSENTIAL TO YOUR CAT'S HEALTH—and your sanity. A bored cat will find ways to "keep busy," and those activities generally result in a frustrated owner. If you've ever returned home to find that your cat used the dining room table to sharpen his claws, or decided the heirloom grandfather clock was more interesting than his scratching post, then you understand that cats need quality exercise to stay out of trouble.

Besides the "good kitty" factor, exercise will improve your cat's circulation, stimulate vital organs, aid digestion, and eliminate harmful toxins from the body. Your cat will feel mentally stimulated and physically satisfied after a quality play session.

Aim to exercise your cat for ten minutes, four times each day. House cats especially require dedicated playtime because they don't burn calories and stimulate their feline instincts by roaming outdoors. It's your job to stoke their curiosity and challenge them with games. A great time to exercise your cat is before mealtime. This way, you cater to your cat's natural cycle: hunt, kill, eat, groom, sleep (see Days 90 and 91). Playtime is your cat's modern-day hunt-and-kill activity.

Not sure where to start? Begin by stocking your kitty's toy chest with safe, stimulating options (see Day 10). Cats love things that dangle, bounce, and move—these actions require chasing and pouncing, which are cats' natural instincts. Use a laser light to rouse a napping cat, or purchase a remote-controlled mouse. Even Ping-Pong balls and wads of crumpled paper are a thrill. The key is that you're involved in the play.

Provide a couple different scratching posts and perches throughout your house so Kitty can play when you're not home.

Cats get a kick out of pawing and pouncing after items dangled from fishing line. Rig your own toys by tying an object or a cat toy to a length of string. Play hard-to-get, and tug on the string and drag the object around the house. You lead—your cat will follow.

Facial Pheromones Can Prevent Scratching

PHEROMONES ARE CHEMICALS produced by scent glands on your cat's face, near his anus, and on his paw pads. Cats use these chemicals as a way of marking their territory and communicating with each other. Facial pheromones, produced along your cat's chin and on his forehead, have a calming effect on cats. Cats rub their chins on the corners of walls, chair legs, and other protruding objects to mark them as friendly territory and communicate comfort.

Synthetic facial pheromones mimic the effects of natural facial pheromones and are available in spray form or in plug-in diffusers. By marking territory (furniture and other hot spots for scratching) with man-made pheromones, your cat catches the scent and associates these areas as already marked. Your cat will determine the territory is "comfortable" by his standards, and will not feel the need to scratch or rub against the object.

Research has shown that cats tend not to urine mark or scratch objects that have been marked with facial pheromones, so spraying them on furniture and other objects may help reduce or eliminate these problems.

Sprays are also useful when traveling. Use the spray on the inside of the carrier to help keep your cat calm. Treat an entire room with a pheromone diffuser. These can be a lifesaver when moving to a new home or introducing another pet to the home. Be sure to follow the manufacturer's instructions carefully.

Cats don't really "smell" pheromones in the way that humans think of smelling. A chemoreceptor structure called the vomeronasal organ, or Jacobson's organ, detects pheromones and other nonvolatile compounds (such as the nepetalactone in catnip). This organ is located near the palate and is part of the accessory olfactory system in cats.

British Shorthair

WHEN ROMAN INVADERS WENT ON conquering missions, they brought their cats along. And those felines were a shorthaired breed now two millennia old. Today, the cats are called British Shorthairs.

Characteristics: This sturdily built, round-faced shorthaired cat took on just about every color and pattern, including colorpoint, thanks to mating with various feral cats that already lived in northern Europe. Tabby markings are very common in this breed. They make calm and loyal companions.

Although the British Shorthair has long appeared in cat shows in the UK, it was not registered in the United States until 1970, and only then in the solid blue original color. Since then, the U.S. registries have expanded to include other colors and patterns of this breed.

History: Perhaps this cat should really be called a Latin Shorthair, because it dates back to Roman times. Who knows why the Romans brought cats on their tours? Perhaps the cats were taken north as a kind of feline equivalent of the Trojan Horse, to terrorize British mice into submission. Whatever the case, the cats remained while the Romans were in northern Europe, for four hundred years, and long stayed their original color, too: solid blue.

feline fun fact > Artist-writer Harrison Weir (see Day 303) championed the British Shorthair and made sure this cat was shown prominently in the very first UK cat competition in 1871.

British Shorthair

Resetting Your Cat's Nocturnal Body Clock

YOUR CAT IS A NIGHT PERSON (er, animal). When the clock strikes midnight, he's on the prowl, ready to play, prance around the house, or exit your abode to find some nocturnal adventure. Well, maybe his clock isn't so precise that an alarm goes off at the stroke of twelve, but after snoozing away the daylight hours, he's bound to feel restless at some point.

You can retrain your cat to be a day-lover (morning cat—that's pushing it). First, understand a cat's natural "program" of events: hunt, kill, eat, groom, and nap. In our modern world, that translates to play/pounce, belly up to the food bowl, lick and preen, then fall asleep a happy cat. (Not a bad life, eh?) Here's how to reset your cat's body clock so he performs these activities during daylight hours, avoiding all that nighttime racket. The key is to start this cycle in the early evening so his nap and your bedtime coincide.

• Remove food bowls in early evening so you can serve a before-bed meal to your cat. (Remember, after eating comes grooming and then *napping*.)

• Play interactive games in the evening so your cat can hunt and kill—then eat once you replace his food bowl.

• Your cat should groom following his dinner, then settle in for a nap just as you're ready to tuck in to bed. Prepare a bowl for midnight snacking in case your cat wakes. Do not succumb to his 2 a.m. cries for playtime. He will eventually learn that it's lights-out until morning.

Taking In a Stray Cat

HER PITIFUL, MEEK MEOW just melts your heart. She's skin and bones, but has a sweet face. You can tell this stray has been fending for herself on the streets for some time. You left the garage door open and in she went. You want to gather her up in your arms and take her inside, give her a bath and a gourmet kitty meal. This baby deserves some serious TLC.

The only problem, well there are several: You already own two cats, and this little stray doesn't come with medical records attached—she may carry a disease such as feline AIDS (FIV) that would fatally harm your indoor cats. You're a socially conscious cat lover, but taking in this stray could be a very bad idea.

Before you jeopardize your household, think "safety first." What are your intentions, here? Do you want to adopt the cat and assimilate her into your home? Do you simply want to make sure she gets medical care and is spayed? Regardless, the first step will be to "trap" her, which sounds inhumane, but you're more or less reeling her in to your care. Do this by placing food in the spot where she knows meals are plentiful, if you've already been offering; if not, place food inside a crate near the spot where you found her. When you see the cat go inside to eat, close the crate door. Provide food and water for her inside the crate, and call the vet immediately.

Your first priority is a thorough checkup for Kitty. She'll need to be checked for internal parasites, rabies, ringworm, fleas, and serious disease such as FIV (feline AIDS). If she is not spayed, either ask your vet to perform the procedure or take the kitty to a shelter or a pet vaccination clinic for a lost-cost or free spay. Commonly, stray cats present with rhinotracheitis, which is feline herpes, a respiratory tract infection that can lead to more serious disease.

If the stray is immunized, spayed, and perfectly healthy aside from the need for human attention, you may decide to adopt her into your home. If you do, there is the issue of acclimating the cat to the other feline veterans of the household (see Day 123). This is a gradual process. Be prepared to put your cat up for adoption if the union between existing cats and this newbie simply will not work. (Remember, who was there first? There are many loving homes that would benefit from adopting a feline friend.)

If you decide not to keep the cat, you can enlist her in a foster program as an alternative to taking her to the shelter; or find a no-kill shelter. If you do decide to welcome the stray into your home, you join a hearty population of cat owners who, when asked how they got their cat, say, "She just showed up one day and decided this was home."

The Colorful Cats of Andrew Lang

SCOTTISH-BORN ANDREW LANG (1844–1912) is best known today for his variously hued collections of fairy tales and folktales from around the world, including his retellings of "Puss in Boots" and several Grimm stories. He wrote several others about cats; all can be read at www.mythfolklore .net/andrewlang/indextitle.htm.

- "The Cat's Elopement" (*The Pink Fairy Book*) is a Japanese tale about two neighboring cats, Gon and Koma, who love each other but are separated by fate.

- "The Colony of Cats" (*The Crimson Fairy Book*) is about a group of cats that rewards a poor girl, Lizina, for living with and taking care of them.

- "The Clever Cat" (*The Orange Fairy Book*) is adapted from a Berber tale, and tells of how said cat, in loyal service to his master, defeats an ogre.

- In "Kisa the Cat" (*The Brown Fairy Book*), an Icelandic story, a princess has been reared with Kisa, a kitten, as her "sister." When the princess grows up, a giant attacks and abducts her. But Kisa appears to care for and ultimately rescue her . . . which breaks the spell that the cat has been under. She, too, turns out to be a princess.

Water Works

CLEAN, FRESH WATER IS ESSENTIAL to life. Water helps prevent many diseases, including kidney and bladder problems, and it flushes out cats' systems, aiding in digestion. Cats will drink about 1¼ to 2½ tablespoons (20 to 40 ml) per pound of body weight per day. This includes water taken in with canned food.

If you notice your cat not drinking enough water (a litter box examination will give clues) or consuming more than normal, he may suffer from urinary blockage (male), an infection, or polydipsia that can snowball into more serious medical conditions such as kidney failure. Carefully monitor your cat's water intake.

If he seems uninterested in the dish you provide, consider experimenting with different dishes or water bowl locations. Try a shallow bowl if your cat won't slurp water from a deep vessel. He may refuse to drink water from a double dish that has compartments for food and water. (Heaven forbid a food chunk spill into his drink.)

If your cat drinks from the bathtub or toilet, but not his dish, he probably prefers running water. You can purchase fountains that provide a steady flow of clean, filtered water. Look for one with adjustable flow rates that is tip-proof and easy to dismantle for cleaning.

Otherwise, be sure to refresh kitty's water bowl several times each day. Also, clean the bowl with soap and warm water daily to prevent bacteria growth.

Training Kitty to Stay Off the Counters

CATS LOVE TO PERCH UP HIGH so they can survey their kingdom and keep an eye on their subjects, even if the kingdom is your living room and you are his subject. Unfortunately, "up high" often includes your kitchen counters. That's not pleasant or sanitary for you, and it's not safe for your cat to be up there with the appliances and the hot stove top. How do you keep him off the counters?

First, provide an alternate perch for your cat if there is room for one. A window ledge or cat tree will allow him to see the area from an approved spot while staying out of your way.

Next, make it unpleasant for him to jump onto the counter. Lay out pieces of cardboard side by side to cover the countertops. Apply wide double-stick tape all over the top of the cardboard. Cats hate stickiness on their paws, so if your cat jumps up, he will immediately jump right back down.

The cardboard "trap" is inconvenient for a couple of weeks, but you can move it out of the way when you need to use the counter and put it back when you're done. If Kitty regresses and returns to the countertop to perch, return the cardboard.

This reminder will refresh his memory and he'll find a cat-appropriate place to hang out.

If you catch your cat in the act, use a spray bottle on "stream" to squirt him, and say "no!" in a low, quiet voice. This is most effective when he can't see where the water is coming from—that is, when he doesn't know that you're the one doling out the punishment. Use this method as a complement to the sticky-cardboard trick.

A third method involves setting up empty cans or other easily knocked over items on the edges of the counter. The bang and clatter of falling cans will scare your cat. Unfortunately, the noise also tends to scare people and other innocent animals. Unless you have nerves of steel, proceed with caution and set up this trap while you are away for the day, relying on alternative keep-off methods for nighttime.

Training your cat to stay off countertops takes time—don't rush it. Give your cat plenty of time to learn the lesson that being on the counter is unpleasant, and he won't want to go up there again.

Burmese

ALL BURMESE CATS TRACE BACK to a single brown shorthair who lived in Rangoon, now known as Yangon. Her name was Wong Mau, and in 1930 she came to the United States, where Dr. Joseph Thompson introduced her to a seal point Siamese. They produced a mixed litter of Siamese and brown kittens. Mating these latter offspring to each other or to their mother equally produced more brown kittens, and the breed began. (Others, which were dark and had colorpointing, led to the emergence of the Tonkinese breed; see Day 320.)

Characteristics: The Burmese is round-faced, with very short fur. In the United States, the only colors accepted in competitions are champagne (a warm beige), platinum (a pinkish pale gray), brown, and blue; other countries permit not only other solid colors but also various tortie tones. (The Malayan is an early term for a Burmese with blue, chocolate, or platinum fur, and is no longer in use by registries.)

The British body type is a little more exotic than the American one. Some modern U.S. Burmese are being bred to have a flatter face, more like a Persian's (this can cause facial deformities such as cleft palate and it is not to be encouraged).

The Burmese is the ideal house cat, tolerant of children and so friendly that it would not survive well outdoors. They love company and live best with a companion cat if you can't be there to serve their emotional needs.

History: Although the Burmese was recognized in the mid-1930s, after eleven years passed, the breed was pulled from registration in the Cat Fanciers Association (CFA), after pressure from Siamese cat breeders who objected to the very brief lineage as being just crossbred Siamese. In 1956, with a few generations of purebred Burmese down the road, the cats were again allowed to enter U.S. shows. Meanwhile, after being introduced into Great Britain in 1947, the Burmese began to branch out into other colors than brown, and then in the 1980s a crossbreeding of Burmese with Chinchilla created the new breed called Burmilla (see Day 103).

feline fun fact > Burmese are so sociable that the males often participate in raising their mate's litter—the "house husbands" of the feline world!

Burmese

Journal Prompts, Part I

FILL UP THE JOURNAL YOU CREATED on Day 25 with more memories. Here are some writing prompts to stoke your creativity:

- How did you celebrate your cat's first birthday?

- What interesting "finds" has your cat presented as a gift to you? (When was the last time you set a mousetrap, thanks to your feline's successful stalking?)

- How did your kitty respond to her first bath?

- How does your kitty "talk" to you when she wants to express happiness, hunger, sadness, frustration, or a need to be alone?

- How do your multiple cats communicate with each other? Which feline is in charge, and how can you tell?

- How did you pick a name for your cat, and what were some runner-up names that didn't make the cut? What do you think about those names now? Would you choose a different name for your cat after getting to know her personality better?

Choosing a Collar

COLLARS ARE MORE THAN JUST A PLACE to hang your cat's ID tag. The wide variety of collars available today let you make a fashion statement to fit your cat's personality.

Nylon webbing is a popular material for cat collars, but other choices include leather, vinyl, cotton, hemp, and elastic. Collars come in an extensive variety of colors and patterns. They can be adorned or decorated with everything from rhinestones to metal studs to faux fur and more. Before purchasing a collar with decorations, check to make sure they are securely attached so that your cat can't scratch them off.

The collar should fit around your cat's neck snugly, allowing enough room to comfortably slip two fingers underneath.

No matter which material you choose for your cat's collar, make sure it is designated a "safety collar" or "breakaway collar." These collars are designed to stretch or come undone if the collar becomes hung up or entangled. Although this feature means you lose the collar and whatever tags are attached, your cat will be able to free himself quickly and safely if he gets stuck on a fence or tree branch and avoid strangulation.

Cats in Classic Literature

CATS NOT ONLY BOUND THROUGH but abound in classic literature. Here are some entertaining examples:

- Lemuel Gulliver feels threatened by a Brobdingnanian (giant) cat in Jonathan Swift's *Gulliver's Travels* (1726), but the cat is actually more frightened of him!

- Elizabeth Gaskell's novel *Cranford* (1851) contains a hilarious passage concerning the attempts by several women to retrieve an accidentally lapped-up piece of valuable lace that had been left to soak in a bowl of milk, to wash it.

- Charles Dickens's *Bleak House* (1853) contains three feline characters, Lady Jane, Mr. Jellyby's cat, and Mr. Vohles's cat.

- *The Master and Margarita* by Mikhail Bulgakov, published in 1973, includes in its cast an enormous black cat named Behemoth, who can talk and play chess.

- P.G. Wodehouse compiled two cat stories into a 1933 collection, "*The Story of Webster*" and "*Cats Will Be Cats*," about the cat Webster and his owner Theodore, a bishop. Theodore sends Webster to live with his nephew Lancelot as a sobering influence on the young man, but Webster returns as dissipated as Lancelot!

- Anne Frank (1921–1945) lived in hiding during World War II with Mouschi the cat, who is chronicled in her famous diary as having had problems with a lack of fresh peat to use for litter.

- American author-editor Peter Gethers's very doglike gray tabby Norton, a Scottish Fold, not only starred in numerous books, beginning with the 1991 *The Cat Who Went to Paris*, but also "authored" *Historical Cats* (1996).

Cats Are Prone to Vomiting

CATS VOMIT MORE THAN MOST PETS, and they do so for different reasons. Hairballs are the most common trigger (see Day 52), but there are many other reasons why your cat may vomit. Sometimes, vomit is not a cause for concern—particularly if your cat chowed down on a bowl of kibble as if he were eating his last meal. If he inhaled his meal a little too fast, his body will remind him to digest. Mother cats may vomit food to give their kittens a predigested meal. This is a natural instinct, and not a red flag that she has gastrointestinal parasites.

You'll know by watching your cat whether her retching is cause for concern. She will look anxious, salivate, and swallow repeatedly. She may pace, or come to you for reassurance and comfort. Call your veterinarian if food is not the reason for your cat's vomiting. Watch out for these warning signs that intestinal parasites, or worse, may be the cause:

- Persistent vomiting
- Sporadic vomiting over a period of days or weeks
- Vomiting blood
- Vomiting feces (sign of intestinal obstruction or abdominal trauma)
- Projectile vomiting
- Vomiting foreign objects

If yours is a multicat household, you feed from a communal dish, and your kitties tend to vomit postmeal, some cats may be overeating. Separate your kitties at feeding time, serve individual portions, and dish out smaller meals. That way, they won't rush to get their share and suffer the digestive consequences.

The Sleepy Cat

WHEN YOUR CAT IS NOT EATING, grooming himself, or playing with his catnip mouse, chances are he's sleeping. Most cats sleep twelve to sixteen hours a day, or more.

Cats are crepuscular, meaning they are most active around dawn and dusk and less active in the middle of the day and the middle of the night. They alternate periods of activity and sleep throughout the day, rather than sleeping in one long stretch. The term *catnap* didn't come from nowhere!

Cats have different stages of sleep, just like humans. Slow-wave sleep is a light sleep. His breathing slows and his muscles relax a little, but he is still somewhat aware of his environment and is easily awakened by the sound of the can opener or the tweet of a nearby bird.

Cats spend about three-quarters of their sleep time in slow-wave sleep and the remainder in deep, rapid-eye-movement (REM) sleep. During REM sleep your cat's eyes move rapidly back and forth. His muscles relax more fully and his breathing slows even more during this critical, restorative period of sleep. In humans, REM sleep is dream sleep, and many experts believe that cats dream, too, during this phase of sleep (see Days 111 and 112).

Waking a cat while he's in deep sleep can provoke a swipe of the claws, so avoid startling him awake with a sudden touch. It's best to leave your cat alone until he wakes up on his own.

Burmilla

THE BURMILLA WAS A GENETIC ACCIDENT, produced in the UK in 1981 when a Chinchilla and a lilac Burmese had a litter that produced four kittens with a silvery coat tipped with black or brown. The owner was so taken with the youngsters' appearance that she encouraged the breeding to continue among her cats.

Characteristics: The body type and face tilt a bit toward the exotic, even while the cat has a muscular, solid body. Like the Burmese, its fur is very short. But unlike the Burmese, its fur is tipped with a darker tone, especially along the spine, and the tail and upper legs usually exhibit tabby stripes. There are often vertical marks above the eyes, separated by a V-shaped patch of darker fur or additional stripes. The eyes are normally green.

Like their Burmese ancestors, they crave company and make affectionate house cats.

History: Although Burmilla cats appear in cat shows that permit unregistered mixed breeds, and they achieved championship status in Great Britain during the 1990s, the Burmilla still awaits full recognition as its own breed with American and other European cat fanciers.

feline fun fact > The super-smart Burmilla is especially adept at opening doors and cabinets to seek objects to play with.

Burmilla

Teaching Children to "Play Nice" with Kitty

CHILDREN LOVE PETS, especially cuddly kittens that are the right size for small hands to hold. Sharing the responsibility of pet ownership with your children can be a valuable experience for them and take some of the load off of you. But don't be fooled by your child's insistence that she'll take care of *everything*, as long as she can have a baby cat to love. Adopting a pet is a family decision. You, ultimately, will be responsible for vet bills, health care issues, supplies, food, and so on.

Before you bring home your new kitten or cat, hold a family meeting and discuss what caring for a cat requires. Help your children understand the responsibilities by relating care and training to their own experiences. Explain that kittens are like babies, and the whole family will help care for this new family member. Pet ownership will provide a lifetime of memories for your children. The key is to set boundaries and assign responsibilities so children understand that Kitty is more than a toy—she's a part of the family that requires care and attention, too. Establish ground rules before Kitty comes home so everyone is prepared. Hold a family meeting and review these key points:

- Discuss the litter box (and why it's important to keep out).

- Explain that your kitty may need private time so that your children don't take your cat's independence personally.

- Discuss how to handle the kitten, and depending on the age of your children, you may need to supervise all kitty–child contact.

- Create a schedule or assign a responsibility to your child, whether it is setting out food at a certain time of day or making sure the water dish is full—little things that give children a sense of ownership.

- Look through cat books together, and discuss different cat traits. Talk about body language and how to tell when Kitty wants to play or be left alone.

- Drive home key points by relating a cat's behaviors to the child's own: "Sometimes you don't want Mom to come into your bedroom because you are busy playing. Kitty will feel that way sometimes, too."

Choosing the Right Cat Litter

IN THE WILD, CATS ELIMINATE WASTE in sand or soil and then bury it. A litter box mimics this natural environment indoors. Historically, litter boxes were filled with ashes, sand, or soil. Today, there are many more sanitary choices available.

Litters come in two basic types: clumping and nonclumping. All litters require at least daily scooping for solid wastes. Many come in scented and unscented versions as well as multicat, low-dust, and nontracking formulas. Although some litters are marked as being flushable, many plumbers advise against flushing any kind of cat litter.

Clumping litters form solid clumps when liquid is introduced, which makes scooping easy. When the litter level gets low, just add more to the box. The downsides to clumping litters are that the particles are very small and thus tend to scatter, and some kinds can be dustier than traditional litters. Be sure to keep clumping litters far away from your cat's food and water. Any kind of moisture will cause it to clump and expand, and you don't want it clumping in your cat's digestive system. This type of litter must be changed and the box cleaned every three to four weeks.

Nonclumping litters come in several varieties. With these litters, liquid wastes are absorbed by the litter and remain in the box until the litter is changed. Thus it is necessary to change and clean the box often, usually weekly.

Traditional clay-based litters have been around the longest and tend to be the least expensive of all the litter options. Clay litter can create a lot of dust, although low-dust options are available.

Silica-based or "crystal" litters are similar to traditional clay-based litters, minus the dust. They are the least like what cats are naturally inclined to use, however, and your cat may need some coaxing to use it.

Plant-based litters are made from pine, wheat, corn, or paper. These are the most "green" of the litter options, because they are made from recycled materials or by-products and are biodegradable. These produce little dust and are the least likely to be tracked around the house.

Veterinarians recommend using unscented, nonclumping clay litter for kittens until they are six months old. Otherwise, you simply need to experiment until you find the litter your cat prefers. Those with hypersensitive noses may not like scented litters because of the smell; those with tender paws will probably not like crystals that can irritate sensitive paws; and cats who lick their paws often may not do well with clumping litters.

Regardless of the type of litter you choose, the litter box should be emptied, scrubbed, and refilled regularly—how often will depend on the type of litter used. Cats will not use a foul litter box, and will choose to do their business elsewhere if they encounter one.

Hey, Diddle, Diddle, and other Nursery Rhymes

Hey, diddle, diddle, the cat and the fiddle,
The cow jumped over the moon.
The little dog laughed to see such fun
And the dish ran away with the spoon.

—Traditional nursery rhyme

CATS ARE WELL REPRESENTED IN traditional nursery rhymes. How many of these do you remember from your days of reading children's books, or being read to? If you have little kiddies—or kitties—of your own, enjoy quality time reading aloud. Here are some favorites:

- Old Mother Hubbard, went to the cupboard, to get her poor dog a bone. In the full-length version of this famous poem, she does quite a bit of shopping, in the course of which she visits a hatter who is too busy feeding his cat to serve her!

- On the other hand, the hapless kitty in "Great A, Little A" is, itself, shut inside a cupboard.

- That fate is perhaps still better than what happens to the cat in "Ding-Dong-Bell," in which Little Johnny Green puts Pussy in the well. Luckily, Little Tommy Stout comes along to pull her out.

- In "Pussy Cat, Pussy Cat, Where Have You Been?" the cat goes to London and there performs a vital service for the queen: catching a mouse he finds beneath a chair (apparently, even royal households had a problem with vermin!).

- Remember the poem about the crooked little man who lived in a crooked little house? He had, you guessed it—a crooked little cat . . . who caught a crooked little mouse!

- Perhaps the cat who makes out best in these little tales is the title character in "Pussy Cat, Pussy Cat, Wilt Thou Be Mine," who is promised that she will do no labor but sit on silk, sew, and eat strawberries with cream and sugar.

Preventing Heartworms: A Fatal Parasite

A SINGLE INFECTED MOSQUITO'S BITE is all it takes for an unprotected cat to get a fatal disease. Mosquitoes are heartworm carriers. If they bite an infected animal, young heartworms called microfilariae enter the mosquito's system. Larvae develop inside the mosquito, and these can be transmitted the next time a mosquito bites another animal.

Heartworms are deadly to cats and dogs, but cats usually do not have microfilariae circulating in their blood. Therefore, it's not a likely that a cat will transfer heartworms to another mosquito. Instead, cats get the parasite directly from mosquitoes, which sucked up the dangerous microfilariae from an infected dog. The parasite is more commonly found in dogs, but because of the comparatively smaller size of a cat's heart, a single adult heartworm can wreak havoc. The good news: *You can protect your cat against heartworms and avoid this parasite completely.*

Symptoms: Because common signs of heartworm infestation are similar to other illnesses, the disease is often not discovered until advanced stages. Your cat may cough and experience respiratory distress or vomiting. Unfortunately, these same symptoms also point to less serious diseases that are easily treated with medications. A cat can suddenly die from heartworms if live heartworms enter pulmonary arteries and obstruct blood flow to the heart, or if heartworms attack the lungs and shut down a cat's respiratory function.

Diagnosis: Diagnosing heartworm in cats is more difficult than in dogs. Your vet will perform antigen and antibody tests. The antigen test only detects female heartworms, so its results are not 100 percent accurate. The antibody test determines whether the cat's immune system has been exposed to the parasite. However, cats with heartworms in places other than the heart (pulmonary arteries, lungs) will test positive in an antigen test. Both tests are necessary to confirm diagnosis of heartworms. Additionally, cats can be tested for normal white blood cells, but this is also not a surefire way to detect heartworm presence because normal white blood cell count is elevated for only the first few months of infestation, and cats with allergies or intestinal parasites also have a higher than normal white blood cell count. X-rays and ultrasounds may be used to detect the size of pulmonary arteries—bloated arties can indicate parasitic presence. With these methods, a vet may actually see heartworms in the cat's body.

Treatment: There is currently no safe and effective medical treatment aside from anti-inflammatory medications or surgery to remove the heartworm.

Prevention: If your cat is not currently taking preventive heartworm medication, get him tested, even if he shows no signs of sickness. Your vet should test your cat annually for heartworms just to make sure he is not infected. FDA-approved monthly heartworm preventives advised by your veterinarian will not eliminate the heartworm infection if it already exists, but it will protect a cat from heartworms.

Hiding Places

CATS LOVE COZY HIDING PLACES, and they're always seeking out new spots to nap. Don't get too worried if you don't see her for a while. She may have found a new secret hiding place where she can enjoy some privacy. However, if your cat misses mealtime or doesn't respond to the rattle of her favorite toy after a couple of tries, she could be stuck somewhere or hiding out because she's sick. That's your clue to start scouring the house. Here are some common hiding spots:

- Under or behind large pieces of furniture, such as beds, sofas, armoires, and chests of drawers
- Inside cabinets
- Inside low drawers, especially those containing clothing or linens
- Behind curtains
- Under blankets or bedclothes
- Under pillows on the bed or sofa
- Behind doors
- Inside boxes or bags
- In the bathtub
- In the space behind the drawer and the back panel of a chest of drawers
- Under the dining table on a chair
- On top of a cabinet or tall piece of furniture
- Inside a reclining chair mechanism
- Behind the toilet (especially on a hot day)

Some hiding places can be dangerous. Always check inside the clothes dryer and other large appliances before closing the door and inside a reclining chair mechanism or sofa bed before closing it. If your cat goes outdoors in cold weather, always knock on the hood before starting the car; cats will sometimes crawl up into the engine compartment for warmth.

California Spangled

WITH A NAME LIKE "California Spangled," one would almost expect such a cat to have sequined fur.

Characteristics: This handsome newcomer to the feline community looks like a jungle beast crossed with a sweet little tabby. The medium-size cat has a wild posture, close to the ground, and an unusually blunt-tipped tail. Its short fur comes in a broad range of tabby colors, from gold through bronze, red, and brown, to charcoal and black. In all cases, the cat is prolifically spotted, with close bars around its legs and tail, and the classic tabby *M* on the forehead. Its eyes tend to be amber.

The California Spangled's complex family tree has worked to its favor to produce highly intelligent, strong cats. Despite its wild appearance, the Spangled has no wildcat blood, and is an affectionate household cat—assuming you can afford to bring it home.

History: The breed was the brainchild of scientist Paul Casey, who, after ten years of interbreeding among eight standard breeds, including Abyssinian and Siamese, produced in the early 1980s the beautiful striped and spotted markings that have become standard to the Spangled.

Early examples of this cat were so expensive and rare that in 1986, the famed Neiman-Marcus department store offered a pair of California Spangled in its "His and Hers" Christmas section, each cat at that time costing more than a thousand dollars. In that same year, the California Spangled was accepted for registration in the United States.

feline fun fact **>** Regardless of whichever color later develops, every California Spangled kitten is born black!

California Spangled

Is Your Cat Dreaming?

CATS CAN SNOOZE MOST OF THE DAY—they never hesitate to make themselves comfortable, whether that means stretching out on a cozy comforter or tucking into a peaceful ball of fluff. Cats enter light sleep and intense REM cycles, when the brain is active and their body responds accordingly. Their paws flex, claws extend and retract, their kitty whiskers twitch, and they mumble softly in meow-gibberish. Cats spend about 30 percent of their sleeping time in deep sleep, when dreaming occurs.

What could your cat be dreaming? Consider his basic instincts. While our house cats aren't wildly chasing down prey, the paw movement in their dreams could be your cat pouncing on his victim.

Cats remember past experiences, and these can surface subconsciously during sleep. This is a good thing, actually. Dreaming is vital to a cat's health. It's a time for data processing and memory storage, for mental replenishment and brain development.

There's great temptation to wake your cat during REM sleep, especially when he is thrashing his paws or meowing as if he's in a heated debate with the family dog. Our natural instinct is to "save" the cat from the bad dream by consoling him: Here, here, mommy's right by your side. Despite activity taking place in the room, a cat in REM is not easily awakened. If you do choose to wake your cat from a nightmare, do so gently by petting him and speaking in a calm, reassuring voice.

Your Cat's Age in Human Years

INDOOR CATS, PROTECTED AGAINST the elements, disease, and predators, typically live fifteen years or even older, which in human years means that they can live to eighty or beyond!

Here is how Kitty's age compares roughly with that of humans:

feline fun fact > The oldest cat ever was Cream Puff, who reached the age of 38. That's 144 in human years.

AGE IN YEARS

CAT	HUMAN
1	15
2	25
3	29
4	34
5	38
6	42
7	46
8	50
9	54
10	58
11	62
12	65
13	69
14	72
15	75
16	78
17	81
18	84
19	87
20	90

Controversy: Melamine in Cat Food

A NUMBER OF UNUSUAL CASES of illness and death in dogs and cats have been linked to pet food. This calls to attention the importance of reading labels and purchasing the highest quality pet food you can afford (see Day 115). In particular, various U.S. Food and Drug Administration investigations have uncovered shipments of wheat gluten and rice protein imported to the United States from China that were contaminated with melamine.

Melamine is a nitrogen-rich industrial chemical used in creating plastics, fire retardants, fertilizers, and colorants, among other things. Because nitrogen is used as a marker for protein content in food product testing, melamine is sometimes illegally added to low-quality food products to make them appear to be higher in protein than they really are.

Although it appears that trace amounts of melamine may not be harmful to humans or animals, the amounts being used in the protein stocks, especially in combination with cyanuric acid, another contaminant, were enough to cause poisoning and in some cases kidney failure and death.

Affected pet foods have been voluntarily recalled in North America, Europe, and South Africa. The contaminants were traced to two protein suppliers in China. Allegedly, the use of melamine to boost protein test readings in food products is an "open secret" in China, and Chinese government officials were at first slow to respond to the crisis.

As a result of the crisis, the FDA has toughened requirements for inspection reports and reporting incidents of contamination.

Canned Food versus Dry Food

DRIED CAT FOOD IS CONVENIENT. It requires no refrigeration and it's easy to scoop out and serve—no gunk, no mess. But is dry food the best option for your cat?

Commercial brands of dry food typically contain about 10 percent water, which means your cat must consume more water to compensate. Wet food can contain as much as 75 percent water, which is an essential element for a cat's bladder and kidney health. Ultimately, you must decide whether your cat drinks enough water freely, and if not, wet food is probably your best bet.

What's more, dry food has a higher magnesium content, which has been connected with FUS (see Day 122).

Dry food has a high degree of fillers. Read the label. Toward the top of the ingredients list, you will find grains such as soy, wheat, corn, and rice, and perhaps even cellulose—wood fiber. Cats that are on a total dry food diet, in essence, are eating carb-heavy diets, which is extremely unnatural for cats. A dry cat food may have as much as 400 percent more carbs than the same flavor in wet food.

Also, think twice before feeding Kitty any products that contain wheat, which is an ingredient in many canned foods with meats shaped into flakes, chunks, or other textures. In unclean manufacturing operations, wheat can be contaminated by melamine, a plastic substance toxic to cats (see Day 114).

Ultimately, you should design your cat's diet around what he would eat in the wild, with modifications to suit modern lifestyles, of course. Cats thrive on meat-, poultry-, or fish-based diets, with only a small amount of grains and vegetables. Avoid gourmet foods gussied up with herbs, vegetables, fruit, and sauces, meant to appeal to *your* sense of sight and smell. Try to avoid dyes, as well; there is no nutritional reason for your cat's food to be colored bright yellow, orange, red, or green; and, to eat it, Kitty will be guided by his sense of smell, not color.

As you evaluate your cat's diet, consider these important points:

Vitamins and minerals: Read your pet food's fine print. A healthy adult cat needs about 30 calories per pound (455 g) of body weight—just ⅓ ounce per pound of cat (or 9 g food per 455 g) of dry food daily, or about 1 ounce per pound (28 g food per 455 g) of canned. (A kitten, pregnant/lactating female, or elderly or ill cat may have special needs; always discuss the diet of such cats with your vet.)

Key ingredients: A quality food should contain real meat, poultry, or fish near the top of its ingredients list, about 20 to 25 percent of the total food content, with few or no grain fillers, few or no plants, about 10 percent fat (which even heavy cats need), and a solid list of feline-friendly vitamins and minerals. Pure fish cat foods, such as tuna or sardines, are fine for an occasional treat, but they lack the vitamin and mineral enrichment of blended flavors. Too much tuna can actually make Kitty sick (see Day 178). Avoid cat foods made with meat or poultry by-products, which can be indigestible refuse, such as beaks, ground bones, and so on.

Alternative diets: Discuss raw food diets thoroughly with your vet, including the question of supplements such as probiotics, and make sure any raw meats you give Kitty are organic, absolutely fresh, and cut into small pieces (do not give your cat packaged ground meats). If you feed your cat cooked non-pet-food meats, such as roasted chicken, give Kitty a feline vitamin and mineral supplement so he doesn't miss out on essential nutrients such as calcium and taurine.

Avoid giving your cat semimoist food and commercially made treats. Pet treats are molded and dyed into artful shapes designed to appeal to humans, and are rife with meat by-products, cereals, and preservatives that are harmful to your pet.

Kitty's First "Mouse"

TINY KITTENS APPRECIATE SOFT, safe toys to cuddle with. This simple-to-make knitted or crocheted "mouse" may well become the toy that your little one carries everywhere and sleeps with during its first few months.

If you don't knit or crochet, this project is a perfect opportunity to learn the basics. A craft book, an online tutorial, or a patient friend can get your needles and hooks clicking in no time. The gauge of the piece doesn't matter. Just be sure to select a smooth wool, acrylic, or cotton yarn; avoid metallic, nylon, or designer yarns with flakes or protruding fibers that could be chewed off or scratch Kitty's mouth.

A "tail" is deliberately excluded from the pattern to prevent your kitten's attempting to ingest it, so please consider your pet's safety and do not add one. Likewise, a solid filler is used instead of polyfill fluff, which could drift out and be eaten if the fabric is punctured. Catnip, unsuitable for young kittens, is not a component of this toy.

MATERIALS

Leftover medium-weight (worsted) yarn (2 grams or less)

1 pair knitting needles, size 6 (4 mm), if knitting

Size F/5 (3.75 mm) or smaller crochet hook, for both knitting and crocheting

Scissors

2 pieces cotton quilt batting or terry cloth (from an old towel), each cut into a square ½ inch (1.3 cm) narrower and ½ inch (1.3 cm) shorter than the knitted shell

Straight pins (optional)

To knit:

1. Cast on 25 stitches.

2. Row 1: Knit.

3. Row 2 and all subsequent rows: Knit (garter stitch) until the piece measures as long as it is wide. The back and front will be identical.

4. Cast off. Snip off the start/end yarns to be no more than 1 inch (2.5 cm) long.

5. Go to "To assemble."

To crochet:

1. Crochet a chain 4 inches (10.2 cm) long.

2. Turn and single crochet across.

3. Chain 1, turn, and single crochet across.

4. Repeat step 3 until the piece is square. Snip off the start/end yarns to be no more than 1 inch (2.5 cm) long.

5. See "To assemble."

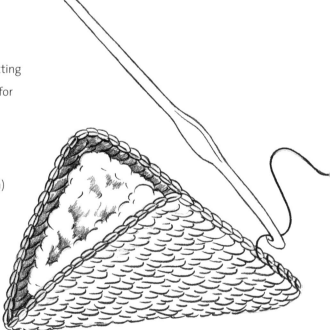

To assemble:

1. Layer the two pieces of batting atop the knitted or crocheted shell, like an open-faced sandwich of two slices of cheese on bread, and then fold on the diagonal, yarn side out, to form a triangle.

2. Holding the folded layers firmly, use a strand of leftover yarn and the crochet hook to single crochet the toy closed from one long point of the triangle around the short point to the other end, to seal the filling inside the toy. Tuck in the snipped yarn ends as you go. (If it is difficult for you to hold the toy together while you crochet, use pins to keep the triangle closed. Remember to remove all the pins afterward!)

3. Clip the crochet yarn strand to within 1 inch (2.5 cm) of the toy, then use the crochet hook to draw it tightly beneath the knitted surface.

Toss to Kitty and enjoy!

Chartreux

MEET FRANCE'S NATIONAL CAT, whose lineage in that country dates back roughly half a millennium. Also known as the "Monastery Cat," this blue shorthair was kept by monks to keep down the rat populations at their monastery, the Grande Chartreuse, located near Grenoble.

Characteristics: Modern-day European litters of Chartreux may contain a variety of short- and longhaired blue kittens, and as a result of all this tampering, this breed is not yet accepted in British registries. In North America, however, there has been greater interest in maintaining the purity of the original French cat, and it is registered there. The French-style Chartreux is stocky and strong, with a range of solid blue fur barely tipped with silver. The eyes are deep amber.

History: The cat's ancestry goes back to the medieval period, when the cat came north from the Middle East on the ships of traders or returning Crusaders. The first modern breeders were sisters, surnamed Léger, who lived in Brittany, where they came across an entire community of naturally purebred Chartreux on the island of Belle-Isle-sur-Mer. Seizing upon this perfect pedigree, the sisters bred and showed them, beginning in 1931.

Chartreux

feline fun fact > The super-dense fur of the Chartreux is water-repellent.

What Your Cat's Ears Are Telling You

YOUR CAT HAS VERY SENSITIVE EARS, capable of hearing about two more octaves higher than yours do. This sensitivity developed so she can detect the presence of mice, birds, and other potential treats, as well as to hear the voices of her kittens. A cat's hearing is so refined that it can judge to a fraction of a second the difference in reception of a noise from one ear to the other, to focus on the exact location of the source. The outer ear can rotate a full 180 degrees to focus on a sound, thanks to ten separate muscles. The same fine-tuning enables your pet, say, to notice while catnapping upstairs the moment you begin to use the can opener downstairs in the kitchen, or to tell from the sound of your car door—not any others' along the street—that you are about to enter your home.

The positioning of a cat's outer ear, called the pinna, says a lot about what a cat is thinking. You can tune in to these ear signals and learn whether your cat is angry, happy, or ready to play defense. Here are a few:

Flattened backward-facing ears indicate an angry cat. The more aggressive the cat, the flatter the ears. This gesture heightens your cat's ability to hear.

Ears flattened sideways is the protective gesture of a cat that is on the defensive or submissive. A frightened cat's ears will be fully flattened toward the sides, to protect its delicate organ.

Erect, alert ears that are cupped forward indicate a happy cat.

A radarlike swivel repositioning can be visible if your cat is trying to identify a new situation or even think through something that is puzzling her. A cat who is feeling confused or uncomfortable may lower her ears to stand out more to the side, looking a bit like the *Star Wars* character Yoda; some reassurance from you may bring them upright again.

Sometimes a cat who has used a paw to wash her ears will forget to flip an inverted ear back into position. Feel free to help out, gently.

Your Cat's Bone Structure

YOUR CAT'S ANATOMY IS UNIQUE to her species, right down to the bone structure deep beneath her fur. Here are some of its interesting features.

Head and throat: The inside of Kitty's nose contains a tightly clustered range of curled bones just above her palate called *turbinates*. These help refine her acute sense of smell (see Day 148 for more about the connection between taste and smell). At the back of the throat, the tongue hangs like a swing from cords of tiny bones called the *hyoid apparatus*. In big wildcats, such as the lion, this area is also encased in a layer of cartilage whose reverberations permit such creatures to roar. All cats, large and small, have very broad cheekbones, which support their powerful jaw muscles.

Torso: Kitty's spine is built for flexibility, especially in the lumbar area between her rib cage and pelvis. This allows her to arch her back, twist her body sharply sideways, and so on. However, in the hip area, called the *sacrum*, the vertebrae are fused together, forming a rigid pelvis. Cup your pet's back just above where her tail begins and you will feel it. (See Days 69 and 70 for more about the tail.)

Chest: Your cat has thirteen pairs of ribs, which are set like rounded bellows along the front of the spine. Look closely: When Kitty breathes, they expand sideways rather than pushing forward toward the belly.

This detail is important in case you must ever give your cat CPR (see Day 290). Your cat has only a vestige of a collarbone. Instead, the ribs and front legs are held together by muscles, which enable Kitty to land from jumps without jolting her vital chest organs.

Legs and paws: A cat's front legs are surprisingly comparable to humans', except for the paws, of course. The rear legs attach to the hips with a ball-and-socket joint that allows for tremendous range of movement; watch how your cat prepares for a spring. The front paws have at least five fingers (some cats have more, called *polydactyly*), the thumb, or *dewclaw*, appearing higher up the leg. Cats have only four toes on each rear leg. The claw of each toe is like a human's fingernail, except cats retract theirs just as a roll-up garage door fits into its frame. Your cat can voluntarily extend or retract her claws. (See Day 127 for more discussion of the skin of your cat's paws, and Day 323 for information about trimming claws.)

Understanding your cat's anatomy will, quite literally, help you recognize her strengths and weaknesses. Wonder why your cat can sniff out a smelly can of tuna from a mile away? Thank her turbinates, which put a human's taste buds to shame.

Famous Cat Haters and Cat Lovers

Cat. *n.* a soft indestructible automaton provided by nature to be kicked when things go wrong in the domestic circle.

　　　　　　　—Ambrose Bierce (1842–1914)

SOME WELL-KNOWN PEOPLE JUST plain hated cats!

Julius Caesar (100–44 BC)
Queen Elizabeth I (1533–1603)
James Boswell (1740–1795)
Giacomo Meyerbeer (1791–1864)
Emily Dickinson (1830–1886), who was distressed that her sister Lavinia's many cats killed birds
Benito Mussolini (1883–1945)
Adolf Hitler (1889–1945)

Others not so much hated as were terrified of them:

French kings **Henry III** (1551–1589) and his brother, **Charles IX** (1550–1574), both of whom would faint at the sight of a cat!
Napoleon Bonaparte (1769–1821)
Alphonse Daudet (1840–1897)
Turkish sultan **Abdül Hamïd** (1842–1918)

On the other hand, there were famous people who adored cats:

Confucius (551–479 BC)
Cleopatra (69–30 BC), who owned a cat named Charmian
Thomas Wolsey (1475–1530), who brought his cat to audiences
Louis Pasteur (1822–1895)
Sarah Bernhardt (1844–1923)
Ellen Terry (1847–1928)
Maurice Ravel (1875–1937), who had a penchant for Siamese cats; his favorite was named Mouni.
Albert Einstein (1879–1955)
Albert Schweitzer (1875–1965)

See Days 324 and 282 for government/religious leaders and literary figures who were feline fanciers.

feline fun fact **>** Rudyard Kipling's "The Sending of Dana Da," in his 1888 collection *In Black and White*, is an amusing a story in which a cat hater was plagued by cats turning up at every imaginable opportunity.

F Is for Feline Diseases

CAT DISEASES ARE NASTY BUSINESS. Their complicated names can be confusing, so here's the scoop on which F is which.

Feline panleukopenia, also known as *feline distemper* or *feline infectious enteritis* (FIE), is caused by a virus. The germs, emitted by an ill cat in his excrement, can live for months at ordinary room temperature; another cat will be infected by oral contact with those wastes or areas they have touched. Although antibiotics may have success, this virus is often deadly, and so its prevention is part of the standard vaccination that vets offer cats against several diseases. This illness attacks the cat's white blood cells, which impairs the cat's immune system. Symptoms may include high fever, vomiting and diarrhea, and weakness. In a pregnant cat, the virus can cause miscarriage or fetal abnormalities.

Feline leukemia virus (FeLV) also affects the cat's immune system, but in a very different way. This is a retrovirus, meaning that the cat's immune system is tripped into attacking the cat's own body when germs are present, leading to a repressed immune system or even the growth of tumors. The disease can lurk undetected in the cat's body and cause health problems down the road. The virus can be passed to other cats via saliva or mucus. FeLV can be prevented by vaccination.

Feline immunodeficiency virus (FIV) is also known as *feline AIDS*. It resembles human HIV but cannot be transmitted to humans. FIV attacks and suppresses the cat's immune system and, like human HIV, can appear dormant for weeks to even years. Then the virus erupts and reduces defense against infection.

The cat does not die of FIV itself, but ultimately of a secondary or an opportunistic infection or tumor that cannot be checked. The virus cannot survive outside the cat unless it enters the bloodstream of a new host. Therefore, apart from contracting it in utero from an infected mother, your cat runs no risk of FIV unless bitten by another cat.

Feline infectious peritonitis (FIP) is caused by a coronavirus. It is very rare, but can be easily spread via cats' body fluids (saliva, urine, stool). There are two varieties, wet and dry. Wet causes fluid to build in the chest and belly, making it difficult to breathe; dry causes pus cells to form in the digestive organs, interfering with the cat's ability to process food. FIP is preventable by vaccination.

Feline urologic syndrome (FUS) refers to several disorders: bladder stones (urolithiasis), urinary tract infections, and urethra blockages. The cat may urinate outside her box or be unable to urinate (and may even appear bloated), or may pass blood in her urine. Any such symptom requires swift treatment to combat infection and restore the normal flow of urine. Your vet may recommend flushing the kidneys with intravenous fluids and/or a diet low in magnesium and high in acid-producing ingredients.

If your cat is an "only child" reared from birth with virtually no contact with other cats or the outdoors, all the above, except for FUS, are highly unlikely to develop. All other cats need to start immunization in kittenhood.

Managing a Multicat Household

WHY CAN'T THEY ALL JUST GET ALONG? Even a harmonious multicat household has its fair share of upsets. Cat "siblings" can develop strong bonds and become best pals, and even so they'll disagree—sometimes aggressively. Then there are cat sibs that can't be in the same room without hissing or instigating a fight. They want nothing to do with each other, ever.

Consider yourself the landlord, the mother cat in charge of this big, happy cat family. Set some ground rules and take time to properly introduce new cats to the clan. Watch for bullying, and know when to intervene if cat play turns into foul play. Here is some advice for maintaining a sane household. We can't promise that all your cats will get along, but they can learn how to be civil.

CAREFUL INTRODUCTIONS

Welcome new cats home gradually. Cats are territorial creatures. And despite claims that cats are independent and not pack animals, try throwing a new feline into the mix without proper introductions and you'll argue that notion. A two-week introduction process with gradual, supervised "meetings" between new cat and the in-house crew eases stress for everyone. Read more about this on Days 8 and 22.

REDUCING DAILY STRESS

The key to avoiding cat spats is to accommodate cats' need for space, privacy, and resources (litter, food, water). If you provide one community food dish and one litter box, the dominant cat may claim these as his territory. If your cats lived in the wild, they would go their separate ways. The key is to provide various territories so each cat can have a small piece of its own turf.

- Set two food bowls in the kitty eating area, and contain the dominant cat for a short time during mealtime if he scares away timid cats.

- Provide two (or more) litter boxes. A dominant cat may leave his waste uncovered to mark his territory. Some cats demand private litter boxes. Observe behavior and set up litter stations to accommodate everyone.

- Create territories with hideouts, cubbies, and perches with many levels. Tall cat trees and cat gyms allow cats to observe their territory from high up, which they prefer.

Cornish Rex

THE SLIM, BAT-EARED CORNISH REX has delightfully wavy fur, a joy to stroke. The curly fur first appeared as a spontaneous mutation, proving that accidents can be a good thing.

Characteristics: This breed has no guard hairs, resulting in its super-thin coat. The fleecy fur comes in all colors, including colorpoint, and is waved everywhere on the cat's body, right down to the tip of its barely furred, pointed tail and wavy whiskers. The Cornish body type is distinctive: long legs, and a curved back and concave belly. The head is small, with a wedge-shaped face, making the cat's eyes and ears look enormous.

It is a myth that the Rex cats do not shed; if allergies are a problem, consider another breed. All Rexes have a slightly higher than usual body temperature but still, because the fur is so short, keep this cat indoors if you live in a cool climate.

History: The product of two domestic shorthairs, this new kitten's shock of wavy hair reminded the breeder of the coat of the special rabbits she also raised. Careful breeding ensued to repeat the effect. The Cornish Rex is the predominant variety in the United States, though American Rexes were crossed with Oriental breeds such as Siamese, creating a variety of physical differences from the British-born Rexes. That's why there are separate classifications for these felines. The U.S. cat registries began to accept the original Cornish Rex breed into their books in 1979.

feline fun fact > The Cornish Rex is very playful and is especially adept at batting at and fetching objects.

Cornish Rex

Story: Preying for Feathers

MY CAT, ERNIE, HAS A THING FOR BIRDS. If he spots one, his ears perk up, his senses sharpen, and his back stiffens ever so slightly. He's on the prowl, but he forgets that he doesn't have wings. His attempts to track down high-flying prey generally leave him frustrated. But for Ernie, it's the thrill of the chase.

One afternoon, I watched Ernie chase a bird in the backyard, and I thought I'd make things easier on him.

I had been cleaning out the house and was about to throw out a genuine feather pillow. The contents were just the reward Ernie deserved! I tore open the pillow at the seams and poured the fluffy feathers into a pile in the yard. Ernie leaped into the down fluff like a child jumping into a pile of leaves. He was in heaven for at least an hour. I couldn't think of a better way to recycle an old pillow.

Your Cat's Skin

THE SKIN BENEATH YOUR CAT'S SOFT coat can shed light on his behavior. For instance, a cat can stand comfortably on hot or cold surfaces, thanks to his leathery paws.

Your cat's skin is very loose on his frame, to provide him with extra flexibility and keep him warm. A cat's skin does not contain any fat, just two layers: the outer *epidermis* and the inner *dermis*. The periodic dropping off of renewing skin cells is what produces dander, a strong allergen for some people.

Cats' skin is similar to our own in some ways. Like ours, a cat's skin is also colored with melanin; the more of this substance the skin contains, the darker it is. But unlike people, cats get a "reverse tan" when they spend lots of time outdoors: A light-colored cat has protective elements in his skin that protects him from the sun, but if he spends a lot of time outdoors, he will actually have lighter skin than an indoor cat of the same fur color. Otherwise, the more melanin, the darker the skin.

Bicolor and striped/spotted cats may have colored areas on their skin, including inside their ears and mouth. If your tabby has brown or black patches on his palate, that is entirely natural. Their paws and nose can range from pale pink to taupe, gray, or brick color, all the way to black. And some cats even have toes of several different colors.

Can your cat sweat? Yes, indeed. The leathery pads of his paws contain highly concentrated eccrine glands that produce moisture if he is hot or agitated. If your cat is leaving damp footprints in hot weather, that's your cue to cool him down.

Other sweat glands prevent fur from drying out. When your cat rubs against surfaces, he is actually marking the spot with tiny secretions called *sebum* from these sweat glands. Sebum is also important for capturing vitamin D from the sun.

Will you notice your cat sweating? Most cats don't appear to have sweat on their fur, but the nearly hairless Sphynx and some very short-haired breeds benefit from periodic wipe-downs to remove oils that gather on the skin's surface.

Cats and Witchcraft

THE DARKER SIDE OF CAT HISTORY involves feline persecution. Yes, we're talking witches, and cats were presumed instruments of evil and sorcery. It was believed that witches were assisted by, could ride on, or could transmute themselves into various animals called *familiars*, and cats topped the list of animals suspected of having such magical qualities. Moreover, cats had a long association with paganism, thanks to their being worshipped in ancient Egypt (see Day 219). Various northern European non-Christian rites, such as witches' Sabbaths, often included cats as sacrifices or symbols; practitioners of devil worship used parts of cats' bodies as ingredients in their brews. It didn't help matters that cats are not mentioned in the Old Testament of the Bible.

The Middle Ages was a time when natural disaster and disease were not understood. Forget about animal psychology. Cats took the blame for all sorts of natural disasters and disease, probably because people noticed cats' sensitivity to weather and the environment. They believed cats must be able to see
the future . . . that the cat was actually a shape-shifted witch.

In 1566, the first witchcraft trial was held in England, during the reign of Queen Elizabeth I (who hated cats). Several hundred witch trials followed within the next several decades, often involving lone or elderly women who happened to live with a cat.

In some cases, the women themselves claimed that their cats could do fantastical things, possibly as a result of the accused witches having had hallucinations from misuse of herbs such as henbane, or even ergot poisoning from contaminated grain.

Well into the 1600s, especially in England, cats were hunted down and burned alive, and suspected witches were drowned in sacks along with their cats. In England, executions of convicted witches continued into the early 1700s. Witch hunts occurred across the continent of Europe as well.

Group hysteria and mob mentality also plays its part in cats' dark history. Shrove Tuesday became a festival day for stoning cats; cats were enthusiastically hung for Lent; and in France, Saint John's Eve was another excuse to murder cats, on that date by means of a bonfire. In Paris, such cat burnings were attended with great pomp by kings.

Today, many people hold superstitions about cats (see Day 16). Many of these beliefs date back centuries, and we keep tidbits of these stories alive by reminding ourselves not to cross the path of a black cat (bad luck). Black cat owners would strongly disagree.

What You Can Catch from Your Cat

IF YOU HAVE THE FLU, GO AHEAD and kiss your cat—he can't catch it. Very few infections can be passed interspecies from humans to cats or vice versa. They are called *zoonotic* illnesses.

The bad news is that the following feline infections could make you ill or even kill you, so it is important to review the list:

- **Rabies**—This potentially fatal disease makes its host's nervous system go haywire and produces excessive salivation, resulting in a vicious, biting cat if the animal is experiencing an active case. A cat may be a carrier without showing any symptoms at all, so even a fleeting nip by a normally good-natured cat is suspect. Read more about rabies on Day 73.

- **Pasteurella**—Causes swelling and inflammation of a bitten area and beyond, which can set in dramatically in a matter of hours

- **Campylobacter enteritis**—A disease of the small intestine; causes severe diarrhea as well as fever and head- and body aches

- **Dysgonic fermenter-2**—Present in the saliva of about 10 percent of cats; can cause illness in people whose spleen has been removed or who have impaired immunity

- **Cat-scratch fever** (bartonellosis)—A mild illness caused by bites or scratches by an infected cat

- **Chlamydiosis**—An upper respiratory and eye infection that can cause conjunctivitis in humans if droplets of saliva or nasal mucus come in contact with the eyes

- **Lyme disease**—Transmitted by ticks that may hitch a ride on your cat's skin; this disease can have serious consequences in an infected person

- **Plague**—Borne by fleas originating on rats, humans can contract it either from a fleabite or from the saliva of a cat who has been infected with plague pneumonia

- **Q fever**—A disease of rural areas, primarily of cattle, but can also be transmitted by inhalation of materials associated with a cat's giving birth, which causes pneumonia in humans

- **Rocky Mountain spotted fever**—Another potentially fatal, tick-borne illness, treatable by antibiotics

- **Salmonellosis**—Cats ingest the salmonella germ via contaminated food or drink, including what they may raid or capture outdoors. The bacteria are transmittable to humans via his excretions.

Cats and humans may share fungal infections or parasites, leading to additional woes. Those include ringworm, giardiasis, toxoplasmosis, and worms (hookworm, roundworm, tapeworm). Avoid transmission with a proper flea control regimen, safe food handling, and hygiene regarding cleaning water bowls, food areas, and litter boxes.

The Apartment Cat

CATS ARE IDEAL APARTMENT COMPANIONS—high-rise, townhouse, no matter what your dwelling, cats can accommodate because they don't need outdoor access for bathroom trips, and they are perfectly happy staying indoors, as long as you keep them entertained with perches and scratch posts.

Cats are quiet, aside from some meowing and an occasional yowl. They're self-cleaning and fairly self-sufficient. They're just not as messy as dogs and other pets. In a way, cats are neat freaks of the animal kingdom, with their fastidious grooming. Many landlords agree, which is why you're more likely to find an apartment complex more accepting of a cat than a dog. (This is also why some dog lovers convert into cat lovers—logistically, feline pets make more sense for individuals who rent.)

Before you move into an apartment building, get the cats-allowed policy in writing. You may be required to pay a monthly pet fee or an additional security deposit. Before moving in, do a damage inspection and make sure the landlord signs a record of pre-existing conditions. Because you will be sharing your apartment with a pet, you can more easily be blamed for wall scratches and carpet stains.

If you will be living above the ground floor, make sure your windows have secure screens to prevent "high-rise syndrome"—your cat's jumping or falling out and injuring herself. And, if you intend to keep Kitty an indoor cat, screen even ground-floor windows.

After you move in, respect that your landlord's flexible pet policy isn't license to let Kitty run free. Be a good neighbor. Never allow your cat to roam the building.

Transport her through the building on a leash (if this is acceptable to other tenants) or in a crate. Ideally, your cat should be spayed or neutered. (This will prevent "spraying" in male cats, which you don't want to deal with in an apartment situation.)

Clean the litter box daily so odors don't leach into the building's hallway. Because you're probably living in close quarters, vacuum regularly and de-hair upholstered furniture (see Day 263) to remove dander that can be overwhelming in small spaces. Speaking of room, your cat will desire privacy and play. Provide these necessities with kitty hideouts and scratching posts. Your indoor cat needs stimulation to stay healthy and happy—and so your apartment remains damage-free.

Finally, recognize that a cats-allowed policy does not mean you should pile a shelter's worth of pets into your apartment unit. Managing a multicat household in close quarters is tricky because of cats' need for personal space. It's really best to keep one or two cats if you know they will be contained in a modest-size apartment.

Be honest with the landlord. Sneaking a cat into your apartment won't be kept secret for long, and you and Kitty may both lose your home. A landlord that does not have a pet policy in place may be able to make concessions for your cat, if you come clean about the living arrangement.

Cymric

THE MANX CAT HAS A longhaired cousin, the Cymric (pronounced KIM rik). Its name is derived from the word *Cymru*, the Celtic term for Wales.

Characteristics: Like the Manx, the Cymric may be entirely tailless, known as a "dimpled rumpy." A "rumpy riser" has a tiny bit of palpable tailbone yet no tail emanates from it. If there is a little bit of tail, that makes the Cymric a "stumpy." One with an almost normal tail is called a "longy." (Only rumpies and rumpy risers are presently acceptable as show cats.) Cymrics have a silky double coat that plushly covers a cobby body whose front legs are on the short side, giving the cats the effect of having their rump in the air (whether they are a rumpy riser or not!).

A litter may produce kittens with a broad range of tail lengths, even of full length, depending on the genes of both parents. Likewise, if both parents are Manxes with a recessive gene for long hair, they may be surprised with shaggy Cymric kittens. On the other hand, tragically, stillborn kittens will result if the embryos inherit the Manx gene from both mother and father.

Probably due to excessive inbreeding, other Cymric kittens may be born not only tailless but also with spinal bifida. Because of such genetic flukes, surviving litters of healthy Cymric cats tend to be small and thus, that much more precious.

History: Although this breed is said to have originated in Canada in the 1960s, when a litter of Manxes included longhaired siblings, the recessive gene was actually traced back to the Isle of Man. The breed is believed to be a spontaneous mutation that may have occurred after a Norwegian Forest Cat or other longhaired cat decided to visit the British Isles and met up with an attractive Manx.

feline fun fact > Cymrics can have a rabbitlike hop to their walk and are often superb jumpers. Maybe not having that excess baggage in their caboose does have its benefits!

Cymric

Name a Godparent for Your Cat

CONSIDER DESIGNATING A GODPARENT for your cat so he will have a "second-in-command" master and you will rest assured that if your health declines, your cat will be in good care. A pet trust is a binding legal document to make sure that your cat receives proper care in the case of your death or disability. This document will ensure that funds will be available to take care of your cat while your will goes through probate or if it is contested. If your situation is not complicated, and you don't want to hire an estate lawyer, these documents are available online and can be downloaded and filed for a very reasonable price.

Be sure to discuss arrangements with your pet's godparent beforehand. You want to make sure it is someone who is not only capable of taking care of your cat, but who also wants to. Create a written list of instructions, including contact information for your cat's vet, where your cat's health and other records are kept, and vital personality information about your pet that the person might not otherwise know, such as that she is allowed to roam outdoors.

Your Cat's Fur

YOUR CAT HAS AS MANY AS two hundred strands of fur per square millimeter of skin. That fur density, which includes three kinds of hair, is what makes your feline friend so irresistibly pettable.

The first layer is a soft undercoat. It is covered by a top coat predominantly on the sides and back, known as *guard hair*, and thicker, blunt *awn hair*. Some hairs, especially along the back and tail, are attached to minute muscles that enable the fur to stand on end when she is agitated. When she is hot, these same muscles lift the fur slightly to cool off your cat. Unlike dogs, cats do not have a layer of fat within their skin, so the guard hairs also fluff when Kitty is cold, literally providing her with a thermal coat.

Length: Long hair is a recessive trait and short hair a dominant one. That means shorthaired cats with the same recessive gene can produce shaggy kittens, and longhaired parents can produce shorthaired kittens (see more about genetics on Day 5).

The Sphynx looks bald but is actually covered in very, very short fur. The curly- or wavy-haired Rex breeds also have short fur that exposes skin.

Color: A solid-color coat is just that. Tipping and shading/smoking mean each hair strand has several bands of color. Tabby markings—spots and stripes—have a wide range of patterns because one gene governs the pattern and another controls the base color.

Pointed fur, dark with melanin, gives protection to light-colored cats living in warmer climates: The darker fur shields their most prominent areas from the sun. Yet the fur on these cats actually gets *lighter* the longer it is exposed to sun. Also, black cats can develop a rusty cast to their fur if they absorb too much sunlight; you might notice this color change if Kitty likes to spend her days on a windowsill.

See Day 5 for more about color.

Grooming and petting: Cats normally clean themselves from head to toe during the day, with special attention to the face after meals. Cats can tell which areas they recently cleaned by the smell and taste of their saliva, which is why cats may wash immediately after you touch them. It's nothing personal—they just want to cover themselves with their own scent again.

Most cats love to be stroked and brushed, because this stimulates the nerves of their hair follicles. For some, however, if the sensation is too intense or the fur is rubbed the wrong way, they may become snappish. Others actually like the static and abrasion of a good stroke in the wrong direction. Listen to and watch your cat's cues for how he likes or dislikes his fur to be touched.

Collect Cat Mail Art

LOOKING FOR A FUN HOBBY? How about collecting postage stamps or vintage/antique postcards that feature cats, or simply framing a pretty one?

Vendors who specialize in postcards and other paper ephemera, postage stamp dealers, and websites dedicated to this ephemera can help you get started. Here are a few of the interesting postage stamps that you may find:

- A series of four depicting a Chartreux, a ginger Maine Coon, a Snowshoe, and a Turkish Van (Guyana)

- A little girl with several cats, in silhouette (Tonga)

- A series of five stamps, each captioned "Thinking of you," featuring a cartoon red tabby (New Zealand)

- A series of five portraits of cats—three kinds of tabbies, a calico, and a bicolor (Malta)

- A photo of a beautiful tabby kitty walking in the grass (Cuba)

- A photo of three tabby kittens leaning together companionably (Republic of Guinea)

- A set of four young animals, two kittens and two puppies (United States)

Cats Getting Busy

So, WHY ARE CATS SUCH industrious breeders? Simply put, the female feline is wired to mate at any time, and her constant cycling improves the odds that male–female contact between two unaltered cats will result in kittens.

Here's the biology behind all of this breeding. Females are seasonally polyestrous, meaning they have repeated heat cycles over the course of a year, until they are bred or spayed. A female's first heat occurs from five to ten months of age, and her cycles continue until she is pregnant or surgically stopped.

Also, female cats are induced ovulators, meaning that their bodies prepare to breed during the actual mating process. A male cat senses a female in heat, and he's prepared to breed.

The activity itself triggers ovulation, so a female's body is primed at the perfect time, unlike humans, who ovulate on a schedule despite outside events.

One good reason to spay your female: You'll keep your home environment sane. During females' heat cycles, they are howling, erratic felines—frustrating for owners, but appealing to male cats who have not been altered (neutered). Males respond by spraying a pungent urine, a primal way of saying, "I think it's time we get together." Constant cycles of this behavior are enough to convince most cat owners that spay and neuter procedures are essential. What's more, the responsibility of caring for a pregnant female and, eventually, her litter is more than most people can or want to manage.

Does Your Cat Really Need a Sitter?

CATS ARE INDEPENDENT, and they can fend for themselves overnight (or longer) if left with food and water, and if they are accustomed to you being gone. Some cats have a Velcro personality and experience separation anxiety if their owners leave for extended periods of time. Others operate just fine without you around. They're thinking: Just leave food, please. And clean my litter box before you go.

No cat is completely self-sufficient. Know her limits. If you will be gone for more than a day, you should enlist a trusted caregiver to drop in and check on Kitty, refresh her water, fill up her food bowl, and play for a while if the cat is an only child.

You never know what can happen at home while you are gone. Your cat may climb inside an open clothes dryer and the door may swing shut behind her; or he may scale a bookshelf and topple its contents—the list goes on. When someone checks in on your cat, you can stop worrying about what trouble your cat is getting into while you are away.

There are also professional cat sitters who will feed and play with your cat, and even help with house chores such as collecting mail and taking out trash. Some cat sitting services offer in-house grooming.

If the alternative is to board your cat at a kennel, many cat owners feel more comfortable leaving Kitty at home in a familiar environment where she will not get stressed. (For more on boarding your cat, see Days 160 and 161.) Another advantage of hiring a professional pet sitter: You can stop asking (i.e., begging) your best friend to take care of Kitty, "just one more time."

Still not sure whether your cat needs supervision while you're on vacation? If you answer yes to any of these questions, enlist a sitter's help.

- Your cat is usually home alone for a few hours at a time—never overnight.

- Your cat has separation anxiety.

- Your cat is an over-groomer that will lick herself raw when she's stressed.

- You own several cats that often do not get along.

- Your cat will not eat if she is stressed.

- Your cat is on medication.

- Your cat is a troublemaker (though sweet!) and frequently gets into household predicaments.

- You will be gone for longer than a couple of nights.

Preparing for a Cat Sitter

Leaving your cat in the care of a cat sitter can be stressful for both you and your cat. Ensure a worry-free vacation for both of you by taking these steps.

- Take time to make sure your cat binder (see Day 81) is up-to-date with your cat's current feeding schedule and amounts, your vet's contact information, and other basic information.

- Set up a time for your cat sitter to get acquainted with your cat and your home before you go away.

- Make sure the cat sitting agreement spells out in writing how often the cat sitter will visit, how long she will stay each time, and exactly what her responsibilities will be (scooping the cat box, feeding and watering, playing, petting, and so on).

- Provide two copies of your travel information, including how you can be reached and when you plan to return. The cat sitter should leave one copy in the binder and take the other with her.

- Provide the name and contact information of a neighbor, friend, or relative who has a key to your home, in case the cat sitter misplaces the key or is otherwise locked out.

- Leave a worn, unwashed T-shirt or other item of clothing out so your cat can snuggle up to something that holds your scent.

- Show the cat sitter where your cat's food, treats, and toys are kept and where her favorite hiding places are.

Devon Rex

THE DEVON REX IS ANOTHER fine product of a spontaneous mutation. Its story is endearing: A wandering cat with curly hair mates with a wiry British Shorthair, and they have one curly-locked kitty. To preserve the correct gene, careful inbreeding was then done with Devon Rexes and other shorthaired breeds.

Characteristics: The Devon Rex has a slightly more rounded yet still wedge-shaped face. Unlike the Cornish Rex, the Devon has a well-developed muzzle rather than its face ending in a sharp point. This breed also has a fuller, heavier torso. Like the Cornish, the Devon has long legs, but they and the tail are also thicker, the latter coming to a rounded end.

The fur comes in every pattern and color, and is so short that it is more like suede than conspicuously wavy, so that it has a ripple to it rather than fully formed curls. However, it is coarser and thicker than the fur of the Cornish Rex, with very short guard hairs. The whiskers and eyebrows are curly.

Due to excessive inbreeding, some Devon Rexes carry a recessive gene called spasticity disorder; because of this tendency, the pedigree of Devons produced at breeders' catteries is carefully recorded. To strengthen the breed, Americans are also mating Devons with Oriental breeds such as Siamese.

Like the Cornish Rex, this cat should be kept indoors in cool climates.

History: The Devon Rex was first registered in 1982.

feline fun fact **>** Perhaps linked genetically in some way to their coiled fur, Devon Rexes and other Rexes have an unusually loud purr.

Devon Rex

Language Skills: Come, Plus Rooms and Furniture

HERE, YOU WILL LEARN TO ASK your cat to come or follow you, and the names of rooms and common pieces of furniture.

1. Start by reinforcing the word *come*. Call your cat by name (let's say, Ginger). "Come Ginger," you say. Give your cat a "come hither" hand signal if you wish.

2. When Ginger approaches without hesitation at the sound of her name, say enthusiastically, "Good Ginger come!" Repeat step 1 from various locations, and while you are walking.

3. Next, stop saying her name and repeat steps 1 and 2, saying only, "Come," while using the hand signal. Repeat until your cat responds correctly to the single word as well as to the silent beckon. Each time your pet gets it right, say: "Good come!"

4. Slowly introduce simple names of rooms, starting with *kitchen*: "Come kitchen," you say as you walk toward and into the room while also using the hand signal. When your cat joins you there, say, "Good come kitchen!" Do the same for *bedroom, bathroom*, and so on. Take your time when introducing new rooms and vocabulary.

> Introduce basic furniture names in the same fashion: Beckon and then point silently to the piece you mean, to lock in the hand gesture. "Come bed" . . . "come table" . . . "come chair." In time, your pet will understand that some terms may refer to similar items in different places.

Your Cat's Whiskers

YOUR CAT'S WHISKERS ARE actually supersensitive hairs with their own set of specialized nerve endings that act like radar devices. By swiveling and twitching her whiskers, your cat can tell where objects or animals are in dim light, or zoom in on changes in the air that may indicate danger. Never clip or twirl your cat's whiskers, because this will impede her ability to get around.

We are most aware of Kitty's facial whiskers, extending from her cheek pads and the areas around her eyes.

But she also has smaller whiskers just behind her wrists. These help her determine just where to set down her paws.

Your cat's whiskers may interfere with her pleasure while she eats if they hit against the side of the bowl. If you notice Kitty is feeling twitchy about dining, try switching her to a flat plate.

Jazz Cats

COOL CATS ARE NATURAL PLAYERS in the jazz music arena. Just think about jazz jargon: *hep cat, scat singing*. And the famous "Kitten on the Keys" was written by Zez Confrey as a jazz piece way back in 1921. Jazz combos from the 1920s to the present day have included cat terms in their group's name; for example, Cats & the Fiddle or Jazz Cats. And of course, rock and other bands also incorporate feline elements into their names, such as the Pussycat Dolls and Cat Power.

Other jazz works and popular songs relating to cats, and their performers, include:

"Ah-Leu-Cha"—Charlie Parker

"Cat-Song"—Laura Nyro

"Chase Me, Charlie"—Noel Coward

"Feline"—Bobby McFerrin

"I Bought Me a Cat"—traditional

"Pussy Willow"—Duke Ellington

"Swingin' dem Cats"—Nat King Cole Trio, Cab Calloway

"The Cat Came Back"—traditional

"The Cat in the Window (The Bird in the Sky)" —Petula Clark

"The Hep Cat's Ball"—Louis Armstrong

"The Pussy Cat Song (Nyow! Nyot Nyow!)" —Jo Stafford and Gordon MacRae

"Tom Cat Blues"—Jelly Roll Morton

"Wholly Cats"—Benny Goodman

"Wild Cat Blues"—Fats Waller

Albums collecting many of the above songs include *Cat Songs* (2000), *Cat-a-Tonic* (2003), *Feline Groovy* (2008), and the jazz album *Jazz Cats: Felix & Other Cats* (2004).

Spaying and Neutering

CATS ARE PROLIFIC BREEDERS. A male and female cat can practically look at each other and kittens are born. Considering the statistics associated with "unexpected pregnancies" among cats (see Day 339), the most responsible decision pet owners make is to spay their females or neuter their males.

Spaying involves removing the uterus, fallopian tubes, and ovaries; neutering is the removal of both testicles. Both procedures are routine and safe. A bonus: Altering surgeries tend to mellow out aggressive males and reduce irritability in females. Rest assured, altering is *not* a personality overhaul. Your cats will still fake attacks on inanimate objects like rubber bands; they'll still be spunky, sweet, independent, and needy. But your spayed female won't be irritable and downright erratic during heat, and your neutered male will stop that putrid spraying business meant to tell feline ladies that he's in mating mode.

Spaying ideally should be performed between five and seven months of age, before her first heat. If the surgery is performed this young, you reduce the chances of developing mammary tumors by 90 percent. Overall, spaying eliminates the change of developing uterine cancers and infections.

Neutering a male is not invasive, and it can eliminate the putrid-smelling spray a male dispenses when he detects a potential female mate. The best time to neuter a male is at six or seven months old, before sexual behavior is ingrained. There is a product on the market called Neutersol, which is injected into the testicle to sterilize dogs and has been used off-label on cats. This product prevents sperm production but does not stop the male cat from making testosterone. So your sterilized male will retain his natural "mating" instincts.

The onetime expense of spaying or neutering your cat will improve the quality of life for both of you. Ultimately, you are investing in the long-term health of your cat, and helping to control the overpopulation of cats.

Word Games

TEACH YOUR CAT *where's* AND got and you have the basis for fun play together.

1. When she is at a short distance from you, ask, "Where's [name]?" while exaggeratedly looking around.

2. Feign delight at seeing her and reach out to "tag" her: "Got [name]!"

3. Repeat in different locations, including when she is in another room and you go in to "find" her. She may begin to come when called, eager to be found (although cats have a proclivity for hiding in plain sight while you search frantically for them!).

4. Introduce yourself or other people, animals, or toys with these terms; for instance, "Where's Mama?" (covering your face with a scarf)— "[Name] got Mama!" (when Kitty reaches for you). Search together for objects you identify aloud, to extend your cat's vocabulary.

5. Play "Where's Hand": Conceal your hand beneath something soft or flexible, then waggle your fingers and ask, "Where's hand?" Kitty will probably pounce on it. Say, "[Name] got hand!" Some cats will hide a paw for you to find; be sure to verbalize what is going on in this variation.

6. Play "Peek-a-boo": Hide behind a piece of furniture or door, then poke your head out: "Peek-a-boo!" If your cat reaches to touch you, say, "[Name] got Mama!" If she hides playfully (perhaps by only hiding her face while the rest of her wriggles visibly in happy anticipation), ask, "Where's [name]?" with mock anxiety, then either call, "Peek-a-boo!" if she emerges on her own, or tap her and say, "Got [name]."

7. Play "Gotcha": This can be done sitting or running. Tap your cat and say, "Gotcha!" Become more specific: "Got ear!" "Got tail!" Kitty may reach out to tap you back. If so, vocalize her action: "[Name] got Mama foot!"

8. Use these terms to comment while your cat plays with toys. A pet who has lost a ball behind a door may only need to be told, "Peek-a-boo ball," to understand where to find it.

9. Play "Fetch": Throw a toy away from your cat and ask, "Where's [toy]?" This may induce her to not just run after but also retrieve it for you. Eventually, you may be able to request toys you haven't thrown, or Kitty will herself initiate a game of fetch. Remember to exclaim, "[Name] got [toy]!" when she picks up the toy.

Egyptian Mau

AN EARTHENWARE STATUE OF A Mau cat was uncovered in an Egyptian tomb that's older than the Bible. The paintings inside portray Mau pursuing prey.

Characteristics: Although this breed looks, as a body type, a lot like its fellow Egyptian, the Abyssinian, it has a special characteristic that sets it apart: its finely spotted, ticked coat. The color range is restricted to date to only four: black, bronze with a beige ground, silver, and smoke (black spots on a silvery white ground). The face and neck display tabby markings, including the famous M.

The Mau may have had very early wild origins to the Felis libyca, and breeders have been taking care to outbreed an innate savage quality that seems to be part of its genetic makeup. Although today's Maus are more civilized than their ancestors, they do not take well to the company of other animals and tend to dislike being passed to another owner once they have bonded with their first. They do best in quiet and stable one-cat households.

History: The Egyptian Mau originated in Cairo, Egypt, and traces back at least three centuries in that region. Many of the modern North American cats of this breed are pure descendants of just three cats brought from Egypt to the United States in 1956 by Nathalie Troubetskoy, although some have been crossbred with other cats. The Egyptian Mau began to be registered as a breed in 1977. In Great Britain, on the other hand, the Egyptian Mau is a very late arrival, introduced to that nation in 1978 and yet to join any association's registry.

feline fun fact > The ancient Egyptian Book of the Dead repeatedly depicts the Mau cat conquering a snake, sometimes with the help of an illustrated knife held in one paw!

Egyptian Mau

Emulating Mama Cat

MOST MOTHER CATS HAVE AN instinctive sense of how to rear their youngsters. Mama cats are able to separate loving their young from using tough love to make sure their kittens obey them. Here are some ways to make Kitty look up to you as an authority. These techniques even work on older cats, as long as you start and stick to these techniques right away.

- *Mama cats discipline their kittens.* They step in immediately if one kitten is hurting another or getting into mischief. One common disciplinary measure is a bop on the nose. This is Mama-speak for "Cut it out!" You can replicate it with not a punch, but blowing on your cat's nose. The sensation is just unpleasant and startling enough to make Kitty hesitate to repeat the action that provoked it. Do this only when you catch your cat in the act of something, because it is meaningless out of context.

- *Mama cats are vigilant.* They are immediately alert to danger. Another Mama-cat communiqué is a distinctive hiss or yowl that means "Freeze!" or "Back off!" From a human throat, it can be as simple as a sharp "Ah!" or tongue-click or whistle. At first, make the sound while physically stopping your cat from the behavior so he associates the sound with your correction.

Use that sound *exclusively* for situations when your cat or an object/individual is in immediate danger (e.g., preparing to leap onto the lit stove or batting at your grandmother's fragile antique vase).

- *Mama cats instruct by rote.* Discipline/redirect Kitty consistently. For example, if you want him to stay off your TV, remove him immediately *every* time he climbs there. Likewise, if you prefer your cat to sit next to rather than on you when you read the newspaper, transfer him to where you wish him to sit, then praise him lavishly whenever he stays or sits willingly in the appointed spot until he clearly associates seeing the newspaper with sitting beside you.

Never pick up your kitten or cat by the nape of the neck. Mama cats know where to hold and how much pressure to safely apply—you don't! If you are unsure about how to safely lift your cat, ask your vet to demonstrate.

Cat's Senses of Smell and Taste

A CAT'S SENSE OF SMELL IS four times stronger than our own. Your cat's supersensitive nose is what directs her to food and helps her distinguish one animal or human from another. Imagine how a can of tuna would smell if its odor were quadrupled. Your cat's fine-tuned olfactory capabilities may also be the reason for her finicky eating habits (see Day 171). She can tell whether food is not completely fresh and, by her standards, the smellier, the better.

A cat's sense of smell is directed by a kind of echo chamber of tiny cylindrical bones located above her palate. Those bones conduct scents into her mouth, and vice versa. In the roof of the mouth lies *Jacobson's organ*, which has specialized scent cells that shoot information to the brain to try to identify the odor. The bones gather the information, and Jacobson's organ decodes it: *Aha! Delicious kibble with clam juice drizzled on top.*

Sometimes, your cat needs to get a better whiff of something and will make an open-mouthed grimace while sniffing, a gesture known as *flehmening*, which means she is engaging this organ to maximize her analysis of a scent, by pressing her tongue to the roof of her mouth. Your cat may do this to other cats, or even to you, to check an identity!

feline fun fact **>** Just what is that attraction cats have for eating plastic grocery bags? She's drawn not to the plastic but to the very thin layer of oil or gelatin that manufacturers put on the bags to help separate them. Protect your cat by keeping these bags out of reach.

Cats on the Tube

BETWEEN CARTOON CATS AND LIVE CATS, television has had its fair share of feline actors. The dates are when each series premiered.

- Early television's *Our Miss Brooks* (1952) starred feline actor Orangey (see Day 289) as Minerva, character Margaret Davis's (Jane Morgan) cat.

- The animated *Courageous Cat and Minute Mouse* (1960) entertained children as a parody of Batman, its superhero animals (both voiced by Dal McKennon) living in a Cat Cave and traveling in a Cat Mobile. The show was the creation of Bob Kane.

- The Hanna-Barbera cartoon *Top Cat* (1961) followed the exploits of a rough-tough gang of New York alley cats whose leader was Top Cat (voiced by Arnold Stang, imitating the style of TV character Sergeant Bilko). When the series was shown in Great Britain, the title was changed to *Boss Cat* to avoid a conflict with the name of a brand of cat food there.

- The long-running *Mr. Rogers' Neighborhood* (Canadian CBC 1962, U.S. NET/PBS 1968) included among its imaginary neighbors Henrietta Pussycat (voiced by Fred Rogers).

- *The Cattanooga Cats* (1969), a Hanna-Barbera collaboration, showcased animated characters Kitty Jo (voiced by Julie Bennett), Groove (Casey Kasem), Country (Bill Callaway), and Scoots (Jim Begg) as rock-and-roll musicians.

- In 1974, the British children's show *Bagpuss* came to the telly, named for its pink and white stuffed cloth cat who could magically come alive.

- The British cartoon *James the Cat* (1984) concerned the eponymous, a penguinlike black and white cat, and his animal neighbors. It was picked up for Iranian TV.

- *Uncle Croc's Block* (1975) had an animated cast that included a cat (voiced by Allen Oppenheimer) who was down to his ninth life—a very good reason to be a "fraidy." But even worse, any time he uttered any number between one and eight, a ghost from his past (of the appropriate life) appeared to beleaguer him.

- *The Secret Lives of Waldo Kitty* (1975) was a play on the timid Walter Mitty character, about a fraidy cat.

- Hello Kitty, a syndicated character of the Japanese company Sanrio, had her own television series in Japan, the United States, and Canada in several different seasons, beginning in 1986. Kitty lived with her parents and her twin sister Mimmy. There is a plethora of commercially produced products tying in to the Hello Kitty image.

There has also been crossover from films to television and vice versa, including the cartoons of Tom (of *Tom and Jerry*), Sylvester, and Heathcliff. See Days 37 and 261 for more about these characters.

Mealtime Etiquette in a Multicat Household

CATS ARE GRAZERS, so many owners leave food out so their felines can munch freely. In multicat households, free-feeding can be problematic when the cat "bosses" dominate the food bowl. You may not realize that one of your less boisterous kitties is underfed at first. Eventually, you will realize that one or more of your shy cats aren't getting their fair share. They may lose weight, or shy away from the food bowl, preferring to find times to eat in private while other cats are not watching.

Here are some tips for making sure that every cat in the house gets a square meal:

- Provide several feeding areas with food and water dishes so cats do not have to battle to get their fair share.

- Observe your cats while they are eating, and keep an eye out for aggressive behavior.

- Take turns feeding cats; confine dominant cats while the others eat.

- If certain cats require a special diet, feed them in a room separate from other cats, and take away food dishes after mealtime to prevent food thieving.

The Embellished Cat

IF YOU ARE HANDY WITH A NEEDLE, you can incorporate cats to your wardrobe, home, and gifts, using a variety of fabrics and embellishments.

Fabric: Choose cat-print fabric for projects. Some prints are realistic, even photographic; others, more stylized. Consider the scale of your intended project before selecting a pattern.

Quilting: Create a cat-themed quilt from a ready-to-use pattern in a quilting book, from a purchased pattern or kit, by using cat appliqués, or by using squares of colored fabrics to reproduce cat patterns. Consider making a template of a cat- or paw-print silhouette to trace, to guide your stitching through the quilt layers; or add embellishments such as embroidery, ribbon, and buttons.

Appliqué: Use cat-shaped cookie cutters or illustrations to sketch cat cutouts you can sew onto fabric. Embellish with ribbon collar and sequined tag, beaded eyes, etc. Or carefully cut the cats from cat-print cloth and appliqué them onto other fabrics; even knitted or crocheted items can be perked up with an appliquéd cat or two.

Embroidery: Cats can be embroidered in counted cross-stitch, crewel, and needlepoint. Try your hand at charting your own illustration or photograph onto graph paper or as a colored table in your word processing software. Experiment with stitches that suggest the texture or smoothness of fur, the button quality of eyes and the nose, and so on. Look for fine, furry yarns to give your project even greater texture.

Exotic Shorthair

IN AN ATTEMPT TO PRODUCE A CAT with a low-maintenance shorter haircut than the original Persian cat, a winning "match" was discovered in two American Shorthairs that were bred together. The result: trim facial fur.

Characteristics: Like the true Persian, the Exotic has a thick neck, broad face, small ears, and "pushed-in" nose, which, combined with its short facial fur, has given rise to its comparison to the teddy bear. It has a cobby body and relatively short tail. The fur ranges through all Persian and all American Shorthair colors and patterns.

Exotic Shorthairs are generally sweet-tempered and quiet cats, and certainly do require less intensive grooming than their Persian relatives.

History: In 1966, this hybrid began to be professionally bred only to its hybrid relatives, to standardize the breed, and in 1971 became the only hybrid registered in the United States. The pedigree is very strictly regulated to make sure that no outbreeding is attempted beyond combinations of Persians, American Shorthairs, or Exotic Shorthairs. Because of the mixed genetic pool, the mating of two Exotic Shorthairs may produce longhaired kittens, which are called "Exotic Longhairs" and may be shown in some competitions as Persians.

Exotic Shorthair

Start a Cat Blog

A CAT BLOG IS A FUN WAY TO share photos and stories of your cat with your friends and family. There are a number of options for creating your own free cat blog that are easy to use, even if you don't have a lot of computer experience.

First, decide on which blogging service you want to use. Blogger, WordPress, and TypePad are just a few. An Internet search on "cat blog" will turn up other options that are more specifically focused on cats. Some services will place a small ad on your blog page in exchange for providing the page for free.

Once you have chosen a service, follow the instructions at the site for setting up an account. You'll need to have a valid email address; this can be your own—you don't need to set up a special one for your cat (unless you want to).

Once you have your account, you can start to set up your page. There are usually different layouts and backgrounds to choose from, and you can upload your cat's photo and write a short bio for her.

Blogging is like writing a diary; each entry is dated. When you post a new entry, it appears at the top of the page and older entries are pushed down. You can usually control the number of posts the page shows at a time. Once posts are pushed off the page, they go into an archive, and visitors to your cat's blog can go back in time by selecting articles out of the archive.

Your posts can be stories, poems, tips, ideas, projects, photos—whatever you like. You can even upload videos and include links to other information on the Internet. You can present the blog from your point of view, or you can write it as if your cat were writing it herself. If you enable the comments feature of your blog, people all over the world can respond to your posts.

Looks Are Everything

CAT COMPETITION JUDGES and breeders have a unique lexicon for describing colors and other characteristics of cats. How many of these terms apply to your feline friends?

Agouti: Also known as "ticked" fur, this is fur that is alternately light and dark along the same hair. It can also refer to the ground color between stripes. Abyssinians and Somalis typically have agouti fur.

Banding: Distinctive bars or rings of color, such as around the throat or tail

Bib: The fur of the chest, sometimes of greater length than surrounding areas

Blaze: A contrasting color that appears on the forehead or runs vertically along the center of the face of some cats

Brindled: Having dark streaks or spots on a tawny or gray ground

Calico: A spotted or patched pattern of three distinctive colors, typically orange and black on white. The Mi-Ke–colored Japanese Bobtail is a calico

Cameo: A cat that has red-tipped white fur.

Cobby: A body type that is sturdy and broad, set low on short legs. A Persian cat, for instance, has a cobby build.

Curl: A cat whose ear tips turn outward

Fold: A cat whose ears turn inward

Kink: A bump or twist in the tail

Laces: White markings on a cat's back legs

Lilac: Also known as frost or lavender, a pinkish gray color especially found in Siamese

Mackerel: Narrow two-toned striped coat; see *tabby*

Necklace: A distinctively different color around the neck

Piebald: A white cat with markings only on his head, legs, and/or tail, such as the Turkish Van

Points: The ears, muzzle (known as the *mask*), paws, and tail, such as in a chocolate-point Siamese that is brown in only those areas. These cats are referred to as being colorpointed.

Ruff: Longer, manelike fur around the neck, such as on a mature Maine Coon

Self: Also known as *solid*, a coat of a single color

Smoke: A cat whose fur is tipped with a darker color

Tabby: A two-tone, striped (known as *mackerel*) or spotted pattern of fur darker than the fur's basic ground color

Tipped: Also known as *shell*, fur that has another color or contrasting tone only at its outer tip

Torbie: Also known as *patched*, a tabby with orange patches

Tortoiseshell: Also known as *tortie*, a black cat with mottled patches of orange and cream

Wirehair: A variation of the American Shorthair that has sharply twisted or bent fur

The Mysterious Cat

SOME PEOPLE VIEW ALL CATS as being a bit mysterious, which makes them ideal sidekicks and leading characters in mystery novels. Take the long-running Cat Who . . . series by Lillian Jackson Braun, which centers on a detective and his two Siamese cats. Other famous feline sleuths include Carole Nelson Douglas's Midnight Louie, Rita Mae Brown's Sneaky Pie, and Garrison Allen's Mycroft. Other feline mystery authors to watch for include Lydia Adamson, Marion Babson, Evan Marshall, Gilbert Morris, Shirley Rousseau, Clea Simon, and Fran Stewart.

For younger readers, Linda Stewart's Sam the Cat series has a hero modeled on famed private eye Philip Marlowe.

Want to get on the case? Look for blogs and online discussion boards that focus on cat mysteries, or ask your local library or bookstore to direct you to suitable authors. Consider joining a reading group of other feline-fancying mystery readers, or start your own by connecting with other readers from local animal organizations.

Tasty Treats for Cats

FOOD IS AN EXCELLENT MOTIVATOR for cats during training, and a tasty token of affection "just because."

You'll find out what taste your cat prefers (fish, chicken, beef, vegetable) through trial and error. Unlike most dogs, who will basically eat what's in front of them as long as it doesn't run away, cats tend to be finicky (see Day 171). They'll let you know what they like.

Dental treats: These snacks work double-duty, removing plaque and cleaning your kitty's pearly whites while rewarding her with a treat.

Low-cal snacks: If you tend to dole out treats generously, opt for a low-calorie treat.

Catnip: Catnip is available in flakes, treats, or grass forms. Fill an interactive toy with catnip flakes, or purchase stuffed toys that are filled with the substance that drives cats crazy (in a good way).

Semimoist and chewy treats: Semimoist and chewy treats are easy on cats with dental issues.

Meat treats: You can purchase meat treats, or portion small bites of "people" meat (chicken, beef) that is not seasoned.

All-natural yums: Tuna flakes, cat grasses, lactose-free milk, and other low-cal treats are healthy for your cat.

There's nothing wrong with treating your cat, but be sure that snacks do not interfere with your cat's appetite for his nutritious kibble. Limit treats to 5 percent of your cat's total food intake, especially if your cat needs to drop some pounds (see Day 206).

Build a Cat Cabana

ENCLOSING YOUR LITTER BOX IN A tailored tent of breathable, washable cotton fabric will not only allow Kitty to dig away without an audience but will also keep the dust where it belongs. Visitors may not even realize the box is there.

First, decide how to suspend a firm surface over your litter box. Remember to leave about 18 inches (45.7 cm) of vertical clearance, so your cat can get into and stand in the box comfortably. A small side table that fits entirely over the box (with a little clearance all around for walking) is ideal. In a multicat household, several boxes can be placed side by side as "stalls" beneath a broader table. A shelf within a taller table is another good spot from which to pitch your tent.

The basic idea is to give your cat movable side flaps for entry and exit, which would not be the case if you used a regular tablecloth.

MATERIALS

Ruler

Several sheets of newspaper and a pencil

Scissors

Straight pins

Cotton or cotton/polyester fabric (quilt fabric is ideal)—see step 1 for how to measure—washed and ironed before measuring

Sewing thread and needle

Iron

1. Make your pattern. Measure the length and width of the table, add 1 inch (2.5 cm) to the width and 1 inch (2.5 cm) to the length, and draw this pattern onto a sheet of newspaper (piece A). For the side flaps, measure the height from the floor to the tabletop and draw one flap (B) for the shorter side of the table and another (C) for the longer side, using the exact width or length of the table for the horizontal measurement and the exact height to the top of the table for the vertical measurement.
(If your table is perfectly square, you do not need to create a pattern piece C; just use pattern piece B for all four flaps.)

Example: for a 20-inch wide x 24-inch long x 18-inch high (50.8 x 61 x 45.7 cm) table:

A = 21 inches x 25 inches (53.3 x 63.5 cm)

B = 20 inches x 18 inches (51 x 45.7 cm) (length x height)

C = 24 inches x 18 inches (61 x 45.7 cm) (length x height)

2. Check your measurements. Cut out the pieces of newspaper and pin B and C to piece A only along the top, then test the fit on the table. If you like, trace an arc around the edge of a saucer at each lower corner of the flaps, to enable you to cut curved rather than square corners.

3. Cut your fabric. When you are satisfied with the way the paper pattern looks, pin it to the fabric, cutting two each of B and C. If the print of the fabric needs to be kept in a particular direction to be viewed correctly, be sure to pin both B and C in the direction their print should hang from the table.

4. Finish all edges. Using the sewing thread and needle, blanket-stitch around every raw edge of fabric. This is tedious, but you will be laundering the cloth often, and this will keep it from raveling.

5. Attach the flaps. Pin the top of each flap to part A, using a ½-inch (1.3 cm) seam allowance all around. Double-check before sewing that this is a good fit for the table (Note: The finished height is deliberately slightly above the floor; you didn't make a mistake), and then sew the seam all along the perimeter. Press the seam allowances toward the underside of the top.

6. Place over the table. Leave one flap open for a day or two, until your cat gets the "hang" of how to enter his cabana.

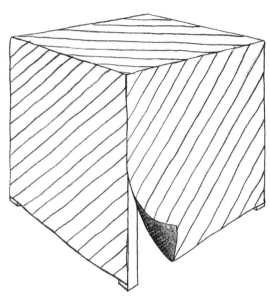

The finished cat cabana fits over a small table.

German Rex

RECOVERED FROM ASHEN RUINS in the bombed-out city of East Berlin, a feral female cat was rescued by a doctor, who called her "little lamb" for her curly locks. Today, she is the great-plus-grandmother of all German Rex cats in Europe.

Characteristics: The German Rex is fine-boned and tall, and has dense, closely curled fur resembling Astrakhan fur, including along its tail. Its whiskers, unlike the Cornish Rex's, are nearly straight, however. The color and pattern possibilities run across just about the entire feline spectrum, from solid-colored Rexes to bicolors and even colorpointed cats.

The German Rex is often playful and quite lively; like the other Rexes, however, its short fur necessitates its being kept indoors in cold climates, for optimum health.

History: Following the rescue of the black-haired kitty known as "little lamb," she was bred extensively throughout Europe, and eventually her ancestors were brought to the United States in 1960 for the same purpose.

Because the German Rex and the Cornish Rex have the same genetic makeup, they can be crossbred to produce offspring with nearly identical characteristics. The true German Rex has longer hair than the Cornish variety, with a slightly heavier body, but so much crossbreeding has occurred over the years that it can be difficult to know whether a Rex cat is entirely German.

German Rex

Boarding Your Cat

IF YOU THINK BOARDING IS FOR THE DOGS, you may reconsider after visiting some posh kennel facilities that treat cats like queens. Also, if you will be away for an extended period of time, kenneling your cat may be the best alternative for safety and health reasons. (See Day 137 to help decide whether you should hire a sitter or leave your cat home alone.) Although cats tend to get stressed out when they are moved from their comfortable territory, some pets stress more when they stay at home and their owners never return. Only you can decide whether your cat will have a better experience in a kennel or at home with a sitter.

If you choose to board your cat, there are many kennel options. Here are some pointers to help you make a decision.

- Investigate the facility carefully before booking a stay for your cat—and book early, especially if you'll need reservations during holidays.

- Talk to your veterinarian and find out whether they offer boarding services, or can suggest a reliable kennel.

- Tour the facility before boarding your cat. How large are the kennels, and do solid partitions separate each unit? Are indoor and outdoor facilities available—will your cat have a "run" to the outdoors? This is important for indoor-outdoor cats that may get stressed if confined for too long.

- Check out the cages. Are they clean? How does the facility smell? Ask how often cages, dishes, and litter boxes are cleaned, and what substances are used to sanitize the kennel.

- What is the feeding schedule, and will they accommodate special food needs?

- Meet the individuals who actually work with the animals. How long have they been working at the kennel?

- What are the kennel's pick-up and drop-off hours? How secure is the kennel?

- Finally, find out whether the facility is accredited by the American Boarding Kennels Association.

If you board your cat, prepare a shot record for the kennel and provide emergency phone numbers and your vet's contact information. If your cat takes medication, neatly write out instructions. Discuss the medication in advance with the kennel to find out whether they can accommodate those needs.

Finally, relax. If you've done your homework, your pet is in good hands. Dropping off Kitty for a stay at the kennel can be an emotional experience, but rest assured, she will fare well without you. And you can travel knowing your cat is safe and sound.

ID Tags

EVEN THE MOST INNOCENT-SEEMING CATS can be very adept at sneaking out between your ankles when you answer the door or carry your groceries inside—all the more reason to add some "jangle" to that collar by attaching an identification charm that contains your contact information.

ID tags are typically made of metal or hard plastic and come in a range of designs, from traditional circles to hearts and even mice shapes. The most common form of ID is a flat, metal medallion that attaches with a ring to a cat's collar. Slide-on tags, which have slits that allow threading through the collar, are a wise choice if your cat is bothered by a tag dangling from her neck, or if she must also wear a license or vaccination tag and the jingling of multiple tags bothers her or you.

Many pet stores have machines that will print tags on the spot, or you can order them over the Internet or by mail. Cat tags tend to be smaller than dog tags, which might limit the amount of information you can include on the tag. If you must omit something from the ID tag, leave off your cat's name. Most don't respond to their name anyway, and an address and a phone number will be more helpful in returning your cat to you than her name. Take advantage of discounts for ordering multiple tags at one time, if you can, because cats lose tags more often than dogs (see Choosing a Collar, Day 99).

When you receive your tags, check them for rough edges by running your finger along the edge. Use a nail file to smooth any rough spots before attaching them to your cat's collar.

Cats in Folk Art

EVERY HOLIDAY, A CAT OWNER somewhere receives a new calendar, coffee mug, or pot holder. Looking for something unique to give this year? Seek out folk art finds at marketplaces and street fairs, museums, antique and vintage shops, and even tag sales. Beautiful wooden pieces, for example, are made in Africa and such countries as Thailand, as well as by Native American carvers; Russian artisans create cat-shaped *matryoshka* (nesting) dolls; Mexico produces charming feline-themed pottery; and "naïf" American art includes many painted images of cats on wood.

Their distinguishing characteristic: They were not mass-produced by machines, but one at a time, by individual craftspeople.

Look for these folk art and artisan items shaped like or depicting cats:

- Hooked or woven rugs
- Paintings, especially on wood
- Quilts and other coverlets
- Wind chimes
- Garden statuary and ornaments, including items designed to scare away birds
- Trivets or tiles
- China, pottery, and ceramics
- Blown, stained, or depression glass
- Tiny painted clay or lead figurines
- Wood carvings or papier-mâché figures

Excessive Grooming: Calming the Trigger

OUR CAT'S CONSTANT LICKING IS beyond high-maintenance. Her intense grooming and obsessive preening is a sign that Kitty is stressed out—her licking releases tension and calms her nerves.

Some cats lick because they're bored. They need more stimulation. Other cats groom like crazy because of medical problems. Their persistent licking is an effort to comfort a painful skin condition or rid it of external parasites. Many cats that present with compulsive grooming have allergies (see Day 227).

How do you know whether your cat is just grooming or displaying an obsessive-compulsive behavior? Over-grooming is more than just clean-paw licking. Cats may pull out tufts of fur, and they often focus on the insides of the thighs, the abdomen, and the groin. You may not catch your cat in the act, but you'll notice the signs. Your cat may develop bald patches, a stripe of thinning hair down her back, or a bare abdomen.

If you notice these signs, immediately take your cat to the vet to rule out medical causes. Conditions that can result in bald patches include hyperthyroidism, allergies, bacterial pyoderma, fleas or flea allergies, mites, ringworm, and inflammatory skin diseases. Your vet will take skin scrapings from affected areas to rule out parasites and fungal infections.

Flea combing the coat and blood testing will tease out diagnoses. If your cat does not present with a medical reason for all the licking, her environment is triggering the crazed licking response.

Never punish your cat for overgrooming. This could worsen the problem. De-stress your cat's life by sticking to a routine—feed, play, and exercise at the same time each day. Consider environmental changes that may trigger her response: moving to a new home, a new baby, adding another animal to the household, home renovations, or a family member leaving the nest. If stress management doesn't work, your vet may recommend appropriate antidepressants or antianxiety medications. This is a last resort and a "bridge" to ease the cat into a less-stressed state of mind.

These breeds are prone to compulsive grooming: Siamese, Burmese, Himalayans, and Abyssinians.

Make a Felt Catnip Toy

THIS SIMPLE CATNIP TOY IS very easy to make, even for those with very little sewing experience. Make a bunch to give as gifts!

MATERIALS

Scissors

2 sheets of felt, one each of two coordinating colors

Sewing machine, or needle and thread

2 tablespoons dried catnip

4 cotton balls

1. Cut one 3-inch x 3-inch (7.6 x 7.6 cm) square out of each color of felt.

2. Cut one 1½-inch (3.8 cm) circle out of each color of felt. Use a small lid or shot glass as a template, if you need one.

3. Center one of the felt circles on a felt square of the other color. Sew the circle to the square. Repeat for the other circle and square pair.

4. Stack the two squares of felt together with the circles on the outside. Sew the squares together edge to edge on three sides, with a ³/₈-inch (1 cm) seam allowance. If you are sewing by hand, be sure to use small stitches.

5. Stuff the opening with the catnip and cotton balls. The cotton balls give the toy more bulk. Sew the remaining side closed.

6. Let your cat enjoy!

Havana Brown

THE HANDSOME Havana Brown is distinctive for its deep brown, solid-colored coat and slender exotic build.

Characteristics: The British version of the Havana is a cat with a solid brown coat and a strongly exotic body structure: long nose, triangular face, and angular build. In the United States, however, the Havana has a shorter nose, a rounder face, and a semicobby body; an alternative color is the green-eyed lilac, the result of mating a Russian Blue to a chocolate-point Siamese. Unlike Siamese, Havanas are born with their final color rather than maturing into it.

History: All-brown Siamese have cropped up in the West from time to time, such as one at a British cat show in 1888. But the Havana's spectacular color in modern times was the result of breeding experiments in the 1950s, which mated a chocolate-point Siamese with a black shorthair whose ancestral line had the seal point gene. The resultant chestnut brown kitten was shown in the UK in 1953.

Across the pond, in that same year, another brown kitten was born, following the same formula, and breeders mated the cats from both sides of the Atlantic to strengthen the coloring of the subsequent offspring. The classic color is a rich, dark brown, with brown whiskers and lime green eyes. As such, the breed was recognized in Great Britain in 1958 (where the cats were first called Chestnut Browns); the first Havana Brown competed in the United States in 1959, and in 1964 the breed joined U.S. registries.

feline fun fact > Havana Browns use their "hands" to explore and play, more than other cats typically do.

Havana Brown

Cat Advocacy: Volunteering at Shelters and Pet Rescues

SPREAD YOUR CAT LOVE TO THE homeless by volunteering at an animal shelter or sponsoring "found" cats through animal foster programs. Organizations like these depend on dedicated individuals who can lend various talents. If you're a number cruncher, find out whether a shelter needs assistance with their books or office duties. If you're a marketing guru, volunteer to run a campaign for the animal program. If you're a bleeding heart with extra room in your house, serve as a foster parent until cats can be adopted by loving families. (This job does require willpower, as we learned on Days 83 and 84.)

If you cannot commit to a regular volunteer schedule, sign up to help with projects or one-time events, such as adoption days. By volunteering, you'll connect with other cat lovers and give back to an organization that relies on caring people to offer their services.

Here is a list of functions a volunteer may fulfill at a shelter:

- Updating the shelter's website
- Taking photographs of new cats and kittens for adoption
- Writing articles for and/or designing the shelter's newsletters
- Greeting visitors
- Helping out on adoption days or at shelter events
- Cleaning cages
- Playing/socializing with cats
- Assisting with mealtime
- Taking on administrative tasks
- Fostering cats

Choosing Harnesses and Leashes

IF YOU PLAN TO TAKE YOUR CAT out on a leash (see Day 176), a harness is a must. Cat collars are made so your pet can slip out of it if he gets caught in any way. Harnesses fit around both the neck and the body, making it impossible for the cat to escape.

The two basic types of harnesses are a figure eight shape and an H shape. The figure eight shape has two loops connected directly to each other; the H shape has two loops connected by a short section of harness material. Many veterinarians recommend the H shape because it distributes tension more evenly between the cat's neck and body. Another option is a cat walking jacket, which has a loop around the neck but a panel of fabric around the body rather than another loop. A walking jacket distributes tension even better. You may have to try several styles before you find one your cat likes, or at least tolerates.

To choose the right size harness, measure your cat around his neck and body, just behind his front legs. The harness should fit snugly, but not be too tight. Make sure you can comfortably slip two fingers underneath the harness loops. Read and follow the harness maker's instructions for putting it on correctly and making adjustments.

Leashes are available in a number of different materials, from nylon to leather to elastic. The pressure on the harness from a heavy leash is uncomfortable for most cats, so choose a light-weight leash. A standard leash (about 6 feet [1.8 m] long) is best for leash training. Once your cat is used to being on a leash, you can consider an adjustable-length, retractable leash if your cat wants to wander farther.

Because harnesses are escape-proof, use a harness *only* when your cat is on the leash. If he gets caught up on a tree branch or fence while in a harness, he could strangle himself.

Cats in Classic Children's Books

HERE IS A CHRONOLOGY OF some of the most beloved cats in children's fiction:

- **Carlo Collodi** (pen name of Carlo Lorenzini) wrote a fablelike situation into his 1883 *The Adventures of Pinocchio*: A wily cat and fox attempt to swindle Pinocchio by pretending to be blind and lame. Later, when they are old, they are genuinely disabled, but Pinocchio won't be tricked twice and refuses to help them.

- **Rudyard Kipling's** "The Cat Who Walked by Himself" is part of his *Just-So Stories* (1902). Although the Cat balks at coming inside to be domesticated, the Woman strikes a deal: If he can make her utter three words of praise, he can enter on his own terms. He complies by entertaining her baby, putting the child to sleep, and then catching mice. The Cat enjoys a bowl of milk and the hearth, and then departs, preferring his independence.

- Minnesota-born **Wanda Gág** (daughter of a Bohemian woodcutter) wrote and illustrated *Millions of Cats* in 1928. It tells the story of an elderly man who goes in search of the prettiest cat for his wife. Of course, every cat is pretty in its own way, and so the couple ended up with . . . you guessed it!

- Puff, a tabby cat, was the feline cast member of the original Dick and Jane readers of **Dr. William S. Gray** that were published for several decades starting in 1930.

- Beginning in 1937, artist-writer **Clare Turlay Newberry** produced beautifully illustrated children's books about cats, such as *Smudge, April's Kittens, Mittens, and Babette*—and even named her daughter Felicia!

- In 1938, **Katherine Hale** published eighteen stories about Orlando, the Marmalade Cat, beginning with that eponymous title, for her own sons, infusing the tales with old-fashioned family values, such as Orlando's wife Grace's housekeeping skills. The cats have three kittens: Pansy, Mable, and Tinkle.

- From 1944 to 1973, Connecticut-born **Esther Averill** wrote a series of cat books, including *The Cat Club, The Fire Cat*, and *The Hotel Cat*, telling a dozen tales in all about the red-scarfed black shorthair Jenny Linsky, who was based on Averill's own cat.

- **Dr. Seuss (Theodore Geisel)** created the revolutionary *The Cat and the Hat* in 1957, whose infectious rhymes engaged early readers in ways never achieved by prose. Its lanky title character appears by magic to amuse two children on a rainy day, and then even cleans the house just before their mother comes home.

- **George Seldes's *The Cricket in Times Square*** (1960) introduced Harry the Cat to child readers.

- British illustrator **Nicola Bayley** is responsible for the artwork of many stunning children's books of the 1980s and '90s, which include *The Windmill Cat, The Mousehole Cat, The Necessary Cat*, and such petite titles as *Polar Bear Cat* and *Copycats*.

Entice a Finicky Cat to Eat

CATS, BY NATURE, ARE PICKY EATERS—they happily let you know whether their meal is not fresh or whether the dining room is not up to par.

Even though your cat's meals may not vary from day to day, one day he may decide he'd rather fast than feast. No matter how many "Here, kitties," you coo to convince him to eat, he simply won't.

First, examine potential reasons why your cat is refusing food. Cats are sensitive to their environment. Has anything changed recently? Did you bring home another cat, or is there a houseguest? Did you recently go on vacation? Are there new sensory disruptions, such as music playing at mealtimes? Is he feeling under the weather (e.g., a stuffy nose will make food seem tasteless)?

Next, try the following to encourage your kitty to eat:

- A new type of wet cat food, preferably with a strong scent
- Wet food, if he eats only dry, or vice versa, or mix the two
- Kitten food

- All-meat "human" baby foods (lamb, chicken, or turkey—avoid pork; no onions or garlic)
- Solid or semisolid food from your hand (carefully)
- A smidge of grated cooked carrots or cooked, pureed sweet potato, pumpkin, or squash
- Lactose-reduced milk, or other dairy or soy-based dairy-style products
- Hard-boiled egg yolk mashed with a little milk or mayonnaise
- A bowl of chicken, turkey, or lamb broth (without onions, garlic, or additives)
- Roasted or boiled chicken, in bite-size pieces
- "Human" tuna, salmon, and other canned fish (or use their juices to make any of the above more attractive)
- A gel-form or chewable vitamin made especially for cats
- All-natural deli meat or sausage (avoid pork and ham, and spices)
- A small taste of other safe "people" food, such as crunchy breakfast cereal

Keeping Your Cat Out of the Potted Plants

UNFORTUNATELY FOR THOSE OF US with green thumbs, some cats find the soil around potted plants irresistible. It's not that they want to make a mess or disturb the plant's roots—it's their natural instinct to dig in dirt. You don't have to give up your plants, though (except for those that could be poisonous; see Day 269). Here are a few options for making potting soil less tempting yet still allow your plants to thrive.

- Cut a circle out of fiberglass screening (available in rolls at the hardware store) to match the circumference of your pot at the soil level. Cut a line from the edge to the center, then cut out a bit of the center to fit around the plant's stem. Fit the screen around the stem and secure it into the soil with landscape pins.

- Cover the surface of the soil with decorative stones. These are available at your nursery and come in a range of colors and sizes. Avoid pea gravel and other very small stones—anything with a size and texture resembling cat litter. Smooth river rock works well and looks good in many environments. Be sure to thoroughly rinse rocks before adding them to the pot to remove any dust or grime left over from the manufacturing process.

- Cover the surface of the soil with tumbled glass (sold as "beach glass") or glass marbles. These materials are often sold in craft stores near the flower arranging supplies and come in a number of colors and finishes.

- If you really don't want to cover your soil with anything, try putting strips of double-stick tape around the edges of the pot. Cats don't like the sticky feeling of the tape, and will usually stay away from places where it is used.

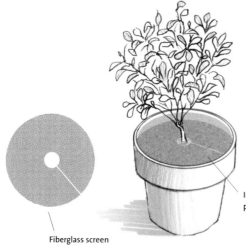

Fiberglass screen

Insert screen in potted plant

Himalayan

THIS CAT HAILS FROM HARVARD—it was a breed experiment in an effort to produce a cat with a puff-ball fur coat. The first Himalayan was named Debutante, a fitting moniker for an Ivy League feline.

Characteristics: The puffy ball of fur known as the Himalayan is actually a Persian—with Siamese-style colorpointing (in fact, it is known in Great Britain and other countries as simply a Colorpoint Longhair or an Exotic Longhair). Himalayans can be blue, chocolate, cream, lilac, red, or seal pointed; they can also be tortie or lynx pointed. Whatever the color of their fur, they should have blue eyes. They are considered far more retiring in temperament than the Siamese.

This class of coloring was first recognized by the British cat fanciers in 1955; two years later, the first American Himalayan show cat was displayed in Calgary, Canada.

History: This cat was deliberately developed quite scientifically by Western breeders rather than emanating from the famous Asian mountain range that inspired its name.

The breed originated in Sweden, in 1922; Americans jumped on the bandwagon in the 1930s, producing the first Himalayan at Harvard Medical School in 1935. The breeders at Harvard began with a female Siamese and a black male Persian, which resulted in black shorthaired kittens. Then they tried a female Persian and a male Siamese, which again created black shorthaired offspring but—aha! They then crossbred the litters, which brought out the longhaired and colorpointed gene.

Since that time, crossbreeding by others to narrow down the desired characteristics continued, such as to preserve the round, flattened face of the Persian rather than narrow the jaw and lengthen the nose to appear Siamese.

feline fun fact **>** Himalayans are born creamy white and do not attain their colorpointed coloring or their full-length coat until they reach maturity.

Himalayan

Story: Lost—Gracie Cat

IT WAS A LAST RESORT—I would do anything to get my lost kitty back, and she had been gone for a good week. I'll tell you all the steps I took first, with no luck, and you'll understand why I was willing to try anything, even that, to lure her back home. My cat, Gracie, was an indoor dweller who occasionally toured the neighborhood, but always returned. Life is good here at home. That's why I panicked when she departed for what I thought was a quick prowl around the block, but the next day, no Gracie.

I calmed myself down, rationalizing that she would return later that evening. But she didn't. The week progressed and I enlisted my address book of friends in a flyer campaign. No phone pole went unmarked. Flyers contained Gracie's photo, description, my contact information, and even an enticing reward. My cat was lost, and I had never felt so lost . . . and helpless. How do you reel in a cat who is on the streets? This is the same cat that cozies up by my pillow each night, and watches TV with the family, and . . . I couldn't imagine her out in the "wilds" of our town.

Horrible thoughts flashed into my mind, interrupting my train of thought at any given moment. At work, at home, with friends, in public . . . a restaurant worker would ask me whether I wanted a side of this-or-that, and I would respond, "Have you seen my cat?" I never imagined I'd be the one hanging the posters and praying for Kitty's swift return. But who does?

I tried everything. I walked the streets of my neighborhood, shaking a can of cat treats. I set my worn pajamas (translation = dirty laundry) on the front porch, along with all of Gracie's cat toys. No results. The posters were still hanging on poles around town, but no one called. Everyone had written off this lost cat business as a done deal. No more Gracie.

But there was one more trick I read about, and finally was willing to try. I guess you could say my "secret weapon" worked like a charm. I "marked" our front porch (not during broad daylight, and very discreetly using a cup of diluted urine). There are a lot of front porches like ours in town; maybe Gracie needed a scent. Who knows? Besides, the tip I read on a lost pet website said this would work.

For Gracie, this gave her a scented "map" home. She made her way onto our front porch and has lived safe and warm inside ever since.

Leash-Training Your Cat

WITH PATIENCE AND PERSISTENCE you can train most cats to tolerate a leash, and maybe even enjoy it. First, understand that leashed cats don't behave like leashed dogs: They don't heel. "Walking" a cat is more like following along behind her as she explores. Cats usually take longer to leash train than dogs, so the earlier you start, the more success you are likely to have. Once you have your expectations in line and have selected your harness and leash (see Day 169), you're ready to start.

First, introduce the harness and leash to her play space or sleeping area. Give her plenty of praise as she sniffs and explores them. After a week or so, when the harness and leash are no longer intriguing new distractions, casually pick her up and fasten her into the harness. If she fights it, calmly back off and try again another day—the idea is to get her to accept the harness, not to associate it with fear or punishment.

If she accepts the harness, praise her and give her a treat and distract her with playtime. Once she is accustomed to the harness, attach a standard lightweight leash (not a retractable one; those are too heavy for training) and allow the leash to trail along behind her while you distract her with playtime. Eventually, pick up your end of the leash and follow her around the house.

Be careful not to tug hard on the leash. Cats tend to respond to this with panic, not compliance. Redirect her as necessary with a toy, treat, or other distraction, or just pick her up and move her.

Don't take her outside on the leash until she is completely comfortable with it in the safety of the house. The many distractions of the world outside can cause her to panic, and you don't want the unfamiliarity of the leash to add to her distress.

Never leave your cat unattended when she is in her harness, because harnesses don't have the emergency escape features that safety collars do, and she could get caught on something out of your sight and not be able to free herself.

Advertising Cats

CATS HAVE SERVED AS EXPERT sales-creatures of everything from pet food to whiskey and tobacco. Be it in print or on television, they are undeniably *purrsuasive*.

Some notable examples:

- Various creatively posed cats advertised Dr. Thomas' Eclectric Oil, a patent medicine of the late 1800s; these are now available as original trade cards and ads, as well as replica prints and cards.

- Dubonnet has included cats in its advertising art and on its wine labels for more than a century, dating back to poster artist Jean Chéret's (1836–1932) acknowledgment of Madame Dubonnet's pet cats in his illustrations for the company.

- Because of their association with yarn, cats were the advertising symbol for several thread companies early in the past century, including the Belgian brand Cat's Selecta; Willimantic, the U.S.'s first cotton sewing machine thread; Corticelli Silk; and J. P. Coats sewing thread.

- Chessie, tucked into bed and asleep, was created in 1933 by Guido Greunwald to promote the smoothness of the ride on the Chesapeake and Ohio Railway. Her slogan was, "Sleep like a kitten." In 1935, her family expanded to include two kittens, and a little late on the scene, after people questioned their parentage, the company gave her a husband, Peake.

- The fluffy white Snowy the kitten was photographed by Harry Whittier Frees in various costumes and poses, to sell Mohawk and Utica sheets in the 1930s and '40s (see also Day 226 for more about his photography).

- Red tabby Morris the Cat debuted in 1969 as the finicky spokescat (voiced by actor John Erwin) for 9Lives cat food after having been rescued as a stray at the Hillsdale, Illinois, Humane Society. He became so famous that he even costarred in the 1973 film *Shamus* and authored several books, including *The Morris Approach: An Insider's Guide to Cat Care* (1980). Journalist Mary Daniels wrote his biography in 1974. Since his demise in 1978, Morris has been played by several look-alikes, all shelter or rescued cats.

feline fun fact > Ralston Purina's "Singing Cat" Meow Mix commercial first aired in 1972. What amused viewers didn't know: The red tabby was actually *choking* on the food, not singing! According to advertising agency executive Jerry Della Femma, the cat's expressions as it coughed gave the crew the brainstorm to substitute perky music and the famous "meow, meow, meow" lyrics to their filmed footage.

Healthy for Humans, Deadly for Cats

TEMPTING THOUGH IT MAY BE TO slip Kitty a taste of people food, some edibles that are safe for humans can cause anything from a tummy upset to death in a cat. Be wary of sharing the following with your pet, and take care how and where you store them:

Aspirin and acetaminophen (such as Tylenol): Toxic to cats; can be fatal.

Cod liver oil and other fish oil: The human dosage of this supplement can cause a vitamin E deficiency called steatitis. Cat-size supplements are available.

Large quantities of liver: Liver is loaded with vitamin A, the excess of which can cause internal hemorrhaging or grow excess bone along the spinal column; also may have a laxative effect.

Milk: Once kittens are weaned, they may be lactose intolerant. If your cat drinks milk, she may experience digestive upset and bloatedness. Try cream, or a lactose-free milk product.

Tuna: Tuna as an occasional treat is fine; do not feed Kitty tuna often. She may develop steatitis.

Bones: Bones, especially from chicken or turkey, can splinter and create harmful shards that your cat may swallow.

Fat and turkey skin: May cause pancreatitis.

Apple or pear seeds, cherry, peach, apricot pits: These contain cyanide and can be fatal in even minute quantities. Bring your cat to a vet immediately. The entire fruit of the cherry is toxic to cats.

Almonds: Same toxicity as apple seeds, etc.

Macadamia nuts: May cause muscle damage in cats.

Nutmeg: May cause seizures or death.

Chocolate: Chocolate contains both caffeine and theobromine, and can cause cardiac distress in a cat, even in a tiny amount.

Onions, shallots, leeks, scallions, chives, garlic: The sulfites in these alliums can make a cat very ill, destroying her red blood cells; do not give Kitty any human foods containing even a small amount of these ingredients, particularly onions.

Avocado: A substance in avocados called persin can cause anything from digestive upset to death.

Green tomatoes, eggplant, peppers, potatoes: All belong to the deadly nightshade family. Potato eyes or green skin are especially dangerous to cats.

Alfalfa: If you use these sprouts on your salad, make sure Kitty doesn't nibble.

Rhubarb: The powerful oxalates in this vegetable can damage your cat's kidneys. Induce vomiting (see Day 192) and then bring her to the vet.

Raisins and grapes: May cause kidney problems in cats.

Salt: Too much salt upsets your cat's electrolyte balance.

Products containing xylitol (a sweetener): This chemical is toxic to cats.

Dog food: The nutritional needs of dogs are different from those of cats. Although Kitty may not become ill from snacking from your pooch's bowl, she is not getting the vitamins and minerals she needs, particularly taurine.

Dealing with Home Flea Infestations

IF KITTY HAS HAD A CASE OF FLEAS (see Day 80), your house is also infested. Flea infestations can get out of control rapidly if not addressed. Each adult female flea can lay up to fifty eggs a day over a period of several weeks, so it's best to start treatment at the first sign of fleas.

Carpets, upholstery, and floorboard crevices are all ripe spots for flea eggs to accumulate until the fleas emerge as larvae, and most homes have an abundance of these hospitable surfaces. Be diligent when cleaning these "hot" zones.

Begin your flea-be-gone regimen with a thorough vacuuming using a high-suction vacuum cleaner. Start with the furniture, including cat beds. Remove any washable fabrics, such as pet blankets, and wash them in hot, soapy water. Remove and vacuum the furniture cushions on all sides. Get into all the crevices of each piece of furniture with the crevice tool. Next, tackle the rugs and floors. Be sure to use the crevice tool to get into all corners of your rooms along the baseboards.

Pay extra attention to any wide cracks in the floorboards if you have hardwood floors. Remove and dispose of the vacuumed-up waste outdoors to avoid reintroducing any fleas that may still be living.

Next, apply a pet-safe flea dust, such as diatomaceous earth or silica gel, following the manufacturer's instructions. Some of these products need to be left on for a few days before vacuuming; others take only a short time to work. Again, remove and dispose of the vacuumed-up waste outdoors. If the number of fleas doesn't appear to be reduced after two treatments, try a pet-safe pesticide-based flea solution, following the manufacturer's instructions. If those products don't seem to be making a dent in the problem, it's time to call a professional exterminator.

The life cycle of a flea can last anywhere from several weeks to more than a year, depending on environmental conditions. Treatment may need to be repeated a number of times to ensure that all of the fleas are eliminated.

Japanese Bobtail

THE JAPANESE BOBTAIL, prized as the model for that country's Maneki Neko (see Day 205), actually began in China. But the handsome breed was quite a traveler, migrating to Japan, where it was highlighted in literature and the arts.

Characteristics: This cat's face is distinctive, with high-set eyes above high cheekbones and a long nose, and it often sports parallel vertical stripes in the center of its forehead. Its tail is only around 2 inches (5 cm) long and is curled tightly against the cat's upper rump, to appear ball-like.

A longhaired version of this cat was first documented in Japan in 1954, but actually this breed did exist as an occasional mutation before that date. These shaggy Bobtails share their shorthaired relatives' short tail and coloring, with the addition of a ruff and ear and toe tufts. Both varieties are known to have a sweet personality and a sweet, melodic voice.

History: Bobtails came to the United States in the aftermath of World War II, when an American brought a pair named Madame Butterfly and Richard to the United States to breed them. Another breeder brought over more, in 1969, and Bobtails flourished in their transplanted environment, accepted as a breed in the United States in 1969. The longhaired variation was finally accepted in 1993.

The classic shorthaired Japanese Bobtail has a small pom-pom of a tail and is predominantly white with patches of red and black, a variety known as mi-ke, which means "three-furred." Legend fancifully has it that the first cats to come to Japan from China were black, the next white, and finally red, which interbred to create the patched effect. Bobtails may be other, solid colors, but not colorpointed or lilac. A Bobtail with only two spots of color on its head has what is called a *van pattern*.

feline fun fact > It is said that Japanese Bobtails were responsible for a kind of Pied Piper miracle in days of old, saving Japan's silk industry by exterminating rats that were ravaging its precious silkworms.

Japanese Bobtail

Yoga: The Cat Pose

IN THE SPIRIT OF BEING ONE with your cat, practice the cat pose to coordinate movement and breath, two qualities that can come in handy while handling everyday stress (related or not to your cats). When executed, the cat pose resembles the back-arching and stretching movement your cat makes when he is frightened or prepared to pounce. The pose teaches you to initiate movement from your center.

Follow these steps to perform the cat pose:

1. Form the neutral position by starting on your hands and knees. Position your hands directly beneath your shoulders and your knees beneath your hips. Your back should form a horizontal, flat line. Gaze at the floor.

2. Press downward into your hands, pushing your shoulders up. When you exhale, sag your shoulders and allow your back to curve inward. Return to the neutral position.

3. Breathe in deeply, and turn your hips into cat tilt as you exhale. Do this by pulling the abdominal muscles back toward the spine, tucking your tailbone down and under, and contracting your rear. Press down with your hands to lift your shoulders; press the middle of your back toward the ceiling, and round your spine upward. This position resembles the arched back of a cat.

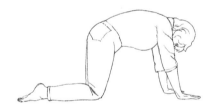

Kneading

YOU ARE RELAXING IN YOUR FAVORITE easy chair, enjoying a cup of coffee with your cat curled up on your lap. You're petting her absentmindedly while dreaming of a massage on an exotic beach when you realize that you *are* getting a massage—from your cat!

The massaging action your cat makes with her front paws is called kneading, or sometimes "making bread" or "making biscuits." She pushes and pulls with her paws, alternating left and right, usually on a soft surface such as a blanket or pillow or your lap.

Some cats manage it without exposing their claws, but others can't help themselves and may deliver a mild scratch or two in the process.

Cats knead to express contentment. It's believed to be a holdover action from kittenhood, when a kitten kneads against her mother's side when nursing. Kneading is a sign of happiness and security and is often a precursor to sleep.

Feline Fables

A Cat was looking at a King, as permitted by the proverb.

"Well," said the monarch, observing her inspection of the royal person, "how do you like me?"

"I can imagine a King," said the Cat, "whom I should like better."

"For example?"

"The King of the Mice."

The sovereign was so pleased with the wit of the reply that he gave her permission to scratch his Prime Minister's eyes out.

—Ambrose Bierce

A fable is a story with a moral, often "peopled" by animals. Some of the most enduring fables from Aesop, the father of the fable, concern cats. A splendid example is "The Cat and Aphrodite," in which a cat so loves a man that she begs Aphrodite to change her into a woman.

Aphrodite complies but then tests the cat by letting loose a mouse when the cat-woman is alone with her lover. The cat forgets herself and pounces on it, destroying the romance! A variation of this story is "The Cat-Maiden," in which the cat is changed into a woman because of a bet Aphrodite has with Zeus, with the same end and moral: "Nature will win out."

Ambrose Bierce, who adapted Aesop's techniques to narratives, continued in the tradition, retelling some of Aesop's (his "The Cat and the Youth" is the Venus story, revisited) plus such tales as "The Sagacious Rat," in which a rat, spying a cat nearby, asks a fellow rat to come along when they exit their hole, courteously requesting that his friend emerge first. The friend is duly pounced upon and carried away, allowing the wise but rather asocial rat to enjoy his foray outside undisturbed.

Does Your Cat Need Vegetables?

CATS ARE CARNIVORES BY NATURE. Although their prey may have dined on grains and vegetables, these elements are only present in small amounts within the creature's digestive system. Apart from nibbling on catnip or related plants (mint, lavender), cats do not eat herbs or vegetables in the wild. So, why do pet food manufacturers add grains such as brown rice, vegetables, herbs, and even fruit to cat food?

Much of this is to appease the owners, who may have been adding whole grains, vegetables, herbs, and fruit to their own diet, and who think Kitty needs to eat likewise. Some people may be vegetarians and vegans, and think the correct balance of non-animal-derived foods will be healthy for their cat. Not so.

Cats need arachidonic acid, which is found only in animal foods, especially fish. Also, vitamin A is found only in animal flesh and eggs.

Beta-carotene, a precursor to that vitamin, also occurs in orange vegetables, such as carrots or squash, which can be given to cats in small quantity (grated raw if carrots, or cooked and pureed if squash). (They create too much roughage in large amounts.)

A diet high in plant material can make Kitty's urine too alkaline, which can cause very painful stones to form in the urinary tract. The fiber in plant matter can cause diarrhea or gas and interfere with your cat's ability to digest both the offensive plant and other, healthier foods.

If you wish to give your cat grains and vegetables, these carbs should comprise no more than 25 percent of his diet and preferably much less, as compared with 30 percent protein and 40 percent fat derived from chicken, turkey, beef, lamb, or fish.

Be particularly skeptical of any pet cookbook that advocates giving your cat considerable quantities of grains or other plant material, and especially books whose ingredient lists include garlic, which is toxic to cats.

Dealing with Cat Urine Odors

CAT URINE ODORS ARE notoriously difficult to remove. The main culprits are urea, a sticky substance that is the body's way of getting rid of nitrogen; urochrome, what gives urine its color; and uric acid, what causes the worst of the odor.

Most cleaning products easily take care of urea and urochrome, but detergents and soaps will not remove uric acid. Uric acid crystallizes and bonds to porous surfaces, such as carpet fibers, which makes is very difficult to remove. When the crystals are dry, humans can't smell them, which fool us into thinking the urine is gone. Cats, however, with their more sensitive noses, can smell the uric acid and will return to the spot to urinate. When the crystals absorb moisture—on a humid day, for example—the odor is released.

To remove uric acid, use a solution specifically formulated to remove cat urine odors. These solutions work by using enzymes to break up the crystals. Carefully follow the manufacturer's directions for best results. Most enzymatic cleaners require several applications to fully remove uric acid, especially if the stain is old. If one product doesn't work, try another with a different formula. Cat owners report varying degrees of success with commercial products; what works in one situation might not work in another.

Never use ammonia or an ammonia-based product to try to remove cat urine. The ammonia smell signals to cats that this is an acceptable place to urinate.

Korat

THE KORAT IS KNOWN AS the good-luck cat in its home country of Thailand. Natives call the silver cat, with its vivid green eyes, Si-siwat.

Characteristics: Korat fur, supersmooth without any undercoat, sheds so little that this breed is considered a good one to try in a household with cat allergies (the allergy is to dander, but the lack of shedding keeps much of the dander on the cat). The hairs are solid blue lightly tipped with silver. Korat kittens may be born with amber eyes, and it can take a few years for their coat to acquire the glossiness prized in adults. Unlike other exotics, their body approaches the cobby build, with a rounder, more heart-shaped face than the Siamese's classic triangle.

This breed likes things quiet and slow, as perhaps its lifestyle is in its native country. They demonstrate acutely sensitive sight, smell, and hearing, and in consequence dislike loud noises.

History: Like its colorpointed cousin the Siamese, the Korat originated along the east coast of Thailand, in Khorat, near Laos, sometime around the 1300s. Some six centuries passed before they ever visited the West, when in 1896 what was possibly a Korat—it was described as a blue Siamese—was shown at a British cat show. (At around that time, reportedly, it was Siam's then king, Chulalongkorn, who gave the Korat cat its name, after the place where it originated.)

Another half century passed until a definitely Korat pair of cats named Nara and Darra were sent to live in the United States in 1959. They had kinked tails tipped with white. Five years later, an example of the breed was shown at a U.S. cat show, and five years after that, the breed was accepted by both Canadian and U.S. cat fanciers. Great Britain kept apace separately, not officially importing Korats until 1972 and then recognizing the breed in 1975.

feline fun fact > In Thailand, brides often receive a Korat as a wedding present, for luck.

Korat

Bringing Home a New (Human) Baby

IT'S IMPORTANT TO INTRODUCE your cat to the sight and sounds of a baby before the real one arrives. That way, your cat will not arch its back and yowl with fear at the sound of the baby's cries—or do worse, and scale the crib.

Once baby comes home, allow your cat into the nursery only while you are supervising. Take time to introduce your cat to the room, and spend time in the nursery with the cat and baby so Kitty isn't suspicious and angry that you dedicate so much time behind the closed door.

Before you bring home your baby, play "mom" with a babydoll. Cuddle with it and talk to it so your cat gets used to the idea of sharing your attention. If a friend has a newborn or older children, ask if you can record real sounds of a baby crying. Play the recording several times a day for your cat before bringing home the real baby.

When the baby is born, ask a family member to bring home one of the baby's swaddling blankets for your cat to smell. It helps to have your personal scent on the blanket, too. You want to familiarize your cat with the new baby's scent before your newborn comes home.

When you arrive home with your new baby, ask a friend to help with the introduction. While you and your spouse enter the house, your friend will hold the baby. Mom and Dad greet the cat first, then the baby is passed to Dad. After a few minutes pass, Mom holds the baby—all the while, attention is paid to the cat (if she is interested).

The key is to make a gradual introduction, assuring that everyone in the household is important and loved. Because your cat was there first, she will likely play the role of protector over the child. You may even discover your cat watching over the baby as if it were her own.

Your Cat and the Law

MANY COMMUNITIES HAVE LAWS regulating pet ownership. You should know what those regulations are so you can stay on the right side of the law. Many cities and towns post their municipal codes online for easy access. Alternatively, contact your city hall or animal control office to find out what you need to do to stay legal.

Common regulations address:

- The number of cats and other animals that can be kept in one household
- Whether pets must be registered and whether they must wear registration tags

- The types of vaccinations your cat must have
- Nuisances and disturbances of the peace, such as noise, digging in neighbors' yards, and excessive odors
- Humane treatment of animals
- Requirements for control and confinement

The last point is especially important to cat owners. More communities are passing laws that make it illegal for cat owners to allow their cats to roam free. Before you let Kitty out, know what the rules are where you live.

Cats in Shakespeare

Purr! the cat is gray. —*King Lear*, act III, scene vi

FORSOOTH! CATS, MOSTLY IN metaphoric allusion, are rife in Shakespeare's works. Screw your courage to the sticking place and peruse:

- The cat, with eyne of burning coal. —*Pericles, Prince of Tyre*, act II, scene v

- What would'st thou have with me? / Good king of cats, nothing but one of your nine lives. —*Romeo and Juliet*, act III, scene i

- They'll take suggestion as a cat laps milk —*The Tempest*, act II, scene i

- The mouse ne'er shunn'd the cat as they did budge. —*Coriolanus*, act I, scene vi

- The cat will mew and dog will have his day. —*Hamlet*, act V, scene i

- I am as melancholy as a gib cat. —*King Henry IV*, part I, act I, scene ii

- If your mother's cat had but kittened, though yourself had never been born. —*King Henry IV*, part I, act III, scene i

- I am as vigilant as a cat to steal cream. —*King Henry IV*, part I, act IV, scene ii

- Playing the mouse in absence of the cat. —*King Henry V*, act I, scene ii

- Thrice the brinded cat hath mew'd. —*Macbeth*, act IV, scene i

- Some, that are mad if they behold a cat. —*Merchant of Venice*, act IV, scene i

- Tear a cat in, to make all split. —*A Midsummer Night's Dream*, act I, scene ii

Protect Your Cat from Poisons

CATS ARE VERY SUSCEPTIBLE TO poisoning due to their liver's inability to process toxins safely out of the body. Even a small amount of a food, chemical, or unsafe plant can make a cat very ill or even kill it. See Days 178 and 269 for more about dangerous foods and plants.

Other items to beware of:

- Drugs and nutritional supplements intended for humans or other animals

- Laundry products, such as detergent, bleach, and fabric softener

- Cleaning products, drain cleaners, and disinfectants, including such "natural" ones as citrus oil–based cleansers and borax. Pine-based products are highly toxic.

- Mothballs—use natural herbs, such as lavender and rosemary, instead.

- Potpourris, scented air fresheners, and essential oils. Use only herbs and flowers that have not been treated with chemicals and that are nontoxic to cats, such as lavender or rose petals.

- Carpet cleaners other than bicarbonate of soda mixed with natural herbs

- Antifreeze is lethal to cats, and its sweet smell is very attractive to them. Clean spills from your garage or driveway, and make sure the container is well out of reach. Fix your car's radiator if it is leaking the fluid.

- Insecticides and rodent poisons. If you have a mouse problem that Kitty is not attending to, use snap-style mousetraps.

- Cocoa bean garden mulch. Chocolate, very toxic to cats, is derived from cocoa.

- Oil, kerosene, lighter fluid, and so on

- Salt or other deicing products

Symptoms of poisoning appear immediately or take several days to appear. If your cat experiences any of the following, he may be poisoned:

- Sudden severe vomiting or diarrhea

- Convulsions or difficulty walking

- Unexpected weakness or lethargy

- Drooling or foaming at the mouth

- A chemical scent to your cat's breath

- Blistering, redness, or swelling of the lips, tongue, or throat, or pawing at the face

- Unconsciousness

Helping a Poisoned Cat

If your cat displays symptoms of being poisoned, first call your vet.

- Noncorrosive materials may be brought back up with syrup of ipecac or a 1:1 solution of hydrogen peroxide in water, but do not induce vomiting if your cat's mouth is blistered or swelling, or an hour or more have passed since the poison was actually ingested.

- A crushed activated charcoal tablet may help absorb toxins, or milk may dilute them. Vinegar or lemon joice in water may neutralize an alkaline; or baking soda in water, neutralize an acid.

Outdoor Cat Enclosures

IF YOUR INDOOR CAT PINES to go outdoors—giving you not-so-subtle hints like meowing by the door or gazing out the window with a pleading look in her eyes—an outdoor cat enclosure might be just the solution to give you peace of mind and your cat fresh air. Just make sure the enclosure is large enough so your cat can play and establish her own territory if she must share the space with other cats.

The simplest way to create a cat enclosure is to screen in an existing porch. If you don't have a suitable porch, you can construct a freestanding kennel out of lumber and screening. Or enclose a lean-to or room addition that can be accessed through an existing door. Some cat owners build elaborate, multistory structures with bridges and tunnels and with multiple access points through doors, windows, or cat doors on each floor of the home.

Whether your structure is simple or complex, make sure it is safe and secure for your cats. It must have at least a partial roof to provide shade and protection from rain. Inspect it to make sure the screening is attached securely and that no nails or screws protrude. Seal any gaps you find; cats can squeeze through tighter places than you might think.

If the floor is dirt, secure hardware cloth to the structure and run it 6 to 8 inches (15.2 to 20.3 cm) under the ground on all sides so your cat cannot dig her way out. Inspect the perimeter regularly to check for signs of digging. Consider placing large stones all around the perimeter on the inside to discourage digging.

Once you have the structure in place, furnish it with cozy places for your cat to perch. Simple shelves can be attached to the walls to provide perches; stagger a number of them to allow your cat some exercise and entertainment. Use wide board lumber to create ramps and bridges from one part of the room to another. Provide a couple of comfy places where Kitty can curl up for her naps, and don't forget a litter box if she won't have free access to where her regular box is.

Before modifying or adding any structures onto your home, be sure to check with your homeowners association (if you have one) and local building department to determine whether there are any regulations you must abide by or permits you need to apply for.

Maine Coon

DURING THE U.S. CIVIL WAR ERA, Maine Coon cats were best-of-show winners at Madison Square Garden and Boston cat shows. Soon after, Americans began preferring imported breeds.

Characteristics: The Maine Coon is best known for having lynxlike tabby markings, but in fact can appear in all colors except colorpoint. It takes about three years for the complete characteristics of the breed to emerge. It is sweet-tempered and an excellent companion for children.

History: America's oldest indigenous cat is related to wild cats native to Maine's woodlands, which met up with Angoras brought to U.S. shores by British sailors. The combined genes created a shaggy, massively built cat equipped to withstand cold weather, with large, round facial features; tufted ears and paws; enormous (and often polydactyl) toes that can almost function as hands; and a thick brush of a tail. (A tightness in the rump may make these noble creatures run with an awkward swish to their rear, as if they are wearing too-tight underclothes.)

Another fifty-odd years passed before the Maine Coon achieved show recognition in its native country. (In 1983, these gentle giants were introduced to the UK, and achieved their recognition in 1994.)

feline fun fact > The Maine Coon has a distinctive chirping voice that belies its huge frame.

Maine Coon

Pet Massage

THERE'S NOTHING MORE RELAXING than a professional massage—it's a mental escape and a time for physical rejuvenation. If your cat is accustomed to being handled, she too will bask in the luxury of a good rubdown from a pet massage therapist. These trained masseuses can address specific pain issues, or simply tickle your cat's fancy by hitting all the "happy spots." Cat massage focuses on the whole body. The cat lies on a bed on her side at first, and gradually the masseuse will rotate her onto her back and other side, working the body in circular motions to release tension and stress. (If you are skeptical, watch the process and how a cat looks after the massage: blissed out as if she woke up from the best nap of her life!)

Massage has many benefits. Cats' muscles get sore over time and their joints can break down over the years. Massage can help prevent this soreness and damage, or alleviate pain if this process has already begun.

Older cats with arthritis and stiffness may have difficulty exercising, leading to further pain and stiffness, which leads to even more inactivity. Massage can diminish pain levels in arthritic cats as well as improve flexibility and range of motion. This helps these cats feel and move better, allowing them to be more active.

Ask the masseuse to teach you some techniques to practice at home so you can provide therapy to your cat in between appointments. Massage is a great bonding activity and health benefit.

Conditions improved by massage include:

- Inactivity due to injury, illness, old age, or obesity
- Poor circulation in muscles
- Sluggish lymphatic system
- Recovery after surgery or injuries
- Arthritis

Kitty Come Home

YOUR HOUSE CAT MADE A grand escape into the wilds of your neighborhood. She's never been outdoors without your supervision, but this time she's on her own. She snuck out at night, and it's morning with still no signs of her return. At what point do you call a wandering cat "lost"? The answer: immediately.

Indoor-outdoor cats that come and go as they please tend to have a schedule—how long they roam before returning home. If your cat is gone longer than usual, take steps to locate your cat and bring her safely home.

First, don't panic. The good news about cats is that they are territorial. They have an uncanny sort of feline GPS that seems to direct them back home—they know their turf. That said, if your cat is gone for an abnormal duration of time, there are several scenarios that might have played out: Your cat got scared and is hiding out or she was picked up by animal control or another cat lover who thinks the cat is "lost."

Here's how to get Kitty back home safely:

Scout your yard. Look under the deck, in the garage, under brush, and other places where your cat could duck and hide. Take a favorite squeaky toy or noisemaker with you and call out to your cat so she will run to you.

Plant strong-scented personal effects outdoors. Dirty laundry, shoes, and other items that carry your scent might lure Kitty back home. Put her litter box and/or favorite toys outdoors. Place a container of smelly canned food or tuna by her usual entrance to the house.

Start advertising. Make a "lost" poster of your cat with a close-up, clear photo so people can view her distinct coat and eye color. Include facts, such as: *Responds to the name Fluffy. Loves tuna snacks. Wears a red collar.* Think of ways for a potential rescuer to identify the cat as yours. Don't forget to provide your contact information. You may consider running a lost-and-found advertisement in the newspaper or on your city's website, if they offer this service.

Call animal control. Also phone the police to find out if your cat is already found. Contact your local animal shelters and area veterinarians. Prepare an accurate description of your cat and drop off flyers.

Canvass the neighborhood. Talk to neighbors, shop owners, pedestrians, anyone who might have information about your lost cat. Bring flyers with you so people can associate your description with a photo.

Keep the faith. Pets are lost for months and still return home to their owners. Be careful when meeting people who respond to your advertisements. Meet individuals who claim to have found your cat in a public place, and never go alone.

25 Cats Named Sam

WHEN PEOPLE THINK OF ANDY WARHOL, images of soup cans and such celebrities as Marilyn Monroe are probably what come to mind.

Born Andrew Warhola in Pennsylvania in 1928, he worked as an award-winning commercial illustrator prior to rocketing to fame for his silk-screened, semiphotographic images depicting iconic American products and famous performers. In 1962, he formed an art-filmmaking studio named the Factory, launching the era of Pop Art, which celebrated the mundane and familiar.

But even before Warhol became a household name, he began painting vividly colored full-length portraits of his numerous cats. Except for one kitty named Hester, every one of this eccentric illustrator's pets was named Sam! In 1954, Warhol privately published the collection as lithographs, in the book *25 Cats Name Sam and One Blue Pussy* [sic].

It featured no text, just calligraphic captions penned by his devoted mother, Julia. (It was she who misspelled the title and, in fact, the small book contains only seventeen feline images.) Warhol would collaborate with his mom on another volume, *Holy Cats*, in 1957, in which Hester and other pets are shown romping in heaven.

Warhol died in 1987 following complications from surgery. But his feline fancy lives on—the 1994 book *Cats, Cats, Cats* collects thirty-nine of his cat illustrations, plus his many Sams now appear on everything from note cards to night-lights (one can't help thinking Warhol would have enjoyed such blatant commercialization!). Another fun commemorative: his nephew James Warhola's children's book, *Uncle Andy's: A Faabbbulous Visit with Andy Warhol*—examine its illustrations to spot the famous twenty-five cats as immortalized by Warhola, an artist in his own right.

Your Cats Need Taurine

TAURINE, THE SHORT NAME for 2-aminoethaneulfonic acid, is an amino acid vital to cats' health. Dogs are able to synthesize it within their own body, but cats need an outside source on a regular basis. For this reason, *do not* feed your dog food to your cat. Commercially prepared cat foods are usually supplemented with the correct amount of taurine per serving.

If your cat does not receive enough taurine, he may develop retinal degeneration, tooth decay, hair loss, heart disorders, and reproductive problems. A cat deficient in this nutrient may go blind.

A cat who eats predominantly "people" foods needs to be given a supplement that contains taurine.

Canned cat foods tend to contain more taurine than do dry, another case for switching Kitty to wet foods (see Day 115). A dry food should contain at least 0.2 percent of the amino acid.

Connecting with Other Cat Owners

CAT OWNERS LOVE TO TALK ABOUT their cats. Owners groups are a great way to meet other cat lovers and share information, tips, and stories.

The Internet makes it easy to connect with other cat owners through email discussion lists and online forums. To join an email discussion list, simply subscribe to a group and you will receive messages sent by everyone involved. You can participate in the discussion by replying to the message, and you can usually adjust your settings for your message to go to an individual or to the whole group.

Online forums, also called message boards, are great Internet venues for reading cat commentary and posting feedback. It's okay to "lurk" on a list or forum—receive and read messages for a while without sending any yourself—to get a feel for it before deciding whether you will stick around and participate.

Discussion lists and forums address such issues as general cat information, breed-specific knowledge, health-related questions, and even pet travel tips. The list goes on—there is more information than you will have time to read! Get started by searching for "cat discussion list" or "cat forum." Narrow your search with additional terms, such as "health" or "vet."

Those without Internet access or who simply prefer to meet other cat owners in person should check with their local humane society, shelter, vet, or breeder. These resources can provide the contact information for local organizations that may interest you. Also, many libraries maintain lists of local organizations. And if you can't find a local organization, why not start one?

Manx

THE MANX CAT IS WELL KNOWN because of its physical handicap, which in the eyes of fanciers makes the breed a sleek and beautiful animal. The Manx has a partial tail, or no tail at all. It may even be missing a final vertebra in its spine. (That's why Manx cats should come with a warning: Handle with care.)

Characteristics: The cat's torso is very short, the most truncated of any breed, with a round rump that is raised a bit in the air, due to a shortness of the forelegs. The chest and face are broad. Although the Manx has a thick double coat, it is a shorthaired cat. It comes in every color and pattern, including colorpoint. The lack of a tail does not impede the Manx from being an adept climber, jumper, and hunter.

As for that spinal defect? Kittens conceived by the mating of two tailless Manxes run the risk of being spontaneously aborted, or if they survive birth may have a severe defect similar to humans' spina bifida, which impairs their lower digestive system. The problem can be averted by only mating an at least partially tailed cat with a tailless one.

History: The Manx cat is native to the UK's isolated Isle of Man, where the tailless breed interbred to perpetuate its unique characteristic. It dates back centuries and yet, owing to a genetic defect that can prove fatal, it is, ironically, not accepted in UK competitions, for fear that lauding the Manx will increase the breed's popularity. In the United States, however, there is no such restriction. The breed was first imported to the U.S. in 1933.

feline fun fact > There is no truth to the rumor that the first Manx resulted from crossing a cat with a rabbit!

Manx

Cat-Friendly Travel Accommodations

PERHAPS THE MOST COMPLICATED ASPECT of traveling with your cat is finding accommodations that appreciate your four-footed friend as much as you do. The good news is that locating a cat-friendly hotel is easier than it used to be. As the pet industry grows by leaps and bounds, other markets recognize that animals are part of the family and marketing their service as pet-friendly can pay off.

Be sure to make reservations in advance. Research hotels and secure arrangements before you depart home. You'll find pet-friendly hotels, highways, outdoor dining, and parks.

Once you decide on accommodations, here are some questions to ask hotel/motel management before you arrive:

- Do you still allow pets—what about cats? (The policy may have changed.)

- How close is the nearest veterinarian? Obtain the name/contact information of the animal care facility.

- What are requirements for litter disposal?

- Do you require a pet deposit?

- Do you require all cat owners to show shot records? (The answer should be yes.)

- Will you provide a cat sleep mat/bed? Some luxury hotels will offer this perk.

Cat Personalities

CATS HAVE A REPUTATION as being aloof loners who reluctantly share their living space with their servants (us). Many first-time cat owners are surprised to find that cats have a range of personalities and varying degrees of tolerance for humans.

Some cats thrive on human attention. These social cats greet you when you come home, and not just because they want to be fed. They curl up on your lap when you watch television and crawl into bed with you at night. They're happiest when they're being petted, and will nudge your hand as a gentle reminder if you neglect your duty and let your hand sit idle. These cats will put up with all kinds of silly games from their humans because they just love being loved.

Other cats are more timid. They scamper off when you reach for them, but love to snuggle up as long as you're not paying too much attention. While reading a book, you may find a napping cat at your feet. Timid cats usually need some coaxing to get them to play, but once they step out of their shell they can be as enthusiastic as any other cat.

Queen cats rule. The queenly cat spends most of her time doing her own thing, ignoring humans around her unless interaction will work to her advantage (for instance, when purring and nuzzling could earn her a taste of lunch-meat that was just extracted from the fridge). Queenly cats can be friendly, but usually on their own terms. Approach them with a tasty treat or a good-feeling brush, but be willing to step away if she's not in the mood.

Lucky Cats: Maneki Neko

THE MANEKI NEKO IS A SYMBOL OF good fortune and typically depicted in illustrations or statues. According to legend, this Asian cat with one upraised paw brings good luck to its owners.

The Maneki Neko, which often resembles a calico-patterned Japanese Bobtail cat, first cropped up in newspapers and other documents of the Meiji period (1868–1912), although the feline charm dates back to the Edo period (1603–1867). According to legend, a feudal lord was saved from a lightning strike by a cat that beckoned him into a humble Buddhist temple. In thanks, the nobleman became the patron of the temple, which became prosperous. The legend became widely known and businesses began to place a Maneki Neko in their entranceway, hoping to attract customers, profits, or simply good luck. The decorative motif quickly found its way into all manner of objects. Today, items as diverse as key chains, porcelain tea sets, quilt block patterns, and fabrics boast a Maneki Neko design. China and Thailand have adopted the image as well, which is why you might see a Maneki Neko statue in some Chinese restaurants, despite its being a Japanese symbol.

The traditional Maneki Neko is frequently shown wearing a collar (often red) and bell or tag, like a house cat, which may have Japanese writing on it. Beneath the collar there may be a kind of neckerchief or bib, a feature of other Japanese spirit statues. Another feature may be the gold coin ornament, a *koban*, which attracts more good luck. An all-black body color is thought to ward off danger or illness.

In Japan, the palm usually faces inward; this position is reversed in Maneki Neko made for export. Various meanings, somewhat contradictory, have been assigned to which arm is raised (in Japan, it is usually the left one); in fact, some Maneki Neko have both arms in the air in a stick-'em-up pose, and it is even possible to find others with a raised knee as well. The higher the "hand," the greater the luck.

In Japan, owners of lost or ill cats leave prayers with images of the Maneki Neko at the Gotoku-Ji temple, said to be the original temple of the above legend, which houses several statues of this spirit figure.

If you or your cat could use a little luck in your life, Asian shops and online sources are sure to have a Maneki Neko to suit your tastes and needs.

The legendary Maneki Neko is a good-luck talisman for its owners.

Fat Cats: Managing Obesity

A FEW EXTRA TREATS, a few extra pounds, what's the difference? Those tasty rewards may be more damaging for our cats' health than we realize. We aren't doing our feline friends any favors by giving in to their pleading meows for just one more morsel, or by supersizing their meals.

Consider this: What humans would consider a slight tipping of the scale—3 pounds (1.4 kg) of extra weight on a cat—is equivalent to about 40 pounds (18 kg) on a human. That's more than a holiday splurge, and the extra pounds can pack on fast (as we all know).

In fact, obesity is the number one feline health problem among house cats, and owners aren't always to blame. Fifty-four percent of all cats are overweight, according to a National Pet Obesity Awareness Day study. Because cats are grazers, owners who keep the food dish full might not realize how much they feed their cats. In multi-cat households, greedy eaters can eat more than their fair share, sneaking food from a finicky feline sibling's bowl. Sedentary cats that prefer to couch surf rather than chase mice don't burn off extra calories from treats.

What if your cat needs to go on a feline slim-fast plan? Here are some useful weight-loss suggestions and tips to help you manage your cat's weight over the long term:

- Stop feeding people food to your cat.

- Choose low-calorie treats.

- Resist the urge to top off your cat's food bowl during the day if you allow her to graze.

- Dry food can contain more carbohydrates than a cat needs. Overweight cats may benefit from a protein-rich diet (achieved by mixing in a portion of moist food) that more closely resembles their naturally carnivorous diet.

- Cats who are stubborn to exercise can be stimulated with interactive toys, such as laser pointers and crinkly toys, or catnip.

- Consider leash training early on to form healthy exercise habits (see Day 176).

Overweight cats have an increased risk of suffering from potentially fatal diseases, including diabetes, liver disease, arthritis, and respiratory problems. Also, cats who are overweight and must go under anesthesia are at a higher risk of complications.

Crochet a Cat

THE FLAT DESIGN CAN BE USED to embellish garments, accessories, and soft furnishings. Finished size: roughly 4 inches (10.2 cm) tall.

MATERIALS

A small quantity (1 gram or less) of worsted-weight yarn (A), plus a very small quantity (about a foot [30 cm]) of pink or red yarn (B)

Crochet hook size E/4 (3.5 mm)

Scissors

To change colors: Holding the last two loops of the stitch on your hook, pull a loop of the new color through to complete the stitch.

To carry the unused color: Hold the unused strand of yarn firmly against the edge of the motif as you double crochet over it.

With yarn A, chain (ch) 4 and slip stitch (sl st) into the first ch.

Body:

Round 1: Ch-3 (counts as first double crochet), then double crochet (dc) 13 stitches into the ring, ending with a sl st into the third ch of the ch-3 that began the round. (14 dc)

Round 2: Ch-5, dc-2 into the next dc, dc into the next four dc, *dc-2 into the next dc, ch-2, dc-2 into the same dc (corner made),* dc into the next three dc, repeat from * to * once, dc into the next three dc, changing to yarn B as you complete the third stitch. With yarn B, carrying yarn A along the top of the last round, dc-2 in the next dc, changing to yarn A as you complete the second dc. Break off yarn B ¾ inch (2 cm) from the motif. Continuing with yarn A, dc-2 into the last dc, sl st into the third ch of the ch-3 that began the round. (equilateral triangle of 8 stitches per side and 7 on the bottom, between ch-2 chains)

Round 3: Ch-3, dc-1 in ch-2 loop, ch-2, dc-2 in ch-2 loop, dc in next eight dc, *dc 8 in ch-2 loop,* dc in next seven dc, repeat from * to * once, dc in next six dc, triple crochet one-third of the way down between the two dc you made in yarn B (this creates the indentation in the top of the heart), dc in the base of the ch-3 st that began the round, sl st into the third ch of the ch-3 that began the round. (triangle of 43 dc in all)

Head:

Row 1: Ch-3, dc in next dc, dc-3 in ch-2 loop, dc in next two dc. Turn. (7 dc)

Row 2: Ch-3, dc in next six dc. Turn. (7 dc)

Row 3 (ears): *Ch-3, then holding the last loop of each stitch on the hook, dc in the next two dc, and yarn over and draw the yarn through all three ch on hook. Ch-1, then sl st-3 evenly down the side of the last dc you just made. Sl st into the base of this dc (i.e., into the top of same dc of previous row).* Sc in the next dc. Sl st into the next dc and repeat from * to *. Ch-1 tightly to secure the yarn and snip off ¾ inch (2 cm) from the crocheted edge. Weave in the loose end.

Whiskers:

Cut two 2-inch (5 cm) strands of yarn A or B and use the hook to draw them through the top of the fourth (center) dc of Row 1 of the head. Center and tie each strand tightly to secure it, then spread out horizontally. Trim ends evenly with the sides of the head.

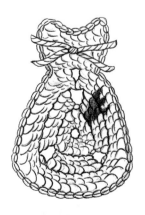

A finished cat with a heart

Munchkin

YOU'VE HEARD OF CATS THAT ACT like dogs, but this breed also resembles a dog—a dachshund, to be exact.

Characteristics: The Munchkin comes in all colors and coat lengths; because the breed is unregulated, anything goes when mating time comes around. There are even longhaired Munchkins whose belly fur literally brushes the ground!

Its limbs are notably short, which can make it difficult for the cat to run, climb, and jump. Considering this liability, the cats should be kept indoors, because outside it would be difficult for them to escape danger.

History: The breed, which was first noticed in the UK in the 1930s, actually reflects a spontaneous abnormality that many cat lovers feel should not be encouraged by deliberate breeding. Consequently, as of this writing, most registries will not accept it. The only U.S. organization that does is the International Cat Association. All current Munchkin show cats in the United States are descendants of a black Munchkin named Blackberry, who in 1981 was adopted as a pregnant stray by Sandra Hochenedel.

The chief characteristic that sets the Munchkin apart is unusually short legs, with the front legs usually bowed, which gives the cat a forward-leaning appearance. A serious concern among cat lovers is that extended breeding of Munchkin to Munchkin will result in other physical deformities or illnesses, although the lumbar problems that have manifested themselves in such dogs as Dachshunds have not developed in cats, whose spines are structured differently. This short-leggedness is a dominant trait, so it takes just one Munchkin in a pair of parent cats to produce Munchkin offspring; some breeders nevertheless seek to continue reproducing the breed.

Munchkin

Journal Prompts, Part II

FILL UP THE JOURNAL YOU CREATED on Day 25 with more memories. Here are some writing prompts to stoke your creativity:

- Describe a vacation with your cat. Where did you stay? How did she respond to her new environment? Share stories about the trip.

- What are your cat's favorite foods? If your cat made your weekly grocery list, what would she request?

- How does your cat mark his territory? What does he consider "within borders"? (Your whole yard, the whole neighborhood, your bed and couch?)

- Have you ever stopped a cat fight? How did you do it—were you scared?

- Do you remember the first day you brought Kitty home?

Honing the Hunting Instinct

CATS ARE NATURAL HUNTERS and like to play in ways that reflect that. Cats need regular physical and mental stimulation to be happy and healthy, and mock hunting will fill both of those needs.

Jumping, pouncing, and swatting at "prey" are all components of hunting play. A useful toy for encouraging these behaviors is a flexible wand with a "birdie" attached to the end with a length of string. The birdie is usually made of feathers or leather strips, or is sometimes a catnip-filled toy. In the better versions, the birdies are replaceable. You hold the wand like a fishing pole and move the birdie around for your cat to chase and jump at. Feather versions move a little more unpredictably than heavier toys, keeping your cat on her toes.

You can encourage pouncing by attaching any cat toy to a long string and pulling it across the floor. Cats love to watch and wait for the right moment to pounce, and will sometimes give you some additional amusement by wiggling their hindquarters right before they pounce.

Treat-filled toys have pouches into which you can tuck a treat, a piece of kibble, or a pinch of fresh catnip. Your cat will use his sense of smell to track down the toy and a bit of brainpower to figure out how to get the treat out. Foraging boxes (see Day 67) can also hone your cat's ability to solve a puzzle.

A Game of "Cat-egories"

BACK IN THE MIDDLE AGES, terms evolved to categorize groups of this or that kind of animal: a gaggle of geese, for instance, or a colony of ants. Genuine examples relating to the cat kingdom include:

- A clowder of cats
- A kindle of kittens
- A pride of lions
- A leap of leopards

Actor-poet James Lipton, in his book *An Exaltation of Larks*, traces such phrases to the fifteenth century, when they were used in hunting jargon.

In our own time, these expressions can serve in a much kinder sport as a jumping-off point for imaginative wordplay; Lipton invented amusing new collective terms in his book (e.g., "a pounce of cats").

The next time you get together with, shall we say, a *lap* of cat lovers, why not make a game of creating additional phrases that have a feline twist to them? Refer to our Friday entries for breeds and to the cat terminology on Day 155 for inspiration. A pad thai of Siamese . . . or patchwork of calicos, anyone?

Cat Rescue: Helping a Choking Cat

IF YOUR CAT IS COUGHING, really hacking and trying to heave, your first instinct is, "Help! Emergency!" Cats often choke on things lying around the house—items such as string or a thread that could be embedded in the carpet or couch and completely invisible to the human eye, or so it seems. Cats find things. And they explore, many times, with their mouths. The most common choking trigger is hair balls. Often, when a cat appears to be choking violently, the hair ball is not in his airway at all. It's in his stomach—he's working hard to, well, "defuzz" his insides.

Important: Make sure your cat is really choking before starting the Heimlich maneuver; otherwise, you could cause serious injury to your cat. If you believe your cat swallowed a dangerous object but his airway is not blocked, take your cat to the vet immediately. If you do perform the Heimlich maneuver, still take your cat to the vet so your pet can be examined for stomach damage or cuts in the throat and mouth.

How do you know whether your cat is really choking, and whether the Heimlich maneuver and/or assistance from your vet is necessary? Some signs include:

- Pawing at the face or throat
- Acting frantic
- Trying to cough (but not severely coughing, as with hair balls)
- Difficulty breathing

Before attempting the Heimlich maneuver, remove your cat's collar, which could be constricting his neck. Examine his mouth, but do not probe around inside with your finger. You can mistake a bone at the back of your cat's throat for an object. Only attempt to remove an object if you can see it. In the case of a string or thread, if you can loosely pull it from the cat's mouth, then do so. If gentle pulls do not free the string from your cat's mouth, then ask someone to drive you to the vet while you hold his mouth shut so he does not ingest the string (and so the string's end remains visible so the vet can reach it).

If you cannot clear the object from your cat's mouth, start the Heimlich maneuver.

- Turn your cat upside down with his back against your chest.
- Hug him by placing both hands, one on top of the other, just below the rib cage.
- Give five deliberate squeezes.
- Stop. Check to see whether the object is visible in the airway. If so, remove it. If not, repeat squeezes.

Make a Cat Christmas Stocking

WHY NOT MAKE A Christmas stocking for Kitty that's shaped like his own paw? Use a holiday-theme novelty cat-print fabric, or other suitable prints or even luxury fabrics such as velvet or brocade.

To embellish: Add braid or tassels around the top opening, add sequins or lace to the body of the fabric before stitching the two halves together, embroider your cat's name on the stocking, and so on.

The stocking will be large enough to hold several toys and treats. Sewer's hint: Read all instructions before cutting into fabric.

MATERIALS

Pencil

Piece of scrap paper, approximately 9 inches x 12 inches (22.9 x 30.5 cm)

Scissors

Fabric, approximately 9 inches x 12 inches (22.9 x 30.5 cm)

Straight pins

Needle and sewing thread to match fabric

Embellishments (optional)

Iron

Ribbon, 4 inches (10 cm) or longer, for hanging the stocking

1. Lay your hand and arm on the piece of paper, palm down, with your fingers curled under in a flattened fist (only the lowest section of each finger should show). Spread your fingers as much as you can, then trace around your hand and arm, using the pencil.

Round the silhouette of your hand into a paw shape. The total length should be about 9 inches (22.9 cm). Draw a straight line across the open arm edge. Cut out the pattern.

2. Fold the fabric in half widthwise, wrong side out, and pin the pattern to it. Make sure that if a printed design has a direction, it faces the right direction. Sketch around the pattern along one wrong side of the cloth, then sketch a 3/8-inch (1 cm) margin all around for the seam allowance. Cut through the double layer of fabric.

3. Working separately with each layer, fold over the seam allowance at the top (straight edge), and pin the edges on the "wrong side" (facing inside) of the fabric. Hemstitch the edge and add any desired embellishments to the "right side" now.

4. Repin the two pieces of cloth together, wrong side out. (Any trimmings will face inside.) Use a running stitch around the remaining seam allowances except for the hemmed top, securing the sides of the hemmed edges with a couple of backstitches for strength.

5. Use scissors to make small snips along the seam allowances every ½ inch (1.3 cm); do not cut into the running stitch. Called "grading the curves," this will help the stocking stay flat when you flip it right side out. If the fabric ravels or sheds fiber easily, such as velvet or brocade, blanket-stitch all raw edges.

6. Turn the stocking right side out, and press flat with an iron.

7. Fold the ribbon in half and use the needle and thread to tack it firmly to the top of the "pinkie" side seam.

8. Fill with goodies.

Nebelung

THIS BREED EARNS POINTS FOR DIVERSITY. It has a German name, and is a descendent of a Russian breed that actually originated in Denver, Colorado.

Characteristics: The Nebelung is so new that it is only sporadically listed with cat registries. Already, however, a standard appearance has been established: a densely furred blue longhair with ear tufts and a plumed tail, and a tendency to pose very upright when seated.

History: The curious thing about the Nebelung is that this new breed was the result of the mating of a blue and a black American Shorthair, back in 1984. The kitty's parents were probably confused, too, by the sight of their shaggy infant son, who was named Siegfried by owner Cora Cobb.

But not so much that they stopped producing kittens, which led to the perpetuation of this surprising re-emergence of a long-forgotten recessive gene, via matings of Siegfried and his sister Brunhilde (the breed name is a riff on either the opera cycle *The Ring* or the saga that inspired it, the *Nibelungenlied*). Subsequent Nebelungs, mated to each other, produce other Nebelungs without any reversion to Shorthairs.

feline fun fact **>** Although the mature Nebelung's eyes are green, the kittens' eyes start out as blue, then turn yellow, before maturing into green.

Nebelung

On the Road with Kitty

IF YOUR CAT WILL ACCOMPANY YOU on a car trip, prepare her for the excursion so she can travel safe and you can stay sane on the journey.

You'll need an appropriately sized carrier (see Day 36). This will keep your cat secure and safe. Also, your cat should be collared and wear ID tags at all times. A microchip ID is excellent backup in case your cat's collar is removed (see Day 358).

The key concern with car travel is motion sickness (though not all cats suffer from the condition). Do not feed your cat food or water several hours before travel. Try a nonprescription product to ease anxiety, but first consult with your vet, or try flower essences, such as Rescue Remedy. Usually, car sickness is spurred by fear of the new environment, not an inner ear problem, as with humans.

The key is to train your cat to accept the car and not be afraid of it. Here are a few tips:

- **Acclimate your cat to car noise.** Lead your leashed cat (see Day 176) and ease her toward the car. Open the door and sit inside, holding her. Turn on the car. Reward her with a treat, and return to the house. Repeat several times, rewarding her each time.

- **Introduce your cat to car motion.** Lead your leashed cat to the car, and turn the car on. Back out of the driveway, then stop the car. Reward her with a treat, then repeat the exercise.

- **Familiarize your cat to travel.** Follow the tips above, then take a drive around the block, always rewarding your cat with tasty treats and praise. Eventually build up to longer trips. The key is repetition. Once your cat identifies the car as safe, she may even claim it as her own—a true sign that a cat is happy and comfortable.

Grooming: Tools and Techniques

CATS ARE PROS AT SELF-GROOMING. Their specialized tongues and flexible bodies are made for keeping fur in tip-top condition. All cats, however, can benefit from a little grooming help from their human companions. Longhaired cats are more prone to mats and tangles and need more human assistance with grooming than shorthaired cats do. Frequent grooming also helps prevent hair balls ingested as part of grooming and cuts down on cat hair tumbleweeds in your house.

Always brush or comb in the direction of hair growth, from head to tail. Start with the coarsest comb and progress to the finest brush. Not all cats will require a cache of grooming tools. Choose the tools best suited for your cat's coat type.

Here are some tools and techniques to help you help your cat look her best:

Wide-toothed combs should be the first step for longhaired cats to start the process of gentle straightening and detangling. When the wide-toothed comb moves easily through your cat's coat, move on to a medium-toothed comb, then a fine-toothed comb. (**Fine-toothed combs** are good for shorthaired cats.)

Flea combs have very fine, closely spaced metal teeth. When the comb picks up a flea, remove it from the comb and squash it with a tissue. For a flea infestation, use an anti-flea treatment (see Day 80).

Wire brushes help remove loose hair on longhaired cats.

Hard-bristled brushes are a good final step for grooming longhaired cats. These help distribute your cat's natural skin oils throughout her coat for a lustrous shine. (**Soft-bristled brushes** are great for shorthaired cats.)

Undercoat rakes and **shedding blades** are for longhaired cats with thick coats. These thin out the coat to help prevent tangling, mats, and hair balls. These are especially useful in the spring, when longhaired cats shed their winter coats.

Rubber curry brushes or **rubber grooming gloves** are good options for cats that won't sit still for a prolonged grooming session or are bothered by pointy bristles. The rubber attracts loose hairs, and the nubs give a mini massage.

Detangling sprays can be helpful if your cat has a lot of tangles. Choose one specifically for cats, because whatever you put on his fur will eventually be ingested (through grooming). Never use conditioners intended for humans, and never try these products on a cat whose fur is matted. Mats require special tools and techniques to remove (see Day 239).

Cats in Ancient Egypt

THE EARLIEST DOMESTIC CATS appear to date all the way back to about 2500 BC, as documented by an image of a collared cat in the tomb of Ti, an employee of the pharaoh, who oversaw the royal animals during Egypt's Fifth Dynasty.

In that culture, male cats were associated with the male sun god Ra, who was believed to transmute into a cat each dawn to subdue the serpent of night. Female cats were thought to be the animal representation of the goddess of the moon as well as fertility and motherhood, Bastet, also known as Bast and Pasht. Cats who lived at Bubastis, where there was a temple dedicated to Bast, were cared for their entire lives as representations of the goddess.

Many cat sculptures and paintings honoring Bastet are preserved in museum collections, some depicting her as a mother cat flanked by tiny kittens. (If she has a human body with a cat's head, she is called Bast, not Bastet.) When standing erect, Bastet is often shown holding a rattlelike musical instrument, called a sistrum, in one hand and an aegis, a shieldlike collar, in the other. In ancient times, a Bastet-worshipping woman who desired children would have worn an amulet of the goddess and her kittens as a good-luck charm.

Other Bastet (entirely feline form of the goddess) sculptures show a naturalistic cat sitting on her haunches, sometimes with tiny gold hoops through her earlobes. Bastet is also depicted as a lioness or a human with a lion's head in some artifacts and paintings: as Sekhmet, her manifestation as the nondomestic goddess of war and pestilence.

Cats were also appreciated purely as cats and for their hunting abilities, and were useful to the Egyptians as protectors of grain silos. They were such superb hunters that Egyptians took cats, rather than dogs, when they went out to snare game birds and the like, using the cats to fetch the prey. Cats were so valuable to ancient Egyptian culture that there were laws preventing their exportation; soldiers were sent to retrieve any that had been smuggled out of the country!

Members of an Egyptian family would shave their eyebrows to mourn the death of a cat, and they would embalm and mummify the remains—sometimes with mummified mice and bowls of milk to carry along to the afterworld.

Museum shops that carry replicas of Egyptian artifacts often have for sale small statues of Bastet or Bast, jewelry with small reproductions of such statuary or goddess-related medallions, and other items that would allow you to honor this ancient tradition in your own life.

Identifying and Treating Common Ear Problems

IF KITTY SHAKES HER HEAD, or scratches and rubs her ears, or you see a dark, crumbly material in her ear, disease or infection could be the culprit. Other symptoms include discharge from the ears, redness or swelling, and an odor. Ear infections are fairly common in cats, and are often spurred by allergies, mites (especially if you notice intense itching), poor hygiene, or simply because ears are a warm, moist environment that is ripe for bacteria formation.

COMMON EAR TROUBLE AND TREATMENT

Ear mites: Look for ear debris that resembles coffee grounds. Your cat will scratch her ears raw, risking harm, if the situation goes on too long. Ear mites spread from cat to cat, so your outdoor roamer may pick up the condition from another feline host. If you have other cats or pets at home, treat all of them for mites. Mite eggs take twenty-one days to hatch, so treatment must last a full cycle to ensure that mites don't reinfest the ear.

Treatment: An ear swab is taken and observed to identify parasites. Clearing up ear mites requires thorough cleaning followed by an ear medication. If scratching and irritation are severe, and your cat is in a great deal of pain, your vet may anesthetize your cat to properly clean the ears. Proper medication will prevent infested ear mite eggs from hatching and penetrating deep into the inner and middle ear, which could cause hearing problems.

Allergies: Ears are often the first sign of an allergy to food or something in the environment (pollens, dust). Look for discharge, redness, swelling, and itching. Another sign that the ear trouble is allergies is if your cat presents with ear trouble during a certain time of year, or after a change in environment.

Treatment: Treat the root of the problem, not just the ear condition. If allergies are suspected, your vet will perform tests (see Day 227) to tease out environmental triggers. Treatment may include regular ear cleaning with a solution, antihistamines, and fatty acid supplements (see Day 255). Corticosteroids in various forms—oral, injectible, or topical—can quell allergy symptoms. Remember, allergies can be controlled but not eradicated.

Foreign objects: If your cat roams outdoors, check her ears daily to look for scratches and wounds. Burrs, plant debris, and other objects may get lodged in the ear.

Treatment: Diligently check your cat's ears after her outdoor romps, and call a vet if you suspect injury or notice a foreign object in the ear canal. Regular ear cleaning will prevent a number of bacterial hosts found in the great outdoors from nesting in your cat's ears.

Bacteria: Ears are warm, protected places that welcome the growth of bacteria and yeast. Although your cat is armed with natural defenses against bacteria, allergies, hormones, or increased ear moisture can offset Kitty's balance and make her prone to bacterial ear infections. You'll smell a bacterial infection, and you'll see it in the form of yellowish discharge.

Treatment: Ear cleaning can clear up a minor infection, but if your cat's ears are a frequent host or the situation is severe, call your vet. Antibiotics may be necessary. Ear infections can spread deep into the ear if not treated properly.

How to Clean Kitty's Ears

Check your cat's ears weekly and look for unusual discharge, beyond the slight waxy build-up found in normal ears. Cats' L-shaped ears can "hook" debris, which can work into the ear and cause infection and irritation. Diligent, weekly cleaning will keep those ears squeaky clean.

1. Collect your supplies: olive oil (warm to the touch) or commercial feline ear cleaner to clean the inner ear; cotton balls and cotton swabs; an eye dropper.

2. Stabilize your cat by holding her in the crook of your arm, using your opposite hand to support her head. Put a few drops of cleaner in her ear and massage the base of the ear for 20 to 30 seconds. This will soften and release any debris. Use a cotton ball to wipe excess fluid. Repeat process for her other ear.

3. Your cat will shake its head and do her part to dislodge more dirt. After she settles down, use a cotton applicator to clean the inside of the ear flat and canal—only ear parts you can see. Do not insert a swab into your cat's ear because you may pack debris further into the ear canal.

Are You and Your Cat Prepared for an Emergency?

THE UNEXPECTED CAN HAPPEN anywhere at any time. Every household should have an emergency plan of action that includes your cat and all other pets.

Medical emergencies are most common. Being prepared can save crucial time when you need to get to the vet. Keep your cat's medical information handy, along with contact information for your vet and an animal hospital (see Day 81). Make sure her carrier is clean and accessible.

Who will care for your cat if you are the one that has a medical emergency? Make arrangements in advance by asking a trusted friend or relative to serve as an emergency cat sitter. If you approach someone who also has a pet, you can help each other as sitters-in-need. Make sure your emergency contact knows where to find your cat's information and how to reach your preferred cat sitter—and also has a key to your home—should you end up in the hospital.

Storms, floods, or other weather situations could limit your ability to get out of your house and leave you without power or other services. When stocking your pantry, don't forget to add extra food and water for your cat, too.

Even if you don't live in an area where forest fires or hurricanes are common, every family should have an evacuation plan. Make sure your cat is part of yours. Your "grab-and-go" kit should include cat food and perhaps a small bag of litter and a litter box.

Finally, although our cats are precious to us, remember that in the event of a house fire, the most important thing is to evacuate—with or without Kitty. Cats are resourceful and many times will escape on their own or survive by finding a relatively safe hiding place. You can purchase stickers for your doors and windows that alert firefighters and other rescue personnel that you have a cat inside, but don't risk your life looking for a cat that may have already escaped danger.

Norwegian Forest Cat

SOME BELIEVE THAT THE ANCESTORS of this deeply furred beauty were Angoras brought north from Turkey by Vikings. Because Norway was so much colder than their native land, they evolved to have a thick undercoat topped with water-resistant guard hairs that can be as long as 5 inches (12.7 cm).

Characteristics: This is a big cat, with a lynx-like look to its face. It sheds its shaggy, uneven winter coat every summer, including its long bib, although it retains ear and toe tufts year-round. The tail is a long plume. The body beneath all that hair is broad and solid with short legs. The heavier bone structure and more pointed muzzle, as well as the thicker quality of the fur, distinguishes this breed from the Maine Coon. The Norwegian comes in many colors except colorpointed, especially tabby, often with a white belly, bib, and/or chin.

History: The Norwegian Forest Cat was shown in its adopted land as early as the 1930s but because the cats did not leave the country for another forty-odd years, it took until the late 1970s for the breed to be registered abroad, in the European FIFé, thanks to the efforts of local cat fancier Carl-Fredrik Nordane. It took until 1994 for an American association to recognize it.

feline fun fact > This cat is an excellent climber, with strong claws, and can even do rock climbing!

Norwegian Forest Cat

Teaching Opposites

CATS ARE AMENABLE TO learning terms about dimension and direction. Sometimes, directionals can even serve as verbs.

Big and little: Gather some items that are similar except for size, then hold a demonstration for Kitty: "*Big* can" (draw out the word *big*) . . . "*Little* can." Contrast yourselves: "Big [your name]" . . . "Little [your cat's name]."

Use the terms more spontaneously: "Big truck" as a large vehicle rumbles by; "[Cat's name] big jump!" when Kitty leaps an appreciable distance; "Big hug" as you give him a hearty embrace.

Refer to his lying down on all four paws as "Big sit." This is useful should you wish him to stay seated, whereas sitting upright enables him to get moving in an instant. Whenever he obeys, be sure to say, "Good big sit."

Kitty will catch on that *big* is a muchness, and *little* is its opposite.

Up and down: Invite your cat to surfaces above him by patting the place and saying, "Up." Point sharply downward or tap your foot and order, "Down." At a staircase, say, "[Name] up stairs," for him to come up with you, and, "[Name] down stairs" for the reverse. (It is a lovely lightbulb-on moment when one day he realizes the *place* called "upstairs" is *up* the *stairs*.)

Use toys to reinforce the terms. Give Kitty's toys simple names, such as *ball* or *mouse*. Place, for instance, the mouse on a higher surface: "Mouse up." If your cat bats it down—or you do this yourself—immediately say, "Mouse down."

Be courteous—ask Kitty's permission before you pick him up: "Pick up [name]?" while making a lifting gesture. If he wriggles to get down, say as you release him, "[Name] down." He will learn in time that *up* and *down* imply vertical motion.

In and out: Conceal, say, a ball inside a box as your cat watches, and say, "Ball in," then tip the toy out and say, "Ball out." Repeat elsewhere, and with different objects. Shut yourself in another room and announce from inside, "[Your name] in." Open the door, step out, and say, "[Your name] out."

Articulate your cat's positions: If he climbs into something, such as a paper bag, announce, "[Name] in." As he exits, say, "[Name] out." If he is allowed outside, when he indicates he wishes to leave, ask: "[Name] out?" then reiterate, "[Name] out," as he actually steps outside. Do the same, using in, when he asks to enter. Use out when you physically remove Kitty from an area in your home, such as a closet. Begin to use it as a command for such situations: "[Name], out!"

Your cat will eventually learn that *in* refers to being inside an enclosure and *out* to being outside one.

Born Free?

SHOULD YOU ALLOW YOUR CAT to roam free outdoors? Few subjects spark more passionate discussion among cat lovers.

Some people argue that cats are meant to roam outdoors, free to hunt and roll around in the grass and explore. By keeping them indoors, they argue, we are preventing them from expressing their true nature. Indoor cats get bored and lazy and tend to gain weight, they say. Barn cats have shelter and companionship and provide a valuable service in helping keep the mouse population in check. And some cats just aren't "people cats"; they do not want to be cooped up in the house with their owners.

Others argue that outdoor cats are exposed to many more dangers than indoor cats, such as other cats or larger predators, traffic, rabies and other diseases, and fleas, ticks, and other parasites.

Frigid temperatures can be deadly for outdoor cats. Outdoor cats that create nuisances, such as digging in neighbors' gardens or stalking a neighbors' bird feeder, are at risk of being caught and turned in to animal control officers or, worse, maimed or killed. Additionally, many communities these days have laws that prohibit cats from being allowed to roam free. Most animal care professionals these days recommend that cats not be allowed to roam free.

Ultimately, only you can make the decision whether your cat will be an indoor cat or an outdoor cat. Understanding the pros and cons of each option will help you make an informed decision.

Felines in Photography

MOST CAT LOVERS TAKE PICTURES of their pets; these books celebrate the work of professional photographers:

- *Cats* by Hanns Reich, editor; text by Eugen Skasa-Weiss (1965)—naturally posed black-and-white feline images from all over the world

- *The Photographed Cat* (1980) and *The Big Book of Cats* (2004) by J.C. Suarès, editor—more black-and-white photos by international photographers

- *The Cat in Photography* by Sally Eauclaire (1990)—again black-and-white, from daguerreotypes to formal portraits, spanning the 1850s through the present, plus essays about photographing cats

- *Cats* by Yann Arthus-Bertrand, photographer, and Danièle Laruelle (1993)—full-color photos, grouped by breed

- *Cats 24/7* (2005) by Rick Smolen and David Elliot Cohen—more than five hundred international images grouped by topic, such as "Cats at Play"

- *Cats* by Caterina Gromis di Trana (2006)— a palm-size Cube Book of tiny, vivid photos indexed by breed

Other notable photographers include:

- Walter Chandoha, creator of a stock photo collection of thousands of cat images, plus his own titles

- Nobuo Honda, whose books include *Exploring Kittens* and *The Contented Cat*

- Hans Silvester, responsible for *The Complete Cats in the Sun* and *Kittens in the Sun*.

- Harry Whittier Frees, whose 1930s *Four Little Kittens* and its sequel featured fuzzy, clothed kittens posed like humans

feline fun fact > *Stuff on My Cat* by Marlo Garza (2006), and more recent sequels and spin-offs, contains photos of just that, cats topped with everything imaginable, from clothing to food to mice.

When Your Cat Is Allergic . . .

LIKE HUMANS, CATS CAN DEVELOP allergies at any time, and display symptoms quite suddenly. Cat allergies can be controlled, but not cured. The key is to identify the culprit and manage your cat's symptoms by altering her environment, food, or exposure to the outdoors, or by administering medications prescribed by a veterinarian, such as cortisone shots or skin treatments.

The three main offenders that cause cat allergies are fleas (see Days 80 and 179), airborne pollens, and food. Generally, vets isolate the cause of allergies by:

- Allergy testing (intradermal or blood testing)
- Eliminating foods or changing your cat's environment (keeping outdoor cats indoors)
- Monitoring reactions to allergy medications

AIRBORNE POLLENS

Inhalant (atopy) allergies are usually seasonal and associated with pollens during certain times of year. (You may be suffering from hay fever, too.) Scratching and hair loss are symptoms, as is excessive licking and pinpoint scabs called military dermatitis.

Solution: Begin a process called avoidance. Consider possible culprits, make a list, and tackle each suspect: pollens, house dust, and molds. Eliminate your cat's exposure to various allergen "hosts" one by one. Note her reaction, and discuss all possible allergens with your vet to establish an avoidance plan of action. Some avoidance ideas:

- Rinse off your cat after outdoor play, and keep your cat indoors when the pollen count is high.
- Keep your cat out of rooms after vacuuming.
- Clean and disinfect humidifiers, and run air conditioning during hot weather.
- Avoid letting your cat play with stuffed toys or sleep on stuffed chairs and sofas that can harbor dust mites.

FOOD

First, know the difference between food allergy and food intolerance. Food allergy symptoms include itching, scratching, and skin irritation. Food intolerance signals include vomiting or diarrhea. Both can be identified with an eliminating diet, applying avoidance principles. The challenge with pinpointing food allergies is that there is usually more than one culprit. Common offenders are ingredients found in pet foods. You can differentiate a food allergy from atopy or fleas by the time of year your cat presents with symptoms, and whether she responds to antihistamines. (If your cat begins itching in the dead of winter, pollen or fleas is unlikely to be the cause.)

Solution: Food trials are the only way to accurately diagnose a food allergy. Buy formulas or make your own with your vet's guidance. Monitor your cat's response to the diet and consult your vet to discuss the next steps.

> In a multicat household, feed the same novel food to all cats when conducting a food trial to make sure they don't swap meals.

Picture Your Cat in Needlework

SAY, "CHEESE!" . . . OR RATHER, "YARN!" From silhouettes to portraits, knitted and crocheted cat images can resemble a particular breed, even a particular cat! The charted designs in this book are a great place to start; others can be found in craft books, or try your hand at charting your own kitty from a photograph.

Knitting: Two easy ways to add cats to knitted pieces: use cross stitch (an X shape) or duplicate stitch (the same V as the knitted stitch) to embroider a charted pattern onto an existing solid background. Actually knitting in the design (a.k.a. the Fair Isle technique) takes more skill but is simple once mastered; this carries unused yarn across the wrong side, looped evenly over the working strand. In all cases, keep in mind that knitted stitches are not perfectly square, which can distort charted designs; look online or in crafts stores for graph paper specially for knitters, if you wish to chart your own kitty. The charts in this book, however, should knit up fine without adjustment. See Days 291 and 319 for a knitted cat-motif hat and scarf set.

Crocheting: Working in single crochet, you can use multiple colors to produce a fully reversible picture! Simply carry the unused colors along the top of the work, within the stitches you are making (as with knitting, check your gauge to be sure your design is not distorting). See Days 207 and 256 for two crocheted cat motifs.

Filet crochet: Using thread or fine yarn, you can make doilies, runners, tablecloths, lace curtains, pillow tops, and even afghans with this technique, which uses open and closed squares to create a single-color, silhouette-style picture. Begin with a chain of 3 chain stitches per square plus 4 extra chains. Row 1: turn and, letting the first 3 chains of the base chain become the first double crochet (dc), follow your charted pattern of choice, using a dc for every vertical bar, and either dc-2 (dark square) or ch-2 (open square) between bars to continue across. Turn and ch-3 to begin each new row.

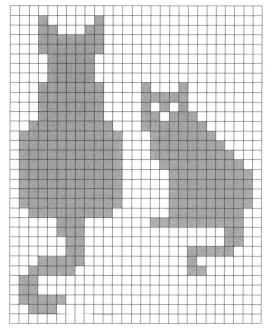

These cats may be knitted, crocheted, beaded, or embroidered. Personalize with stripes, patches, or colorpointing.

Ocicat

THE OCICAT CAME ABOUT BY A Michigan breeder's accident.

Characteristics: The Ocicat's fur is heavily ticked, with several distinct bands of color. Ocicats have a forehead *M* and their tail ends in a dark tip. Although the original Ocicats had brown spots, they can come in different hues, from golden to lilac to blue. For show cats, the eyes may be any color but blue.

History: The Ocicat originated in 1964, when a breeder tried to produce an Aby-pointed Siamese by mating a ruddy Abyssinian male to a seal-point Siamese, but that didn't quite work out—the litter included a gold-brown spotted, cream-base-coated cat. This cat was dubbed Ocicat because of the spots' resemblance to an ocelot's.

The breed was finally recognized in the United States in 1987; it still is not registered in the UK, which regards it as being too much a fluke mixture of other breeds' genes.

Although the Ocicat has a wild appearance, covered with small spots and often with lynxlike tips to the ears, it does not have a wild ancestry. It is accepted for pedigree with occasional matings with Abyssinians to preserve the breed.

feline fun fact > The Ocicat is renowned for its doglike disposition; it can be leash trained, fetches, and likes to follow its owner around.

Ocicat

Story: Life with the Cat Pack

OLIVER WAS ALWAYS A LAID-BACK cool-cat, like a dog, really. He was the only child for some time, even though I had always wanted a pair—and particularly an orange tabby cat. Then I found Pixie on a construction site near my apartment. She was stuck in a haphazard stack of two-by-four lumber that littered the site. Her orange coat blended right in with the landscape. Maybe I was looking for her, after all. I knew she wasn't someone else's pet. Our neighborhood is a notorious stomping ground for strays, and this one had found herself in quite a predicament. I decided to trap her and take her to the vet.

I knew I couldn't just wrap her in a blanket and tuck her into the cozy chair in my living room, though this is what she deserved! What if she had leukemia or feline AIDS (FIV)? She could sneeze on Oliver and infect him; they definitely couldn't share a water bowl or be in contact with one another until Pixie was vaccinated.

While Pixie was at the vet, I weighed the pros and cons of taking in another cat. Frankly, Oliver was quite happy on his own, and I didn't want to disturb the peace. I also recognized that Pixie's homecoming would not be a weekend stay. I'm a committed owner, and the decision to keep Pixie meant possibly fifteen years of being a mother to two felines. I decided to adopt Pixie and integrate her into the household, but under one condition: If Oliver began peeing outside the box or scratching himself to death—showing me that he was not into this "sharing thing"—then I would put Pixie up for adoption.

There are rules for integrating cats into a household, and there's good reason to segregate the newbie for some time. We didn't follow any of those rules, and we paid for it by dealing with dueling cats for two months. Oliver dominated Pixie, told her who was boss. If Pixie was sleeping soundly on the couch, Oliver would approach her and eye her down, give her the look. Pixie would leave the couch and retreat to the other room. Watching a pecking order evolve was a real education. We learned how to create a fair playground for both cats, and eventually they became friends, even taking naps together. (Pixie still gets the short end of the stick at mealtimes, but we've learned to feed her in another room from Oliver.)

The multicat house dynamic has grown more interesting since then. Last year we added a six-week kitten to our pack. Robinson mirrors Oliver's every step, treats him like a big brother. The boys sometimes gang up on Pixie, but she has plenty of hiding spots where she retreats for privacy. And she's my girl, so she makes up in the special attention department. Other times, the three cats coexist peacefully in our living room, taking their assigned posts on the couch and chairs (Oliver giving instructions, of course). Turns out, three is not a crowd.

Accommodating Cats with Disabilities

CATS WITH DISABILITIES BRING just as much joy to our lives as their more able-bodied friends. Most cats can compensate for a lost limb, blindness, or deafness, whether their condition results from an injury or they were born that way. A few commonsense accommodations will help them enjoy life to the fullest.

A cat who has recently lost a leg will need time to heal and adjust. Curb your desire to carry him everywhere; allow him to develop the muscles in his other legs and learn how to maneuver and jump without the lost leg. Cats that have lost a rear leg may not be able to jump as high, and those who have lost a front leg may have difficulty getting down from high places. Most cats will be almost as agile as they were with four legs.

Blind cats rely on not only their other senses to get around, but also their memory of where objects are. With a blind cat, do not leave obstacles, such as bags or packages, where he does not expect them to be. Don't move his food and water bowls or litter box; he uses these objects and their scent to help orient himself. Blind cats are easily disoriented, so avoid picking him up and moving him; if you must, set him down near his food or litter so he knows where he is. Talk to him before touching him to avoid startling him.

Deaf cats are easily startled and sometimes act defensively in response. To avoid a scratch or a bite, make sure he sees you before you reach out to pet him or pick him up.

Felix the Cat

WHO IS THAT WHITE-MASKED BLACK CAT? It's Felix, beloved all over the world as the Charlie Chaplin of cats!

Felix first appeared in 1917 as Master Tom in the silent *The Tale of Thomas Kat* by filmmaker Pat Sullivan, and then starred two years later in *Feline Follies*, such a hit that *The Musical Mews* was released just a week later. Felix was renamed the following month, when he starred in Sullivan's *The Adventures of Felix*.

In 1923, Felix transitioned into a comic strip syndicated to 250-odd newspapers worldwide. That same year, a short, *Felix in Hollywood*, introduced the wisecracking feline to such celebrities as Charlie Chaplin.

Artist Joe Oriolo's Felix doll was so popular that Lindbergh brought one along during his landmark flight. The hit song of 1923 was Paul Whiteman band's "Felix Kept on Walking."

The rise of Mickey Mouse in "talkies" placed Felix in the shadows for a while, but in 1928 it was a papier-mâché model of Felix, placed on a phonograph turntable, who was one of early TV's first stars. Beginning in 1953, Oriolo produced more than two hundred five-minute Felix flicks for television, voiced by Jack Mercer.

Joe's son Don wrote and produced *Felix the Cat, the Movie* (1991), which has another life on the Disney Channel. Modern Felix licensing spans everything from hamburger promotions to a Japanese musical. Felix keeps on walking, indeed!

Basic Eye Care

IF YOU NOTICE YOUR CAT'S EYES are red, irritated, watering, half-closed, or contain discolored discharge, call your vet. Your cat may blink excessively, or her pupils may change in size. She may paw or rub at her eye, or simply hold her eye(s) shut. Common eye problems include conjunctivitis (pinkeye), cataracts, glaucoma, upper respiratory infections, and scratches from cat fights or injuries while roaming outdoors. Do not wait to diagnose and treat an eye problem—it will not clear up on its own.

Keep Kitty's peepers clear of mucus at all times. Some cats are prone to "tearstains," which actually kill bacteria that can cause eye infections. You'll notice these stains as "eye goop" from normal tears that collect at the corners of your cat's eyes. You can purchase tearstain remover products, or use a damp cloth and clean the fur surrounding the eye area daily. Longhaired cats' fur can cover the eyes. Trim back unruly tufts using blunt-nosed scissors. Before bathing your cat, protect her eyes by applying an ophthalmic ointment under the top lid. Use sterile eyewash and wipes for regular cleaning.

Ever gaze into your cat's eyes at night and wonder why they appear as green orbs? Cats have an additional reflective layer behind the retina, called the tapetum. It reflects incoming light and bounces it off the cones, amplifying existing light to improve vision. Your cats have superb night vision—but, like humans, they cannot see in complete darkness. Normal vision for a cat is 20/100 (much keener than our own 20/20). However, cats have trouble seeing close-up objects. They rely on their sense of smell for close encounters. Also, cats have a third eyelid called the nictitating membrane in the corner of each eye. This acts as a protective membrane when your cat is dehydrated, suffering from an infection, is stressed, or is sedated.

Cats and Chemicals

CATS ARE FASTIDIOUS GROOMERS, licking their paws and entire body—anywhere their tongue can reach. Any substance that sticks to their fur can be ingested—a scary thought when you consider the products we may use to clean. Because cats' bodies are much smaller than ours, they have a very low tolerance for common chemicals.

Household cleaners: Avoid using household chemicals when she is around, and keep her away when you are spraying cleaners or sprinkling powders. (Make sure she stays away until the cleaners have been wiped up and dried.) Better yet, seek out products that are labeled "pet safe."

In the garage: Beware of automobile engine antifreeze. Even drops of it can be lethal to cats. The problem is, cats are drawn to the sweet taste of traditional ethylene glycol antifreeze. Check for spills and drips near the car and clean them up immediately. Ask for the new formulas that use propylene glycol next time you change your antifreeze. They are less toxic.

Outdoors: Lawns can be dangerous grounds for cats if fertilizers and pesticides are used. Insect repellents, rock salt, and salt-free deicers can create problems, too. If your cat goes outdoors, consider forgoing these treatments or choose pet-safe alternatives.

Oriental Longhair

TIPPING US OFF TO ITS EASTERN ANCESTRY with its facial structure and Oriental build, the Oriental Longhair has a semi-longhaired coat, thanks to a family tree rich with longhaired cats.

Characteristics: The coat is silky and fine, and not as long as that of other longhaired breeds, with a slimmer, feathery plumed tail. Cats kept indoors, or those living in a warm climate, will have a slightly shorter coat. The colors can be solid black, white, or lilac, red-ticked tabby, blue tortie/tabby, or black smoke. Due to this breed's mixed heritage, the rare colorpointed kitten may occur.

History: The Oriental Longhair is also known as the Mandarin. This breed is related to the Oriental Shorthair (see Day 243), which evolved through a different mixture of the same parentage in separate incidents across the Atlantic from each other.

In the UK, the first Oriental Longhairs were parented by an Abyssinian and a Siamese during the 1970s; a decade later, in the United States, the breed began as a crossing of an Oriental Shorthair and a Balinese.

Oriental Longhair

Coping with the Loss of a Pet

LOSING YOUR BEST FRIEND is heartbreaking. Your cat loved you unconditionally for years. You told her everything—she listened. You can't imagine home without the pitter-patter of paws scurrying across the kitchen floor at mealtime, or that lump of fur curled at the foot of your bed every night.

When your cat passes away, the emotional stress and grieving period is not unlike losing a human best friend. You may not have anticipated the death, or your cat's declining health may have taken place over a period of several very difficult years. Either way, there's no real way to plan for the death of a pet, at least emotionally. You can contemplate those what-if scenarios: What if Kitty's injury or illness hinders her quality of life? What emotional or financial cost can I bear? At what point is euthanasia a sensible option? (see Day 253) No one wants to dwell on depressing scenarios, but by considering these hypothetical situations while your pet is healthy, you will be better equipped to manage some of the tough decisions you confront at the end of a pet's life.

If you are dealing with the loss of a long-loved cat, take time and allow yourself to work through the grieving process. Each of us responds differently to tragedy. Don't beat yourself up for feeling empty or lost. But also focus on positive aspects of life and create a strategy to move on. Finally, celebrate your pet. You'll never forget the memories, and there are ways to pay respect to your cat and memorialize her.

Seek support from family, friends, fellow pet owners, your vet, and even a psychologist if you feel like you've fallen into a depression that you can't shake alone.

Following are some consoling tips to help you through this difficult time:

Plan in advance, if at all possible. Discuss options with your vet before an illness spirals into dire straits. Consider your feelings on euthanasia, and your health-care budget. If your kitten is very young, check into pet health insurance options to see whether this coverage makes sense for your feline.

Take your time. Wallow a little—or a lot. No one expects you to put on a happy face immediately after losing your best friend. Talk to supportive friends and family members. Write in a journal, or give in to a nice, long cry.

Celebrate your cat. Arrange a memorial ceremony and invite family and close friends. Invite loved ones over to share coffee and memories, and look through favorite cat photos. Tell stories.

Console surviving pets. Other household pets—cats and dogs—may get depressed when they lose one of their siblings. Help them ease through their own animal grieving by spending extra time with them. Play with them. Let them get used to a household with one fewer pet. Talk to your vet if you are concerned that one of your pets may be clinically depressed.

Removing Mats from Fur

MATS ARE WADDED-UP TANGLES, or "rats," of fur in a cat's coat and are unsightly and uncomfortable for your longhaired cat. Worse, mats can be hospitable places for fleas and ticks to hide and can also trap dirt, bacteria, and fungi. If the mats are left too long, they can pull on the skin and cause sores and even tears in your cat's skin. Regular grooming (see Day 218) can help prevent matting, but even the most pampered cats can get an occasional mat.

It's important to start removing the mat as soon as you see it to prevent it from growing and hardening. Patience and persistence are key to success, and special care must be taken not to cut or tear your cat's thin skin. You may need a helper to keep your cat still while you work on the mat.

Specialty grooming tools such as detangling and dematting combs and mat splitters have steel blades that can help break up mats. The blades are set such so they cut away from your cat's skin; follow the manufacturer's instructions for using them so that you position the tool correctly. Never use scissors to cut out a mat; a wiggly cat can make it easy to slip and cut the skin.

Small mats can sometimes be gently teased apart with your fingers or the tip of a comb, then brushed out with a wire brush or wide-toothed comb. Removing larger mats can be tricky. It can be difficult to distinguish the mat from the skin underneath, and you want to be careful not to pull on the skin. If the mat is close to the skin, place a comb between your cat's skin and the mat to help protect the skin from the tool and from pulling.

To remove a mat, start at the mat's edge and work on a small section at a time. Use a mat splitter to break up the mat into smaller pieces, and then work on each of these small pieces in turn with a detangling or dematting comb. If these tools aren't doing the trick, you may need to use electric clippers with a comb attachment to protect the skin—but be aware that most cats react to clippers as if they were a vacuum cleaner, so clippers should be your last do-it-yourself resort. It is likely that it will take a number of short sessions over a period of days to completely remove the mat, even with the most patient cat.

For very large mats or mats that are so close to the skin that you can't get under them, or if the skin shows signs of sores or damage, take your cat to a professional groomer or the vet to have them removed.

Tales of Tom Kitten

BEATRIX POTTER (1866–1943), perhaps best known for **The Tale of Peter Rabbit**, wrote many stories about animals, inspired largely by her own and neighbors' pets and animals she met at her farm in Sawrey, in England's Lake District. Although in life she was more of a "dog person," cats appear in quite a few of her books. Potter fondly referred to kittens and children alike by the term "Pickles," dedicating **The Tale of Tom Kitten** to "all Pickles—especially those that get upon me garden wall," clearly referring to feline clamberers!

In **The Tale of Tom Kitten**, set at Potter's farm, Tom and his two sisters, Moppet and Mittens, are forced into fancy clothing by their mother,

Tabitha Twitchit, to impress her imminent tea guests. They go out, lose the clothing to the Puddle-Duck family, and come home filthy.

The Roly-Poly Pudding, later retitled **The Tale of Samuel Whiskers** (dedicated to Potter's late pet rat!), is about two rats who plot to turn Tom into a pudding. Luckily, he is rescued and scrubbed clean by his mother.

The Tale of Ginger and Pickles is set in a village shop run by a tomcat, Ginger, and a terrier named Pickles. The feline cast includes Tom and his two siblings. And if you look at the picture showing the end of Smithy Lane, you can even see a tiny illustration of Beatrix Potter herself!

Cat Acne

A BREAKOUT OF BLACKHEADS on your cat's chin may be linked to stress. Poor grooming habits and, some say, also certain foods may trigger acne. Acne could also signal a weak immune system or the onset of other skin diseases, such as ringworm or atopic dermatitis (allergies). Irritating blackheads cause cats to scratch under their chins and lips. Like frustrated humans who pop their zits, cats essentially do the same thing by scratching their chin and lip area.

Feline acne is stubborn. The infection is limited to the chin area, and it may appear once in a cat's life or for the life of the cat. (Acne-prone humans can relate!) Cats of all ages and breeds can get acne. You can control, but not cure, feline acne. But first, your vet will rule out other skin disorders by collecting "skin scrapings," performing a skin biopsy, or taking culture and sensitivity tests.

Topical treatments that contain benzoyl peroxide (3 percent or less) can break down excess oils to prevent blackheads from forming. Topical vitamin A (0.05 percent Retin-A) is also used, but the drying formula may irritate some cats. Oral medications and, in severe cases, an anti-inflammatory medication such as prednisone may control the situation initially. Never use human-grade acne medication on your cat.

Acne flare-ups can be triggered by allergic reactions, so consider switching your cat's food bowls to stainless steel or china. (Plastic may contain irritant dyes or retain bacteria.) Finally, regularly clean your cat's chin—and tell her she's beautiful.

Holiday Decorating with Cats in Mind

HOLIDAY DECORATING IS A GREAT WAY to create a festive atmosphere at home. For cats, however, many items used in holiday decorating can be dangerous.

- Keep candles and oil lamps well out of your cat's reach. An errant swish of the tail could hurt your cat, spill hot wax or oil, or cause a fire. Also, a cat may not understand not to poke her paw into a flame to try to catch it.

- Feathers on costumes and decorations should be kept away from your cat. The dyes used on decorative feathers are not always safe for consumption.

- Christmas trees can be irresistible for some cats, whereas others will leave it alone. If you must have a tree and your cat is one that can't help himself from climbing it, you'll need to keep him out of the room until the season is over or do what some creative cat owners do: Suspend it upside down from the ceiling!

- The water in a live Christmas tree stand might draw his attention. Avoid using chemical tree preservatives, or better yet, use a tree stand that has a closed water receptacle.

- Ribbon, tinsel, and plastic Easter basket "grass" can all be dangerous if swallowed. Keep these items out of your cat's reach.

- Delicate and fragile items should be placed where your cat can't get to them. Use museum putty to keep breakables in place if there's a chance your cat might knock into them.

(For more on dangerous plants, see Day 269.)

Oriental Shorthair

THIS ANGULAR CAT ORIGINATED IN Thailand, by way of the Middle East. Although the original breed traveled even farther west to the UK and the United States, around the turn of the last century, crossbreeding with British or American Shorthairs altered its appearance somewhat in subsequent Western generations.

Characteristics: The Oriental Shorthair is basically a Siamese cat that is not colorpointed and that has green eyes. After that, anything goes—a solid coat, tabby or tortie markings, ticking. There are, in fact, more than fifty colors, thanks to the cats' broad-based ancestry. A particularly splendid variety is the Oriental Ebony, an all-black cat with vivid green eyes, which must have black parents to qualify for registration. Oriental blues are born to brown and lilac parents; shaded and tipped colorings emerge from mating Siamese with Chinchilla Persians; and on it goes. Unlike Siamese kittens, Oriental Shorthairs are born with their adult color, so at least breeders know what to expect right from the start.

History: This breed's evolution is complicated. In casual matings with non-Siamese, many color variations emerged naturally. Then, during the 1950s, a British breeder's experimentations resulted in a variety of solid-colored cats with a Siamese build. The first cat of this kind had all-brown fur with green eyes, which resulted in its being called a Havana, after the cigar, then a Chestnut Brown Foreign.

Another British breeder, in the 1960s, took a different direction, trying to create an all-white Siamese with blue eyes, and succeeded; these were registered in that country as Foreign White. To add to the confusion, in North America, variants of the Siamese developed with all manner of markings and patterns as well as solid colors, and their collective breed was finally registered as the catchall Oriental Shorthair in that same year.

In 1978, patterned cats of this build were recognized as Oriental Spotted Tabbies. Then, the UK's Governing Council of the Cat Fancy put its paw down and declared all such non-Siamese-colored Siamese to be Foreign Shorthairs. They are slowly coming around to calling the cats by the U.S. designation, Oriental Shorthair, yet for the British, incredibly, every different color is registered as a separate breed. And that's a lot of breeds!

feline fun fact > All-white, blue-eyed Oriental Shorthairs, unusually, miss getting the gene that causes many other all-white cats to be deaf.

Oriental Shorthair

Cat Acupuncture

ACUPUNCTURE IS THE USE OF fine needles inserted into specific points on the body for therapeutic purposes. This ancient technique originated in the Far East. It is based on the principle that there are specific energetic pathways (meridians) throughout the body, which connect all the internal organs and structures. When the flow of chi energy along one or more of these meridians is obstructed, the result may be an imbalance in energy, or disease. By stimulating key acupuncture points in the body with needles, an acupuncturist seeks to restore balance to the normal energy flow along the meridians and, consequently, to holistically balance the body.

Acupuncturists believe that imbalances in chi are the root of disease. Acupuncture in animals works the same way it does in humans and can be used to support any disease or health condition. Acupuncture can be used for any pet and is most appropriate for pets that are sensitive to drugs, pets that are not a good candidate for surgery or other invasive techniques, and senior pets to help restore their life force energy and prevent degenerative diseases.

See the resources on page 317 for more information on finding a veterinarian licensed in acupuncture.

Living with an Older Cat

OLDER CATS MAY NOT BE AS mobile as their younger counterparts, and may require accommodations to help them age gracefully. Here are some ways to help:

• As your cat ages, his ability to jump is affected, as is his ability to climb down from a perch. You won't catch him on the kitchen counter as often, but he may not be able to easily jump up to his favorite window seat, either. Consider placing boxes, steps, or even a ramp nearby so your cat can access his favorite places.

• Older cats may have trouble keeping up with their self-grooming. Be sure to build in extra grooming time for older cats to keep their coats healthy and prevent hair balls.

• An elderly cat may not be able to climb into and out of a litter box as easily as he grows older. If he seems to have trouble, switch to a box with lower sides so it is easier to access.

• Elderly cats also may have trouble controlling their bladder. Consider adding extra litter boxes so one is always close by. If bladder control continues to be a problem, consult your vet for treatment options.

• An older cat's diet may need to be adjusted for his lower activity level and changing metabolism and appetite. If you notice your cat gaining or losing weight, consult your vet.

• Exercise is extremely important for keeping older cats healthy and active within their abilities. He may not chase the laser pointer anymore, but he can still be tempted to bat at a ball on a string or play with a catnip-filled toy mouse. Be prepared to get down on the ground and pick up the slack as the more active playmate.

Fantastical Cats

"You don't mean to say there's an Invisible Cat at large in the world?" said Kemp.

—H.G. Wells, *The Invisible Man* (1897)

HORROR STORIES, FANTASY, and science fiction have their fair share of magical and spooky felines, especially for child readers. Here are a few worth watching out for (and in some cases, really watching out!).

- **Edgar Allan Poe's** 1840 story "The Black Cat" is a classic tale of horror, in which a man murders his cat, Pluto, then kills his wife and hides her body within a wall, not realizing another cat who is the literally spitting image of Pluto has also been trapped inside.

- **Jerome K. Jerome's** *Three Men in a Boat (To Say Nothing of the Dog)* (1889) recounts, in one chapter, the dog Montmorency's run-in with a large black tom. The cat is so intimidating that afterward one only needs to say "Cat" to the dog, and he cringes.

- In **H.G. Wells's** *The Invisible Man*, an experiment to make a cat invisible fails, because its green eyes continue to glow in the dark.

- **E.F. Benson**, best known for his Lucia series, also wrote many ghost stories, including the feline horror tales "The Case of Frank Hampden" (1920) and "The Cat" (1930).

- **Stephen Vincent Benét's** "The King of the Cats" (1929) is the story of a superb musician, M. Tibault, who conducts orchestras with his tail.

- **Dorothy L. Sayers**, famous for her Peter Wimsey books, wrote "The Cyprian Cat," about a witch who assumes the guise of a cat to terrorize an ailurophobe.

- **Lloyd Alexander** has written several feline fantasy novels for kids: *Time Cat* (1963), *The Cat Who Wished to Be a Man* (1973), *How the Cat Swallowed Thunder* (2000), and *Dream-of-Jade: The Emperor's Cat* (2005).

- In the 1980s, **Fay Sampson** created a Celtic fantasy series for children, concerning a medieval white cat named Pangur Bán (see Day 282).

- **Terry Brooks's** Magical Kingdom of Landover series, begun in 1987 with *Magical Kingdom for Sale—Sold!* includes a Prism Cat, Edgewood Dirk, who is really a fairy.

- British writer **Terry Pratchett** features a blue British Shorthair, Greebo, in his Discworld series, beginning with *Wyrd Sisters* (1989), and also a white witch's cat named You. He is also the author of *Amazing Maurice and His Educated Rodents* (2001).

- Editor **Ellen Datlow's** 1996 *Twists of the Tale: An Anthology of Cat Horror* is a collection of short works by twenty-four storytellers, including Joyce Carol Oates and William S. Burroughs.

Dealing with Dandruff

IF YOUR CAT IS SHEDDING DANDRUFF, the cause may simply be dry skin. The lower back and base of a cat's tail are subject to dry skin. Common triggers range from the environment to diet and even bath-time upsets.

- During dry, winter months, skin loses moisture and needs extra TLC. Comb out flakes with a fine-toothed comb.

- If your cat is on a low-fat diet, skin can flake from lack of oils and fats in the skin. Consider supplementing his diet with "good fats" (see Day 255).

- An older or obese cat may have difficulty grooming himself and will develop greasy, flaky skin. Help with the grooming by giving him regular baths and combing out flakes.

- Always rinse shampoo out of your cat's coat completely during a bath, until suds disappear. Use a moisturizing shampoo and follow with a conditioner. Choose pet shampoos designed to comfort dry skin.

- If bathwater is too hot, dry skin is also likely to develop—your cat's skin responds the same way yours does after a long, hot soak. Bathe your cat with tepid water. If your hands dry out while bathing your cat, the water is probably too hot.

If dandruff is persistent, consult your veterinarian. Dry skin may be a sign of a more serious problem, such as mange, flea allergy (see Day 227), ringworm, or seborrhea (see Day 255). Heavy dandruff can also signal hyperthyroidism or diabetes.

Providing for Your Outdoor Cat…Outdoors

IF YOUR CAT IS AN OUTDOOR CAT, you still must provide for her needs and comfort. Domesticated cats are not able to fend for themselves, no matter how independent they may seem.

Protect from exposure to the elements. Although cats have fur to help keep them warm, they require shelter from the wet, cold, and wind in the winter. In the summer, they need protection from rain, heat, and direct sun. Provide a commercially made cat house or build one yourself. Place the shelter in a spot that receives sun in the winter and is shady in the summer. Face the opening away from prevailing winds, and line the bottom with straw for insulation.

Make fresh, clean water available at all times. Puddle or stream water can contain unhealthy substances or parasites. Keep water by the shelter—she'll recognize this is her "safe zone" where she can find protection from elements and a cool drink when she is thirsty.

Monitor outdoor food bowls. Keep them free of insects. Set out food in the morning, when nocturnal scavengers such as raccoons are less likely to get into it. Put out only as much as your cat will eat at a sitting. Excess food attracts insects and other animals. Ideally, mealtime should take place indoors.

Choose pet-safe yard and garage products. Rock salt and other deicers can irritate your cat's paws and are dangerous if ingested. If your cat goes out in areas where these products are used, clean her paws each time she comes back inside.

Persian

PERSIAN CATS WERE CONSIDERED luxury items—an aristocrat's cat. Today, it is one of the most popular breeds.

Characteristics: Persians have a very round face with a distinctive horizontal indentation between their eyes and nose, called the *break*. From the cat's profile, its nose should be aligned with its forehead and chin. Extreme versions of this profile have been encouraged by some breeders (see "Peke Face," Day 348), but they are frowned upon for traditional competition.

The fur is deep, with a long ruff, and requires regular maintenance to remove tangles. This cat must be kept indoors, to keep the fur clean and unmatted. Persians come in more than sixty colors; in America, the colorpointed variety is called a Himalayan (see Day 173); in Great Britain, this is a Colorpoint Longhair. Some colors are favored over others (the British still prefer blues), and in most copper eyes are to be expected; white Persians may have odd eyes, one blue and one copper. A pure black Persian without any white or rust is rare and therefore very valued. In some countries, such as Canada, a solid-colored chocolate or lilac Persian is referred to as a Kashmir. Persians are generally placid and expect to be pampered; they would rather sit around looking regal than tear up the house.

History: Before the early 1600s, all cats in Western Europe were shorthairs. But then travelers began to import longhaired cats, beginning with the introduction of Persians—from Persia, now called Iran—to Italy in 1620. In their native land, these cats were considered luxury items, owned only by aristocrats. During that same period, cats were also imported to France from Angor (now Ankara), Turkey. For about two centuries, Europeans thought the two breeds were the same.

With the advent of cat shows in the late 1800s (see Day 12), the Persian and Turkish Angora (see Day 327) began to be classed separately. Standards for the Persian emerged: a more cobby, heavier frame; a heavier coat; and the dead-giveaway "pushed-in" face. Today, each color remains a separate breed in Great Britain, where the cats are collectively called Longhairs rather than Persians. In the United States, there is one breed, the Persian, which can come in many color. The U.S. strain is even chunkier and rounder than the British one.

Persian

Pet Travel Documents

WHEN TRAVELING WITH YOUR CAT by plane, train, or other public transportation, you will be asked to show health papers for her (see Day 326 for how to make your pet's "passport"). If you are staying within your home country, you will probably need only a valid health certificate from your vet's office. A health certificate is valid for only thirty days, so if you're going to be traveling longer, be sure to locate a vet at your destination who will agree to see you and your cat and issue a new health certificate.

Other papers and regulations come into play if you are traveling outside your home country, and sometimes even to certain regions in your own country. The destination country may require a visa for your cat, and some countries require up to six months of quarantine. It is essential to do your homework and learn the requirements and make arrangements before traveling with your cat, so you don't find yourself having to leave your four-footed travel companion at the gate. The Internet can be very handy for finding preliminary information, but regulations can change. Always call the consulate of your destination country to confirm whether your pet requires a visa or other paperwork.

Understanding Euthanasia

ENDING A LIFE IS A SERIOUS MATTER, and should never be done for convenience. If you are moving to a new house and cannot take Kitty along, if she has scratched or bitten someone or is soiling your home, if she resolutely doesn't get along with other animals or the new baby, or if you cannot afford to feed her or take care of a non-fatal medical problem that she has developed—please find your pet a new home or bring her to a no-kill shelter.

With medication and care, cats may live comfortably for a long time even with terminal conditions such as cancer. If, on the other hand, Kitty is clearly in distress from a disease that cannot be cured or an injury that cannot heal, or her overall health is failing to the degree that her quality of life has diminished irreparably, it may be time to end her struggle. She may even indicate to you that something new is desperately wrong, by withdrawing from you or hiding in an unaccustomed place, by suddenly losing the ability to walk, or by becoming difficult to wake.

If it is not an emergency situation, discuss the matter with your family and friends, other cat owners, your vet, and/or a spiritual adviser, to help you come to a decision. Euthanasia may be the most humane course of action to take eventually if not immediately, and it helps to have a clear mind about it before an emergency develops. Ask your vet whether he or she is willing to make a house call in such a circumstance (yes, some do), to let your pet be disturbed as little as possible within her home surroundings. If you need to go to the vet's office with your cat, bring along a friend or relative for moral support, if you like.

The procedure itself is swift, either by a single injection or by the use of a sedative first. It takes virtually seconds for your cat to quite literally "go to sleep" and then stop breathing; relatively speaking, this is a kind and gentle release. However, be aware that your pet may soil herself as her body relaxes, so if you wish to hold her, it would be practical to cuddle her on a towel or fleece mat on the examination table rather than in your lap. Ask your vet to let you have some alone time with her before and/or afterward, if you need to say a personal good-bye.

Consider whether you would like to bury your cat in your garden or in some other significant spot, or whether you would prefer to have her cremated (which the vet can handle for you). Especially if children have been close to Kitty, a memorial ceremony would be a fitting tribute to your pet and help bring about closure to her human companions. See Days 237 and 238 for more about dealing with loss.

Hartsdale Pet Cemetery and Crematory is the oldest such establishment in the world, located in Westchester County, New York. It was started in 1896 by veterinarian Samuel Johnson, who offered his own apple orchard as the final resting place for a friend's dog. Today, nearly seventy thousand pets snuggle together there into eternity.

Feline Flicks—Live Action

BREAK OUT THE POPCORN for these feline favorites:

- Pyewacket, witch Kim Novak's cat in **Bell, Book and Candle** (1958), won a Patsy Award (an animal star's "Oscar").

- In six James Bond films, beginning with **From Russia with Love** (1963), Bond's arch-enemy Ernst Stavio Blofield is shown stroking a white Persian cat.

- **The Incredible Journey** (1963) sends a cat and two dogs on a two-hundred-mile trip in search of their owners. Sequels **Homeward Bound** (1993) and **Homeward Bound II** (1996) give them voiceover speech (voiced by Sally Field).

- **The Three Lives of Thomasina** (1964) is the story of a little girl who holds her vet father responsible when her cat dies.

- In **That Darn Cat!** (1965 and 1997), DC, short for Darn Cat, helps the FBI find a kidnapped woman. The original DC won a Patsy Award.

- Witch Angela Lansbury has a black cat, Cosmic Creepers, in **Bedknobs and Broomsticks** (1971).

- In **Harry and Tonto** (1974), Art Carney hits the road with his cat to go cross-country when evicted from their NYC apartment. Tonto won a Patsy Award.

- In **The Cat from Outer Space** (1978), a feline alien lands on Earth and is able to communicate with humans with the aid of his magical collar.

- Jones the cat appears in both **Alien** (1979) and **Aliens** (a.k.a. **Alien 2**, 1986).

- Stephen King's **Cat's Eye** (1985) is three horror tales linked to a single tabby cat.

- **Koneko Monogatari** (a.k.a. **The Adventures of Milo and Otis** [1986]) is about a cat and a dog who endure numerous obstacles to reunite.

- **Chacun Cherce son Chat** (a.k.a. **When the Cat's Away** [1996]) is based on a real-life story about a lost cat.

- In **Austin Powers: International Man of Mystery** (1997) and two sequels, Mr. Bigglesworth is a Sphynx ("hairless") cat belonging to the bald Dr. Evil (Mike Myers), a parody of the Persian cat in Bond films (see above).

- In **Stuart Little** (1999), mouse Stuart is threatened by white house cat Snowbell (voiced by Nathan Lane). They return in **Stuart Little 2** (2002) and 3 (2008).

- **Cats & Dogs** (2001) is an espionage thriller about feline attempts to steal a serum to cure humans' allergies to dogs. (Do not confuse with **The Truth about Cats and Dogs** [1996], a romance about a veterinarian.)

- In **Catwoman** (2004), Patience Philips (Halle Berry) dies and is brought back to life as a woman by day but a cat by night.

- The **Cats of Mirikitani** (2006) is a documentary about an eighty-year-old homeless Japanese artist who loves and paints endless portraits of cats.

Essential Elements for Coat and Skin

JUST AS THERE ARE DIETS designed to give humans glossy hair, vibrant skin, and a dewy glow, cats can also benefit if their diets contain vital supplements, namely fatty acids.

Fatty acids, omega-3 and omega-6, are important players in the health of a cat's skin, coat, and other body systems. They've even been known to improve inhalant allergies (see Day 220). Your cat produces some of these "good fats" on his own, but he will need an extra boost to obtain necessary "essential" fatty acids. (What is essential for cats may not be required for dogs or other pets. For instance, cats need arachidonic acid [AA], but dogs do not.)

It's important to know the various types of omega-3 and omega-6 fatty acids so you will understand the contents of over-the-counter fatty acid supplements (see "Fatty Acids" below). To enhance a cat's coat, look for fatty acid supplements with linoleic acid (LA) and gamma-linolenic acid (GLA), which are both omega-6s, and eicosapentaenoic acid (EPA), an omega-3. Cats with seborrhea, or dry scaly skin, are deficient in LA, so look for supplements with high LA content.

Choose a supplement with a ratio of omega-6 to omega-3 of 10-to-1 or 5-to-1. Discuss supplementation with your vet. Because fatty acid supplements increase a cat's need for antioxidants, look for supplements that also contain vitamin E to provide antioxidants.

Vitamin A, niacin, biotin, and zinc also help maintain a cat's skin and hair health. Most commercial cat foods contain the proper amounts of these nutrients, or they would not pass feeding trials.

Guide to Fatty Acids

Fatty acids will improve your cat's skin and coat.

OMEGA-3:

Alpha-linolenic acid (ALA)

Eicosapentaenoic acid (EPA)

Docosahexaenoic acid (DHA)

OMEGA-6:

Linoleic acid (LA)

Gamma-linolenic acid (GLA)

Dihomo-gamma-linolenic acid (DGLA)

Arachidonic acid (AA)

Make a Paw-Print Granny Square

THE FINISHED SIZE OF EACH worsted-weight motif is approximately 5 inches (12.7 cm) square and consumes 1 gram of yarn.

The pattern could be used for a single square in chunky or doubled cotton yarn, suitable for serving as a dishcloth or washcloth, or could be made in multiples for larger items. You could even work with a finer yarn and smaller hook to make individual coasters.

If you wish to make a table runner, pillow cover, afghan, or bedspread, first sketch a chart of the intended shape, "walking" the prints along one side or opposite sides, filling in with motifs worked entirely in yarn A. Then crochet the corresponding quantity of each motif (for a solid-color square, work the total double crochets and chains indicated for each round) and sew together. A comfortable size for a worsted-weight afghan is nine by twelve squares.

MATERIALS

Worsted-weight yarn, for the background (A)

Contrasting worsted-weight yarn, for the paw print (B)

Crochet hook size G/6 (4 mm)

Scissors

Yarn needle, to sew motifs together (optional)

To change colors (XC): Holding the last two loops of the stitch on your hook, pull a loop of the new color through to complete the stitch.

To carry the unused color: Hold the unused strand of yarn firmly against the edge of the motif as you double crochet over it. Always cut yarn B at the end of a round, to avoid stretching the yarn along the back to the next round.

Count stitches as you work. Be sure to double crochet into the easy-to-miss first stitch after the ch-2 corner chain of the previous row.

With yarn A, chain (ch) 4 and slipstitch (sl st) into the first ch to form a loop.

Round 1: With yarn A, ch-3, double crochet (dc) 4 in ring, *ch-2, dc-5 in ring, *repeat from * to *. Ch-1, then switch to yarn B to ch-1. With yarn B, dc-5 in ring (XC to yarn A on last dc), ch-2, sl st into third ch of ch-3 that began the round. Cut yarn B ¾ inch (1.9 cm) from the motif and weave in the end. (4 sets of 5 stitches [st] between ch-2 loops, counting first ch-3 as a dc)

Round 2: With yarn A, ch-3, dc in next dc (XC to yarn B as you finish dc). With yarn B, dc in next three dc, then dc-1 in ch-2 loop (XC to yarn A on last dc). With yarn A, dc-1 in ch-2 loop (XC to yarn B as you finish dc). With yarn B, ch-2, dc-2 in same ch-2 loop, then dc in next two dc (XC to yarn A on last dc). With yarn A, dc-1 (XC to yarn B as you finish dc). With yarn B, dc in next two dc, and dc-2 in ch-2 loop (XC to yarn A on last dc). With yarn A, ch-2, dc-1 in same ch-2 loop (XC to yarn B as you finish dc). With yarn B, dc-1 in ch-3 loop, then dc in next three dc (XC to yarn A on last dc). With yarn A, dc in next two dc (XC to yarn B on last dc). With yarn B, dc-2, ch-2, dc-2 in ch-2 loop (corner made), dc in next five dc, work corner (XC to yarn A on last dc). Sl st with yarn A into third ch of ch-3 that began the round. Cut yarn B ¾ inch (1.9 cm) from the motif and weave in the end. (9 st between ch-2 loops, counting first ch-3 as a dc)

Round 3: With yarn A, ch-3 and dc-2 into next dc (XC to yarn B on last dc). *With yarn B, dc into next two dc, holding back last loop of each dc on the hook, then draw yarn B through all three loops on hook. Dc into next two dc, again holding back the last loop of each dc (XC to yarn A as you draw yarn A through all three loops on hook).* With yarn A, dc-2 in the next dc, work corner, dc once more in ch-2 loop (XC to yarn B as you finish dc). With yarn B, repeat from * to * once. With yarn A, dc-3 in next dc (XC to yarn B on last dc). With yarn B, repeat from * to *. With yarn A, dc-1 in ch-2 loop, work corner, then dc-2 in next dc (XC to yarn B on last dc). Repeat from * to *. With yarn A, dc 2 in next dc, dc in next three dc, work corner, dc in next dc (XC to yarn B on last dc). With yarn B, dc in next seven dc (XC to yarn A on last dc). With yarn A, dc in next dc, work corner, dc in next 2 dc, then sl st with yarn A into third ch of ch-3 that began the round. Cut yarn B ¾ inch (1.9 cm) from the motif and weave in the end. (13 st between ch-2 loops)

Note: If crocheting a solid-color motif to use between paw-print motifs, work this round plain with dc-13 straight across each side, with dc-2, ch-2, dc-2 corners.

Round 4: With yarn A, ch-3, dc in every dc, and work corners as above, then sl st with yarn A into third ch of ch-3 that began the round. (17 dc between ch-2 loops)

Round 5: With yarn A, ch-3 and then dc into every dc around, working each corner as follows: dc-2, ch-3, dc-2. Sl st into third ch of ch-3 that began the round, and make an extra tight chain on the hook to secure the yarn. Cut yarn A ¾ inch (1.9 cm) from the motif and weave in the end. (21 dc between ch-2 loops)

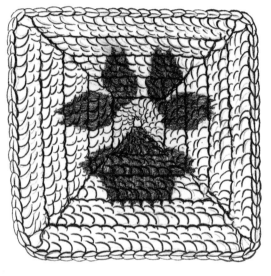

A finished paw-print granny square

Ragdoll

THE RAGDOLL WAS SO NAMED FOR its propensity to flop limply and comfortably in its owner's arms. The claim that the first Ragdolls were the result of their mother's sustaining a car accident is genetically impossible; that is, they would not have produced further generations with the limp characteristic. What is more likely the case is that breeder Ann Baker focused on mating cats that had a docile nature and a tendency to sprawl when relaxed.

feline fun fact > It is not true that the Ragdoll can feel no pain. The rumor got started because of the breed's unprotesting nature.

Characteristics: Ragdolls are large and broad-chested, with a semi-longhaired coat and a thick tail. They bear a passing resemblance to hardy Maine Coons, but they are so easygoing and nonaggressive that it is dangerous for them to be allowed outdoors, where predators might strike. Like Maine Coons, they don't develop their full coat for several years; unlike Coons, even the color of their coat isn't definite until they are at least two years old. They typically have blue eyes, and come in three kinds of point patterns: full colorpoint, bicolor, and white-mitted, the latter of which extends to boots up the rear legs. Bicolors have a distinctive upside-down V of white from their forehead to their chin.

Ragdolls need some help to keep their long, silky fur from developing tangles, and in the spring when they shed their heavy winter coat (to prevent hair balls). Aside from their need for extra grooming, they make wonderful, even-tempered pets that can put up with a lot from children.

History: The breed first appeared in California in the 1960s, the result of a mating between a white longhair and a Birman. They began to be recognized for competition in 1965, but a number of other countries have yet to fall into line, finding the cats' lineage too controversial.

Ragdoll

Teach Hello and Good-Bye

MANY CATS HAVE A DISTINCTIVE TRILL used for greeting. Get into the habit of greeting your cat when you wake up or when you enter your home: "Hi, [name]!" But also prepare him for your leaving your home, by saying, "Bye-bye, [name]," or some such term. You might want to add, "[Your name] out," as you leave.

Good-bye serves to cue your pet that you are going to be away consciously, of your own free will, as well as to underscore that until you arrive to say "Hi," you will not be there with him—no use calling or searching for you. It's not fair for you to disappear without warning him. (Unlike dogs, cats usually deal with an owner's absence well, but if you are regularly away for some time, consider getting your cat a feline companion or leaving the radio on softly for him.)

Perfect Paw Landings: Why Cats Land on Their Feet

CATS HAVE AN AMAZING ABILITY to right themselves midair and land on their feet almost every time. They can jump, or fall, from heights that some humans would not dare scale, and *still* land on their paws. This is one reason cats are said to have nine lives—they often emerge unscathed from situations that would leave other animals seriously injured. How do cats do it?

Two mechanisms are at play in these perfect landings: a *righting reflex* and a *skeletal structure* that can absorb the shock of impact. As your cat falls, the vestibular, or balance, organs in his inner ears help him determine which way is up. He turns his head so it is right side up and pointed toward the ground, then brings his front legs and upper body into alignment with his head. Finally, he twists his flexible spine to bring his rear legs into place and touches down. His body structure is such that the impact of landing is absorbed by his paw pads and joints in the legs and shoulders.

Although cats have this ability, they can still suffer injuries from a bad fall—and those aren't necessarily when a cat lands after a major drop. Short falls are especially dangerous because a cat doesn't have time to complete the righting maneuver before he hits the ground. And although there are miraculous tales of cats surviving falls from balconies or windows many stories high, such cats often sustain broken bones and internal injuries. If your cat falls from a height higher than he can jump, bring him to the vet.

The phrase "he landed on his feet" has come to apply to humans who have been able to emerge okay from an unfavorable position.

Comical Cats

A NUMBER OF CATS have rocketed to fame from the pen of cartoonists. These illustrators demonstrate a special gift for capturing with a few lines and conversational balloons or captions uniquely feline traits that may never quite surface in real-life photos of cats.

George Herriman first drew Krazy Kat as an unimportant character in a 1910 comic strip titled *Dingbat Family*; interest in the cat grew, and in 1918 the strip was renamed *Krazy Kat*. Like Felix (see Day 233), the slightly subversive Krazy Kat used slang and commented on current events.

Everyone knows Garfield, an orange and black lasagna-loving tabby "frequently mistaken for a meatloaf," who was created in 1978 by Jim Davis.

In these cartoons, *Garfield* lives with a cartoonist named Jon Arbuckle, and has a pink kitty girlfriend, Arlene, and a diminutive nephew, Nermal. A parody of Garfield, Bill the Cat is the local orange tabby in artist Berkeley Breathed's *Bloom County*, a comic strip that ran from 1980 to 1989.

George Gately introduced the ginger *Heathcliff* to the comic strip world in 1973. The strip expanded to include the Catillac Cats, a gang of alley cats headed by a character named Riff-Raff. Heathcliff (voiced by Mel Blanc) had his own television series for several years, beginning in 1984.

Caring for Mother Cat

Your FEMALE CAT WON'T EAT her food, and she is leaving evident signs of her upset stomach around the house. She's pudgier than usual, and her apathetic attitude lately strays far from her usual attention-craving self. You visit the vet to confirm your suspicions (yes, cats do get morning sickness). Guess who's going to be a mom? Unplanned or not, your new duties include caring for mother cat, and she has special needs.

No acrobatics: Mama cat will benefit from light exercise; a little playtime is a good thing (see Day 87). But prevent her from jumping up to high places, climbing, or rabble-rousing with other cats in the house. That said, keep her inside.

Serve gourmet: Continue serving up her usual portions of premium food during the first four weeks of pregnancy. Ensure that she cleans her plate and doesn't get full of treats that might prevent her from consuming necessary vitamins to support a healthy pregnancy. During the second half of pregnancy, gradually switch her to the highest quality food possible and a higher-protein diet (see Day 66 for tips on changing food). If she has trouble finishing a full portion, serve smaller meals several times a day. Discuss specific mealtime portions with your veterinarian.

Prenatal checkups: The Queen—breeding terminology for Mama Cat—needs her first prenatal checkup a few weeks after mating. At that time, discuss diet, nutrition, and medical needs with the vet.

She will need another prenatal checkup one week before her estimated delivery date. At this time, your vet will discuss delivery and newborn care.

Prepare a kittening box: A strong cardboard box with a removable lid, or a plastic storage container, can serve as a kittening container. Commercial kitten boxes are also available. Talk to your vet about suitable options.

Study up on Birthing 101: You may not plan to be the birth coach, but in case your vet does not arrive at the time of delivery, brush up on these basics so you can help Mama Cat through labor. There are three stages of labor: 1) The cat's cervix dilates and the birth canal opens; 2) kittens are born; 3) mother delivers the placenta. The first stage may last twelve hours or longer.

You'll know it's kitten time when Mama Cat begins panting and rhythmic purring that will increase as delivery time approaches. Your cat may pace, vomit, dig, strain, and cry out. Take your cat to the kittening box and sit with her. She needs her "mother" now to comfort her (that means you). During actual labor, resist the temptation to interfere. Assistance is only necessary if mother is giving attention to one kitten and another requires her care—either severing the cord or removing the fluid sack. Learn these procedures from your vet in case of emergency.

Removing Cat Hair from Upholstery

THE EVIDENCE THAT YOUR CATS claim the sofa while you are not home is matted to the upholstery. You may not mind a little extra hair in the house, but don't be surprised if houseguests decline your offer to sit down and make themselves comfortable. Depending on the upholstery material, de-hairing a sofa can be a real challenge. Even a high-powered vacuum can fail at the job. However, a basic dry sponge purchased at a pet supply store can do the trick. Lightly wipe the sponge across upholstery to collect fur.

(Make sure the sponge is dry or damp and well wrung out.) A damp rag will perform the same duty. Invest in sticky lint rollers, which you can find at hardware, grocery, and drugstores. These tape-covered tools are useful for a quick cleanup. Roll the sticky cylinder across the upholstered surface, removing tape layers periodically to regain sticking power. If the couch is for casual use, take a clean sneaker and sweep the rubber-soled bottom over cushions and seats. The rubber and friction pick up hair that seems to magnetize to upholstery.

Russian Blue

NOT LITERALLY BLUE, these affectionate Oriental-build shorthairs have bright green eyes and a cool gray double coat tipped with silver.

Characteristics: In the mid-1900s, breeders began experimenting with crossing the Blue with a Siamese for a more pronounced angularity, or with a blue Finnish cat for a darker coat. These experiments have led to there being slightly different breed characteristics among competition and breeders.

Russian Blue

For example, the British prefer their Blues to have blue paws, but in the United States the paws should be more mauve. Variations in body color include Russian White and Russian Black, produced by crossbreeding with solid-color non-blue cats.

History: The breed is believed to have begun in very northern Russia, in the vicinity of the port of Arkhangelsk (Archangel). The icy climate led to the cats' genetic adaptation of a thick coat rather than a longhaired one.

Sailors began bringing the cats to the West in the mid-1800s. The breed was introduced to the United States in 1900, where it was initially called a Maltese. In Great Britain, a Russian Blue, dubbed an "Archangel Cat," was presented as a creature of interest at the Crystal Palace in 1875, and the first Blue appeared in a British cat show in 1880. Until 1939, however, the cat was known in the United Kingdom as a Foreign Shorthair, encompassing other breeds; that year, however, Russian Blue became the official name there and in the U.S., as a subcategory of Foreign Shorthairs.

Story: Love at First Sight

IN AN ATTEMPT TO GIVE "Aunt Lori" the perfect Christmas gift, my niece and nephew, ages three and ten at the time, decided that a kitty was just what I needed. I had recently returned to Ohio after nearly six years of living in Hawaii and a drawn-out breakup, and the little house I purchased was cute but a little lonely.

Thankfully, my niece and nephew didn't show up at my doorstep with a shaking, meowing box. On a snowy night in December, my sister and her kids took me to the no-kill shelter to find a kitty present. There were so many cats there—more than one hundred furry, lonely cats curled in their nooks and cages, strutted on overhead ledges, and timidly stirred as we took in the scene. Some were quite bold, figure-eighting through our legs. I was overwhelmed. Each cat was cuter than the last, and they all needed a good home. I had no idea how I would ever settle on just one.

I spent some time just wandering, petting the cats. Shorthair, longhair, black, calico, tabby, white, old, young . . . what a decision to make.

On my second pass through, a pair of green eyes at about eye level caught my attention. A small tabby was huddled in the back of a closed cage with her little head on her paws, looking all cute and sad. I asked the shelter volunteer about this kitty. What was her story? She told me the tabby had been at the shelter for only a couple of days, that she was friendly but a little overwhelmed by the shelter experience. (This, I understood.) I asked if I could remove the kitty from her cage. When I picked her up and cradled her in my arms, and she looked at me with saucer-size eyes and purred so hard that she started drooling, I knew she was the one.

My niece and nephew seconded my choice. Fiona had not been spayed yet, so she had to stay at the shelter for another ten days before I could pick her up and bring her to her new home. Like most cats, she was timid the first few days, but when she did finally come out to say "hi," she curled right up in my lap. And she's been there ever since.

Cats and Milk

CATS ARE KNOWN FOR THEIR love of milk, or so we assume. Everywhere, cats are depicted happily lapping up saucers of milk and licking their chops before lying down for a nap. Although cats love the taste of milk, most adult cats are lactose intolerant and can't properly digest it.

Like other young mammals, kittens produce a high level of lactase, the enzyme that breaks down lactose so it can be digested. Milk is rich in lactose, a carbohydrate that provides energy and nutrition to growing bodies. But once a kitten reaches the age where she can be weaned, typically six to eight weeks or so, she usually starts to lose her ability to digest lactose. Ingesting milk can lead to intestinal upset and diarrhea.

Some cats retain their ability to digest lactose as they become adults, but almost all retain their love of the taste of milk, even if it makes them sick. Very small amounts of milk or milk products, such as a lick or two off a yogurt lid, on special occasions won't harm most cats. But if your cat shows any signs of discomfort after ingesting milk, avoid giving it to him, or look for a milk substitute for cats at the pet store.

Contrary to popular belief, milk does not contain any special nutrients that cats need that cannot be obtained from a properly formulated commercial cat food.

Cats in Classical Music

> There are two means of refuge from the miseries of life: music and cats.
>
> —Albert Schweitzer (1875–1965)

THE 1816 PREMIERE OF *Il barbiere di sivilgia* was plagued with mishaps, including the unlucky appearance of a real cat onstage. In 1825, music from another 1816 Rossini opera, Otello, was used to create the humorous "Duetto Buffo di due Gatti" (Cat Duet).

Some other classical vocal works that concern cats:

- "Die Katze lässt das Mausen nicht" (Cats Won't Stop Chasing Mice), one of the pieces in J.S. Bach's *Schweigt Stille, Plaudert Nicht* (ca. 1732)

- Domenico Scarlatti's 1739 "Cat's Fugue," inspired by his cat's walking on the keyboard

- Frédéric Chopin's "Valse Brillante in F Major", Op. 34, No. 3, a.k.a. the "Cat Waltz" (1838), which had a similar inspiration

- Jacques Offenbach's 1858 opéra-bouffe titled *La Chatte Metamorphosée en Femme* (from Aesop's fable about Aphrodite; see Day 310)

- Modest Mussorgsky's "The Cat Sailor," one of his *Nursery Songs* (1872)

- Gilbert and Sullivan's 1879 *The Pirates of Penzance's* policemen's chorus, "With cat-like tread." (The "cat" sung about in the 1878 *HMS Pinafore*, however, refers to a cat o'nine tails.)

- César Cui's *Puss in Boots* (1913), which has been recorded under its German title, *Der Gestiefelte Kater*

- Igor Stravinsky's four-song *Berceuses du Chat* (1917)

- Aaron Copland's *The Cat and the Mouse* (1920), his very first published piece

- Ravel's 1924 *L'Enfant et les Sortilèges*, which contains a "Duo miaulé" for its feline characters Chatte and Chat. Its libretto is by Colette (see Day 275).

- Benjamin Britten's 1941 operetta *Paul Bunyan*, whose libretto by poet W.H. Auden includes two cats, Moppet and Poppet

- "A Monk and His Cat," a setting of the poem "Pangur Bán" (see Day 282) from Samuel Barber's *Knoxville: Summer of 1915* (1948)

- Leroy Anderson's 1950 "The Waltzing Cat," a favorite of pops orchestras, which uses the string section to imitate meows

- Ernst von Dohnányi's Nocturne "Cats on the Roof" from *Three Singular Pieces for Piano*, Op. 44 (1951)

- Alan Hovhaness's 1977 Sonata Op. 301 for piano is known as "Fred the Cat." The composer is also responsible for Sonata Op. 366, again for piano, called "Hiroshige's Cat Bathing."

- Hans Werner Henze's 1983 *Die Englische Katze* (The English Cat), based on a Balzac story, "Les peines de coeur d'une chatte anglaise"

- William Bolcom's piano rag "Tabby Cat Walk" (1999)

Keep Off: Beware These Cat-Unfriendly Plants

ALTHOUGH MOST CULINARY HERBS are safe to grow or display around cats, quite a few other common house and garden plants could cause distress or even death if your pet ingests them.

Even the prettiest flowers may be dangerous: The powerful acids in lilies can burn your cat's mouth and throat, the saponins in carnations can damage his digestive system, the digitalis in foxgloves can stop your cat's heart, the alkaloids in daffodils can cause convulsions, and hydrangeas contain cyanide! Also, everyday greenery, such as yew or privet, can kill a cat almost instantly if nibbled. And most bulbs are also poisonous. Even runoff water from toxic plants can be poisonous (including if licked off paws). Holiday plants such as holly and mistletoe are extremely toxic to cats, too.

The good news is that there are attractive non-toxic alternatives, such as coleus, phlox, hibiscus, dahlias, geraniums, and forsythia; and many edible herbs, such as lavender, can be easily grown indoors for their flowers and scent, even if you don't plan to cook with them.

But take a moment now to check your home for the plants listed here and transfer them to a cat-free room, hang them away from any furniture your cat could climb, or remove them entirely if they cannot be safeguarded.

An additional concern is pesticides that may have been sprayed on purchased floral arrangements and plants. Again, place purchased greenery well out of reach of your pet, or obtain them from a florist who grows them organically.

As for dried arrangements or potpourris, make sure that they, too, are organically grown and have not been mixed/coated with toxic essential oils. Move or remove if your cat is ingesting any of the material. Even a nontoxic herb such as lavender could prove fatal to a cat if a needle-sharp length of stem is snapped off and ingested.

See Day 192 for what to do if your cat eats a poisonous substance.

TOXIC PLANTS

Alliums (lily, onion, garlic), *Allium carinatum*
Aloe vera, *Aloe barbadensis*
Amaryllis, *Hippeastrum*
Anemone, *Coronaria var. cyanea*
Angelica, *Angelica archangelica*
Arnica, *Arnica montana*
Arum lily, *Zantedeschia aethiopica*
Autumn crocus, *Colchicum autumnale*
Azalea, *Rhododendron* sp.
Baby's breath, *Gypsophila repens*
Bay, laurel, *Laurus nobilis*
Blue cohosh, *Caulophyllum thalictroides*
Boxwood, *Buxus sempervirens*
Buttercup, *Ranunculus*
Calla lily, *Zantedeschia aethiopica*
Carnation, *Dianthus caryophyllus*
Celandine, *Ranunculus ficaria*
Christmas rose, *Helleborus niger*
Comfrey, *Symphytum officinale*
Cyclamen, *Cyclamen hederifolium*
Daffodil, *Narcissus pseudo*
Deadly nightshade, *Atropina belladonna*
Delphinium, *Delphinium*
Elephant ear, *Alocasia macrorrhiza*

Foxglove, *Digitalis purpurea L.*
Gladiola, *Gladiolus palustris*
Holly, *Ilex aquifolium*
Hydrangea, *Hydrangea serrata*
Iris, *Iris tenax*
Ivy, *Hedera*
Jack-in-the-pulpit, *Arisaema griffithii*
Jonquil, *Narcissus jonquilla*
Larkspur, *Delphinium*
Lily-of-the-valley, *Convallaria majalis*
Mistletoe, *Viscum album*
Mountain laurel, *Kalmia latifolia*
Myrtle, *Myrtus communis*
Narcissus, *Narcissus papyraceus*
Oleander, *Nerium oleander L.*
Pennyroyal, *Pulecium*
Peony, *Paeonia*
Philodendron, *Philodendron xanadu*
Poinsettia, *Euphorbia pulcherrima*
Potato, *Solanum tuberosum*
Privet, *Ligustrum* spp.
Rhododendron, *Rhododendron*
Rose geranium, *Pelargonium graveolens*
Rue, *Ruta graveolens L.*
Saint John's wort, *Hypericum perforatum*
Sassafras, *Sassafras albidum*
Shamrock, *Oxalis triangularis* ssp.
Sweet pea, *Lathyrus odoratus*
Taro, *Colocasia esculenta*
Tobacco, *Nicotiana alata*
Tuberose, *Polianthes*
Wisteria, *Wisteria floribunda*
Yew, *Taxus canadensis*
Zebra plant, *Aphelandra squarrosa louisae*
Zinnia, *Chrysogonum peruvianum L.*

The Office Cat

CATS ARE GREAT WORKPLACE COMPANIONS. If you work alone, your cat plays the role of a sympathetic (and always willing to listen) coworker—and probably the boss, but one who gives you plenty of autonomy. After all, your cat needs his privacy, too. Cats in an office can provide a welcome dose of warm-fuzzy that is shown to reduce stress.

Cats are easy to get along with in the workplace because they are relatively low-maintenance, do not require walks, and won't bark at the mail carrier. In fact, they often become quite famous in their role as a working cat. Shop cats attract fans who stop in special just to see Kitty.

Some progressive companies host bring your pet to work days, which may be chaotic if the workplace becomes a pet zoo of cats, dogs, hamsters, and who knows what else. These "holidays" are fun for everyone, but the same ground rules (below) apply whether a pet is making a cameo appearance in the office or will work there full time. Also, decide whether a pet-filled office would be exciting or traumatic for your cat. Cats like to claim territory, so your feline may operate better if she is an office regular, and the one-and-only.

If you own the company, and you're more than a company of one, consider whether employees will truly benefit from having a cat around the office. If your top salesperson is severely allergic to cats, you may have to decide what's more important.

If Kitty will be a fixture in the work environment, supply him with "work" to stay busy: kitty condos, scratching posts, window perches, and places to hide. Ideally, you should assign a cat zone in the office—Kitty doesn't need an entire cubicle, but he will require a private place to eat, use his litter box, and nap. Aside from litter box duties, carpets, window treatments, and other pet-dander traps require special attention.

Before Kitty's first day on the job, take these steps to prepare:

- Immunize your cat; retain a file containing shot records for your cat, and others if you allow employees to bring pets to work.

- Flea control is a must.

- Remove poisonous plants, hide electrical cords and wires, secure toxic substances such as correction fluid, and follow the cat-proofing steps in Day 85.

- Groom and bathe your cat regularly.

- Prepare Kitty's "cubicle" with a litter box and food and water bowls.

Scottish Fold

ROUND-EYED AND ROUND-EARED, the Scottish Fold looks like a furry owl.

Characteristics: The Scottish Fold is available in shorthaired and longhaired varieties. Both have a round face with small, tightly curled ears tipped fully forward, with a single or double crease, to cup the top of the head. Some Folds are born with straight ears and are called Pink-Eared Folds. They have a cobby body and a less flexible tail than other breeds. The fur comes in most colors and patterns, except for lilac, chocolate, and colorpoint; bicolor or tortie Folds are common.

Scottish Folds are prone to ear mange and deafness. Beware of mating a Scottish Fold to another Fold; this may produce kittens with various forms of bone deformities, including excessive cartilage in their paws or a tail with fused vertebrae.

History: Like the American Curl, whose ears fold in the opposite direction (see Day 40), this breed began as a spontaneous mutation. In 1961, a white cat named Susie was born with folded ears, on the McRae family's farm in Scotland. Susie bore a kitten with the same characteristic named Snooks, who was given to the neighbors. Snooks continued the line by producing Snowball, again with folded ears. This turned out to be a dominant characteristic: Mating a straight-eared cat with a fold-eared cat has a 50 percent chance of producing fold-eared kittens and, in fact, keeps the breed healthy.

Folds were imported to the United States in 1970, and registration followed in 1973, with full championship status in 1978. However, in the United Kingdom, recognition of this breed has had a rocky history; some organizations fear that various ear maladies often associated with the breed will be perpetuated if it is lauded as a show cat. The Cat Association of Britain did finally register the breed in 1983.

feline fun fact > Scottish Fold kittens are born with straight ears, but the ears begin to turn forward in about a month's time.

Scottish Fold

Story: Kitty Stonehenge

MY CAT ALICE HAS A peculiar relationship with her toys. Selecting only stuffed animals, she carries them about the house in her mouth while vocalizing in several pitches, as if carrying on both sides of a conversation: hers and her "pet's."

She has definite favorites, which she knows by name: Mouse, followed by Puppy, Birdie, Duck, and Lion. Others are occasionally corralled for a play session but otherwise piled by Alice at the foot of the stairs . . . with exceptions; for example, Rabbit is for some reason confined to the parlor, except for brief forays into the kitchen.

The favorites, however, perform special active duties. Alice frequently deputizes one or another to stay by my chair or just outside a room I am in: She deposits the toy, then takes off to attend to other business while Lion, say, fills in for her (and, I imagine, reports back to her later!). Also, if I am busy, she will bring me a toy, with great vocal ceremony, and if I don't thank her and also acknowledge the specific toy ("Thank you, Alice. Thank you, Mouse"), she will carry it away and make her entrance again, more insistently ("You didn't *look*!"). She also takes the chosen few upstairs to bed and then back downstairs in the morning. On a busy day, ever-patient Mouse may be toted up and down the stairs a half-dozen times . . . unless participating in what I call Kitty Stonehenge.

A few years ago, I began to notice deliberate arrangements of Alice's toys. Sometimes they are placed along an invisible straight line, occasionally in an equilateral triangle. Some displays indicate a delightful sense of humor, such as when Alice posed her toy Kitty as if it were running after Mouse, with Puppy in pursuit of Kitty. One repeating motif is one toy set at the exact center of our staircase—but, several times, she has sat Mouse rear end outward at the exact center of the top step, to moon anyone approaching from below!

I have never caught her in the act of making such arrangements. They just appear, perfectly placed, rather like crop circles—and, as with crop circles, often involving a perspective that is bafflingly accurate—the toys impeccably equidistant from one another (usually about a foot [30.5 cm] apart).

She has recently enlarged her repertoire to include three-dimensional lineups involving both the stairs and the hallway, and has begun experimenting with arcs. I am looking forward to what she may come up with next, perhaps becoming able to count beyond her apparent ceiling of four.

Until then, her present creative endeavors continue to fascinate. Thank you, Alice. (Thank you, Mouse.)

Climbing Cats

CATS ARE NATURAL CLIMBERS, thanks to their claw structure and fearless attitude. They will identify potential penthouse views in your home—a bookshelf, countertop, windowsill—and scale their way to the top to take in their surroundings. Cats treat their perches like watch towers. They enjoy keeping an eye on their housemates. Between cats' adept climbing and jumping, they can be inventive in reaching unusual places, such as the top of your overhead kitchen cabinets.

Kittens are well known for climbing everything they can sink their claws into: curtains, furniture, even your pant legs. Kittens usually grow out of the climb-everything phase; in the meantime, the best solution is to keep curtains tied up out of reach and to redirect their attention when they attempt to scale your furniture (or you).

Provide your cat with a cat tree or other approved climbing structure. Make it appealing to her by giving her treats and affection when she uses it, rub catnip on it for adult cats. When she has her own special perch she can climb to, she'll be less likely to climb other things.

It's a good idea to protect your breakables by moving them to enclosed places or using museum putty to affix them to the shelves. Museum putty is safe for furniture and objects and helps prevent them from being knocked over (although a Maine Coon and delicate porcelain will never be a good match).

As for that popular image of cats being rescued from a tree by the friendly fire department, true, some cats do love to climb trees. And it's much easier for them to climb up than to climb down. Most cats will eventually figure out how to get themselves down, though, so don't panic unless your cat has been up there all day and hasn't shown any signs of trying to get down.

The Cat-Books Connection

If you want to write, keep a cat.
—Aldous Huxley (1894–1963)

MANY AUTHORS HAVE FOUND inspiration in their feline pet(s), from Victor Hugo to Edgar Allan Poe to Mark Twain (whose numerous cats included Beelzebub and Buffalo Bill).

Colette adored cats and lived with an assortment named Franchette, Kapok, Kiki-la-Doucette, Kro, La Toutou, Mini-mini, Minionne, Muscat, One and Only, Saha, Toune, Zwerg, and La Chatte Dernière (literally, her last cat). She wrote the libretto for the opera *L'Enfant et les Sortilèges* (see Day 268), which includes a duet for cats; she also wrote Kiki into her story *Sept Dialogues de Bêtes (Seven Animal Dialogues)* and Saha into *La Chatte*, about a Russian Blue. Other Colette works that contain discussion of cats include *La Paix Chez les Bêtes (Peace at Home with Animals)* and her various Claudine novels.

Ernest Hemingway loved cats; his museum estate in Key West, Florida, now cares for about sixty, many of them polydactyl, all descendants of a six-toed cat named Snowball, given to the writer by a ship's captain. In Hemingway's short story "A Cat in the Rain," a bickering American couple in Italy takes in a stray tortie.

Managing Feline Diabetes

THE ROOTS OF FELINE DIABETES are similar to those of their owners: A sedentary lifestyle, weight gain, and eventually obesity result in a chronic disease that must be managed carefully. Type 1 diabetes, diabetes mellitus, is the inability to produce or properly use insulin, which regulates the glucose levels in blood. The disease can affect cats of any breed, age, or sex, but is more common in males. Other causes of diabetes besides obesity include genetics, pancreatic disease, hormonal imbalances, and certain medications.

Excessive urination is the most obvious symptom of feline type 1 diabetes. Cats may also display an increased appetite, weight loss, change in coat, and lethargy. As the disease advances, other more serious symptoms can present, including liver disease or bacterial infections. A veterinarian can confirm diabetes by examining the cat for clinical signs, taking a medical history, and doing lab tests. A fructosamine test will identify blood sugar levels.

With today's technology, a cat with diabetes can live a long, happy life, and the daily regimen for maintaining blood sugar levels is relatively convenient and painless for your cat. Treatment requires giving insulin injections one or two times each day. A small number of cats can be treated with medication and a modified diet. The shots will not harm your cat; the needles are small, and the injections will become part of your cat's daily ritual. Your vet will recommend the type of insulin and dosage, and the regimen may require adjustment as your cat's blood sugar levels rise and fall over time.

Regular glucose checks can be performed at home or by your vet. Periodic testing is critical to ensure that the proper level of insulin is being administered.

Commit to this four-pronged approach to managing diabetes—consistency is key—and your cat will live a fulfilling life.

The Diabetes Regimen

Administer insulin: Your vet will prescribe the proper dosage based on your cat's weight. Be consistent with injection time.

Maintain a healthy diet: Limit snacks and control weight gain (see Day 206).

Exercise regularly: Rouse your cat from her nap routine by enticing her with interactive toys to encourage play.

Monitor the disease: Regular visits to the veterinarian for glucose testing is critical. Establishing proper insulin dosage may take several months. As you monitor your cat at home, watch for signs of hypoglycemia, which is triggered by insulin overdose, excessive activity, or a missed meal. Keep food or corn syrup handy.

You Moved: Helping Kitty Adjust

LARGE BOXES, PACKING CHAOS, strange new territory—moving is tough on cats that do not adapt to change as easily as do humans, or even dogs, for that matter. Because of cats' territorial nature, a complete change in habitat is frustrating and scary. Leaving the house they rule (sorry, dear owner) and getting plopped into a different environment is downright traumatic for some cats. You can ease the transition by downplaying the moving preparation process and gradually introducing Kitty to her new home.

Pack early and with stealth. You can't hide the boxes, but you can designate a packing zone away from your cat's perch and food/litter areas. As you pack, stack boxes in a designated room. Or, during packing, assign your cat to a safe room away from boxes and chaos. Place a scratching post or kitty hideaway in the room so she can stay occupied, and so she recognizes that that is her territory as you prepare for the move.

Contain with care. On moving day, place your cat in a safe room, such as the bathroom, where she won't escape or jump into an open box. Post a "Do Not Open" sign on the door. Movers will be entering and exiting your house—doors will be propped wide open so they can usher out boxes and furniture. Keeping Kitty in a safe room will prevent her from making her own move far away from the madness at your house.

Travel safe. Prepare a cat carrier by lining it with a blanket and putting a toy or a bit of catnip inside. If your cat is prone to motion sickness, avoid giving her food or water several hours before departure.

Help Kitty settle. Immediately designate a safe room where your cat can stay as you unload and unpack boxes. Place her crate in the room, and leave behind a towel or shirt that carries your scent. This comforting touch will make her feel more at ease. Gradually introduce your cat to other rooms in the house. Avoid letting her roam freely. You'll be unpacking potentially harmful items.

Tour the neighborhood. If your cat is an outdoor roamer, help her get to know the new neighborhood, but wait a few weeks before you allow her to go solo. At first, let your cat out for brief, supervised romps in a contained area, if possible. Try using a leash to walk her around your property, and give her time to sniff out the new surroundings. Plant a tasty treat in your backyard so she associates your new property with good things. Over time, your cat will recognize your new home as her territory.

Your cat should sport a collar and tags with your address and phone number in case she gets lost. Microchip your cat so she can be identified if the collar falls off. (Read more about this on Day 358.)

Siamese

THE SIAMESE IS ONE OF the royal cats of Thailand, and throughout history they were introduced as "gift cats" to consuls in various countries, including England and the United States.

Characteristics: Initially the breed did not thrive in the West, but breeders persevered. Four colorpoint varieties developed, predominantly the seal point. The others are lilac, chocolate, and blue. All Siamese have blue eyes, a long nose within a wedge-shaped face, a thin tail, and a slim, angular foreign build. They tend to enjoy clambering up to high places. Siamese are notoriously vocal, especially when in heat.

The original show standards in Great Britain back in 1889 actually called for kinked tails and crossed eyes (the first UK Siamese champion, Wankee, had a kinked tail), but these are being bred out as undesirable. American Siamese tend to have a more streamlined, angular body and thinner tail than those living abroad, with ears set low on the sides of the head; some U.S. Siamese breeders also attempt to perpetuate the tendency toward an "apple" (round) head, which is frowned upon in Great Britain.

History: King Chulalongkorn of Siam (1868–1910), the country's most beloved king, loved cats and commissioned the creation of the *Smud Khoi of Cats*, a special copy of a fourteenth-century book of cat verse that discussed the Siamese and also the Korat (see Day 187). This book can be found in Bangkok's National Museum. This king is also responsible for sending a pair of his Siamese palace cats, Pho and Mia, to Great Britain as a gift to the consul-general Owen Gould, in 1884.

Siamese cats had already arrived in England (they were first shown in Crystal Palace in 1871), but the gift cats were considered to be superior, having been raised with care in the palace of the king. This more robust breed appeared at the London Cat Show in 1885. Meanwhile, the first Siamese to reach the United States were similarly a gift to the American consul, David Stickles, in 1878; he gave the cats to the wife of President Rutherford B. Hayes.

feline fun fact > Legend has it that the kinked tail developed because Siamese ladies at court would store their rings on the slender cat's tail, and the tail angled itself to keep the jewelry from slipping off.

Siamese

Story: The Cat Christmas Party

I ALWAYS HOLD MY HOLIDAY PARTY at the beginning of January. I never expected to have extra feline guests, but in the year 2000 there must have been some telepathic thread among my friends that said, "Cats!!!" Maybe it was millennium fever?

It all started on the morning of the party when my friends Louis and Doug phoned to ask if they could bring their very "doggy" Maine Coon, Seth, who enjoyed travel and already knew my apartment and my four female cats—I had cat-sat for him previously in my home a number of times. I said, Sure—bring him over.

As other guests began arriving, my next-door neighbors knocked with their just-acquired-for-Christmas twin male tabby kittens, Clousseau and Cato, in tow. My girls were up for it, accustomed to meeting other cats without a fuss. The boys immediately began exploring my apartment, a mirror image to theirs. My youngest, Clara, became distressed when one of them started to climb along a shelf filled with china—she had just been taught not to go there, and she paced the floor in front of the cabinet, nearly wringing her hands from the anxiety. I assured her that the situation was under control. Otherwise, things went swimmingly.

Another knock at the door—there was my downstairs neighbor, with her new Chartreux kitten, Millena, named for the new millennium, who joined the party but preferred shyly to stay close by her owner on the sofa.

At the height of the party, enter Louis and Doug, with Seth at his doggiest—not only on a leash but also sporting a striped sweater knitted by Doug's sister! Now, that brought the house down! Once we took pictures of him, they removed the sweater so he wouldn't overheat indoors. Seth quickly took in the situation, the kittens from next door hero-worshiping him on sight, and all seven cats—the boys and my four, excepting Millena—piled into my bedroom of their own accord, to play with the girls' assortment of cat toys and romp on the bed, while the humans continued partying in the living and dining area. It was kind of like kids retiring to a resident child's room to play video games away from the adults.

Come time for Seth's departure, of course he didn't want to go. In addition, reminded in the company of his own species that he was, in fact, a cat, he also struggled mightily against being dressed again in his sweater.

Years later, the humans who were there still speak about the Cat Christmas Party, and for all I know, the cats who attended do, too.

The Buzz about Raw Food Diets

As CONSUMERS GROW increasingly interested in organic products and health foods, the market for natural pet foods has expanded. We also hear more about raw diets for our pets. What exactly does this mean, and should you consider such a diet for your cat?

Raw food diets consist of mainly of ground raw meat, organs, and bones, along with dietary supplements. The diet may also include small bits of raw vegetables and nuts or seeds. Recipes are carefully formulated to ensure that meals meet all nutritional requirements. Cat owners prepare the recipes at home using a meat grinder, and usually make large enough batches to feed their cats for several days. Leftovers are frozen and thawed as needed.

Raw food advocates say that these diets are closest to what cats would eat in the wild. Cats are obligate carnivores, which means that meat is a substantial and necessary part of their diet. Their digestive systems are optimized for this kind of diet.

Raw food advocates often cite research done by Francis M. Pottenger Jr. in the 1930s and 1940s suggesting that raw meat diets were much healthier for cats than cooked meat diets.

Skeptics counter the raw food argument with the point that at the time of Pottenger's study, the importance of taurine to the feline diet (see Day 199) had not yet been discovered. Taurine in raw food is destroyed by the cooking process. Cats fed a diet of cooked meat or commercial cat food supplemented with taurine can be just as healthy as those on a raw diet.

Before exploring a raw food diet for your cat, be sure to consult with your vet for information and advice. Cats have very specific nutritional needs that differ from those of humans. Raw food diets must be carefully prepared and stored to ensure that your cat does not miss out on essential nutrients.

Cats in Verse

there s a dance in the old dame yet
toujours gai toujours gai

> —Mehitabel, in Don Marquis's
> *archy and mehitabel* (1927)

CATS HAVE BEEN CELEBRATED in verse for centuries:

- Verses about Pangur Bán were written on a copy of Saint Paul's Epistles by an anonymous eighth-century seminarian perhaps grown bored with his task: "Hunting mice is his delight, / Hunting words I sit all night."

- Geoffrey Chaucer (1343–1400) wrote about cats in the "Mauciples Tale" and in his prologue to "The Wife of Bath's Tale," both in *Canterbury Tales*.

- Jonathan Swift (1667–1745) wrote about a naughty cat in his "A Fable of the Widow and Her Cat."

- Christopher Smart (1722–1771), while he was confined in Bedlam, composed a poem in which he celebrated his cat Jeoffry as being God's servant.

- Commemorative verses are plentiful, including Thomas Gray's (1716–1771) "Ode: On the Death of a favorite cat drowned in a tub of gold fishes"; Thomas Hardy's (1840–1928) "Last Words to a Dumb Friend"; and Louis MacNiece's (1907–1963) "The Death of a Cat."

- William Cowper (1731–1800) wrote a poem describing a cat's accidentally being shut into a drawer in "The Retired Cat."

- Oliver Herford (1863–1935) is the author of the delightful *A Kitten's Garden of Verses*.

- Lewis Carroll's tail-shaped "The Mouse's Tale," from *Alice's Adventures in Wonderland* (see Day 338) describes how a family of mice was destroyed by the collaborative efforts of a cat and dog.

- The archy and mehitabel writings of Don Marquis, begun as newspaper columns in 1916, were first collected into book form in 1927. Mehitabel is an alley cat who left a pampered existence to go off with a Maltese, and who claims she was Cleopatra in a past life.

- William Butler Yeats's (1865–1939) "The Cat and the Moon" explored the mystical relationship of his black cat Minnaloushe and the heavenly body.

- American poet Amy Lowell (1874–1925) wrote a detailed portrait of her cat in "To Winky."

- In addition to his famous four-line "The Kitten," Ogden Nash (1902–1971) also wrote "The Cat" about a caterwauling pet.

- Stevie (Florence Margaret) Smith (1902–1991) wrote several cat poems, including "The Galloping Cat" and "The Singing Cat."

- In "Charlemagne," from *The Golden Gate*, Indian author Vikram Seth (1952–) pays tribute to other celebrated cats, including the abovementioned Pangur Bán and Jeoffry.

Care for That Cheshire Grin

DENTAL CARE FOR CATS is more sophisticated today, with feline root canals, crowns, and even braces. Some veterinarians specialize in dentistry, though visiting a board-certified vet for a routine teeth cleaning is not necessary. Basic feline dental care should include periodic oral exams and cleanings by your veterinarian. (Groomers also offer teeth brushing services.) At home, you should brush your cat's teeth on a regular basis. Once a week is a realistic target.

Don't cringe—a home teeth cleaning can be a positive, even a bonding, experience for you and your cat. The key is to gradually introduce cleaning tools to your cat, and keep a playful attitude as if you're engaging in a game.

First, gather the proper tools to perform the task. You'll need a quality pet toothpaste. These come in flavored varieties; look for the veterinarian-recommended ingredients chlorhexidine, sodium hexametaphosphate, or zinc gluconate. Do not use human toothpaste because it may upset your cat's delicate stomach. Next, gather a pet toothbrush suitable for cats. These brushes are smaller than human toothbrushes, and they have ultrasoft bristles and are ergonomically designed to fit into your cat's mouth.

Now you're ready to introduce your cat to the toothpaste and start the cleaning process.

1. Let your cat lick some toothpaste off your finger to get a taste of it. Praise her and give her a treat. Continue just this step for a few days until your cat is accustomed to the flavor.

2. Squeeze a dollop of paste onto your finger and rub it on your cat's gums and teeth so she gets used to the idea of your hand being in her mouth. Complete the exercise by giving your cat a tasty treat or reward (interactive toy).

3. Introduce your cat to the dental brush. Squeeze paste onto the brush and allow your cat to lick it off. Praise her and give her a treat or playtime. Continue this for several days before actually brushing her teeth.

4. You're ready to brush your cat's teeth, and by now she understands the tools involved and will not be frightened by the process. Use a coaxing, upbeat voice and treat the process as you would a game. Lift her lip gently and place the brush at a 45-degree angle to the gumline. Gently brush the upper canine teeth. It's not necessary to brush the inside (backs) of the teeth because your cat's saliva keeps those surfaces relatively plaque-free. When you're finished brushing, praise your cat and give her another reward.

feline fun fact **>** For amusing parodies of classic poems rewritten to concern cats, read Henry Beard's *Poetry for Cats: The Definitive Anthology of Distinguished Feline Verse* (1994). Pieces range from an excerpt from "Beocat" to "Meowl," a takeoff of Allen Ginsberg's Howl.

Sew a Cat-Print Apron

CRAFT STORES AND QUILT SUPPLY shops sell cunning cat fabric prints ideal for the kitchen—you might even find one featuring feline chefs!

MATERIALS

1 yard (0.9 m) 44-inch (1.1 m) wide cat-print broadcloth, washed in cold water, dried, and ironed before cutting

Scissors

Ruler and a pencil

Straight pins

Coordinating thread and a sewing needle

Iron and ironing board

Cut out the pieces

1. Measure 22 inches (55.9 cm) along the selvage of the cloth and cut completely across the 44-inch (1.1 m) width, for the main portion of the apron.

2. On the remaining 14-inch (35.6 cm) length of fabric, measure 5 inches (12.7 cm) along the selvage and cut completely across, for the apron's sash. Test the sash around your waist; if you need to add extra fabric, do so from what remains. (Sew on any additional sash fabric with a ½-inch (1.3 cm) seam allowance.)

Assemble the apron

1. Trim the selvage areas of the apron body and sash of any manufacturers' text or pinholes. Make sure the length is even along all the cut edges; trim, if necessary. With the ruler and straight pins, turn in a ¼-inch (6 mm) doubled hem along each side and the bottom of the apron body, pinning as you go, so that the raw ends are completely enclosed. Use the needle and thread to hemstitch the three sides.

2. With a long piece of doubled thread (at least 4 feet [1.2 m] long before folding in half), sew a running stitch across, ½ inch (1.3 cm) from the top of the apron body. Gather the fabric by pulling on the thread, until the top of the apron body is 20 inches (50.8 cm) wide, and knot the end of the thread to the fabric so it won't slip. Even out the gathers and use a pin vertically to mark the center of the top.

3. Fold the sash portion in half along its width and pin the center of the apron portion to it, right sides facing. Pin the rest of the gathered body to the edge to each side of the center, matching the edges. On the wrong side, with the gathers facing you as you work, sew a ½-inch (1.3 cm) -wide seam along the gathered apron body/sash section.

4. Fold the sash portion in half along its length, right side out, over the portion just pinned, and pin into place, folding in a ½-inch (1.3 cm) seam allowance and concealing the gathered seam allowance of the apron body within the sash.

5. Continue to pin the folded sash all the way to its ends, again folding in a ½-inch (1.3 cm) seam allowance on each side. Press, making sure the sash fabric is aligned squarely upon itself.

6. Use the needle and thread to sew the seams closed, using a fine whipstitch along the edges of the sash and along the back joining of the sash to the apron body.

7. Press all seams and hems again.

Siberian Forest

THIS RARE BREED WAS BUILT to withstand cold weather. Like the Norwegian Forest and the Maine Coon, the Siberian Forest is large, deeply furred, and muscular.

Characteristics: The Siberian Forest is less cobby in build than its Western cousins, and has large, tufted ears. Like the Norwegian Forest, its fur is water-repellent, and it sheds its winter coat in spring. Most Siberian Forests have fur in the golden or brown family, darker at the tips than near the skin.

History: Although these cats were entered into British cat shows at the turn of the last century, like the Maine Coon they were too rustic to be deemed elegant by cat fanciers, and fell into disinterest as far as registration and competition were concerned. The first modern Siberian Forests to be registered in the West, Mussa and Tima, were brought to Berlin in 1987; their kittens were subsequently registered in various European countries.

Separately, in 1990, several U.S. breeders decided to import the breed from Siberia, to breed them within the United States.

Because this is such a rare breed in the Western Hemisphere, be sure to ask to see the cat's pedigree papers if you attempt to obtain one. The resemblance to other indigenous shaggy breeds is so acute that some cat associations balk at granting the Siberian Forest full championship status, for fear of counterfeits.

feline fun fact > Although the Siberian Forest looks wild and tough, it is temperamentally quite shy.

Siberian Forest

Strange Cravings: The Foods Our Felines Love

IT'S A GOOD THING YOUR CAT doesn't make the grocery list. If she could accompany you on shopping trips, she would paw the most unusual ingredients from shelves. Who knows why cats develop a taste for certain salad dressings or vegetables many humans don't like (beets)?

Has your cat ever enjoyed a plate of spaghetti— or any of these un-catlike foods?

- Soggy greens with cucumber and tomato, soaked in oil and vinegar dressing
- Watermelon
- Cantaloupe
- Pizza slices (and crust)
- Sunday breakfast: bacon, grits, pancakes with syrup
- Shredded wheat flakes
- Steamed broccoli
- Grapefruit
- Tomato sauce
- Coffee
- Raspberries
- Beets
- Edamame

The Attraction of Catnip

CATNIP (*Nepeta cataria*), sometimes also called catmint or catwort, is a member of the mint family. It is native to southwestern Asia, but has naturalized in temperate climates around the world. Why is it so irresistible to cats?

The leaves, stems, and seedpods of the catnip plant contain a chemical called nepetalactone. This chemical triggers a reaction that will vary from cat to cat. To some, it is stimulating, and they may jump around or play vigorously when they have it. To others, it is relaxing, and they may "space out" or roll around lazily on the ground. Still others have no reaction at all. Young kittens, those under the age of two to three months, usually don't react, nor does about a quarter of adult cats. The ability to detect nepetalactone is a genetically controlled trait, and some cats don't have the gene.

Catnip is not harmful or addictive to cats, but many experts recommend limiting use to once or twice a week. Cats that are continuously exposed to catnip may become desensitized to it. Also, catnip should not be given to cats that are behaving aggressively; it may increase their aggression. (See Day 74 for how to grow and dry your own catnip.)

> Like pheromones (see Day 88), nepetalactone is sensed by the vomeronasal organ, not the olfactory bulb, and thus is not really "smelled" in the way that humans smell things.

Star Quality

WHAT DEVOTEE OF THE FILM *Breakfast at Tiffany's* hasn't been struck by the strong presence of Holly Golightly's cat, named simply Cat? Cat was portrayed by one of Hollywood's most widely demanded professional feline actors, Orangey.

Orangey, a male marmalade tabby trained by animal wrangler/owner Frank Inn for the 1961 role, already had ten years' experience under his collar by the time Truman Capote's quirky novel came to the screen. Orangey was the first cat to play the title role in any movie, the 1951 *Rhubarb* (his film debut), which concerns a cat who is bequeathed a baseball team by his eccentric owner. For his performances in *Rhubarb* and *Breakfast at Tiffany's*, Orangey became the first and only cat to ever win two Patsy Awards, Hollywood's animal equivalent of an Oscar. And remember the fugitive cat in the 1959 *Diary of Anne Frank*? Ach, ja, that was Orangey, too.

Trainer Inn received three Patsys of his own for putting Orangey through his paces in *Rhubarb*, *The Incredible Shrinking Man* (1957), and *Diary of Anne Frank*. Although Orangey was reportedly difficult to work with—in his book *Great Cats: The Who's Who of Famous Felines*, J. C. Suarès notes that one particular film take required that dogs be posted off camera at all the exits from the studio, to prevent Orangey from stalking off the set!—they clearly had a special chemistry as a working team.

Casting directors aren't that particular about the gender of household pets, so Orangey "cross-furred" as a kitty named Minerva, in the 1950s series *Our Miss Brooks*. Again, Inn was responsible for his "in."

Cat Rescue: Feline CPR

IF YOUR CAT STOPS BREATHING, you can attempt to jump-start his breathing with cardiopulmonary resuscitation (CPR). Although CPR does not restart a stopped heart, it can keep your cat alive until he receives proper veterinary care. First, look for signals that your cat is not breathing. It is dangerous to give CPR to a cat (or human) that is breathing normally or has a pulse. Place your hand on the left side of the chest and determine whether the heart is still beating. If your cat is choking on an object that is obstructing his airway, perform the Heimlich maneuver first (see Day 213).

CPR is similar for humans and animals. First, call your vet or an emergency animal hospital. Then, follow the ABCs of CPR: airway, breathing, and circulation.

Airway: Make sure your cat's throat and mouth are clear. Open your cat's mouth, but do not place your fingers inside, because an unresponsive cat may bite on instinct. If the airway is blocked, lay your cat on his side and gently tilt back his head to extend the neck and head. Pull the tongue out of your cat's mouth. Perform a "finger sweep" to clear away foreign materials or vomit. If you identify a foreign object, proceed with the Heimlich maneuver.

Breathing: If your cat is breathing, call your vet. If not, after ensuring that the airway is open, begin rescue breathing. (Always be on guard for biting, which is instinct even if a cat is unresponsive.)

1. Straighten the neck and head, but be careful not to overextend.

2. Place your hand around his nose and lips and hold the muzzle closed.

3. Place your mouth over the cat's closed muzzle (mouth and nose), forming a seal.

4. Give four or five quick breaths, exhaling forcefully.

5. Check for breathing by placing your ear to his muzzle and watching his chest for any rise-and-fall motion.

6. If breathing has not resumed, repeat the rescue breathing sequence. Give twenty to thirty breaths per minute.

7. Check for a heartbeat. If there is none, begin cardiac compressions while continuing rescue breathing. Alternate between breaths and compressions.

Find out whether your veterinary hospital offers transportation services. If not, assign a friend or family member as "driver" in case of emergency.

Circulation: Place your pet on his right side on a hard surface, such as the floor or ground, to perform cardiac compressions. This will provide the support your cat needs, and the compressions will be more effective. Kneel next to Kitty and place the palm or fingertips of one hand over the ribs where his raised elbow meets the left side of his chest. (This is different from human CPR, where the recipient is positioned face up.) Working at arm's length with your elbow's locked, compress the left side of Kitty's chest downward by about 1 inch (2.5 cm), twice per second. Check for a heartbeat; continue until you reach a veterinary hospital.

Place your mouth over the cat's muzzle. Give four or five breaths, exhaling forcefully.

If there is no breath, begin cardiac compressions while continuing rescue breathing.

Knit a Cat-Motif Hat

FOR BEGINNER KNITTERS, this cap knits up quickly in stockinette stitch, and is a companion piece to a cat-motif scarf (see Day 319). The cat design is worked right into the background in Fair Isle stitch.

This pattern depicts one cat, using the chart on page 253; alternatively, you might wish to work two facing cats (by flopping the chart for one of them) a few stitches apart. Or, if you prefer, use other cat charts in this book to make an all-around border of cat faces, paw prints, or seated cats, in a single color or in different colors, markings, and/or breeds.

You may wish to choose a background color that will also serve for the cat's eyes, such as yellow or gold for black cats, or blue for Siamese.

The hat is sized to fit the average head of an adult, with a gauge of 11 stitches per 2 inches (5.1 cm) in width.

MATERIALS

6-ounce (170.1 g) skein worsted-weight yarn in a solid color (A)

Small ball worsted-weight, angora, or mohair-blend yarn (B)

Small amount worsted-weight yarn, in suitable color for eyes (optional) (C)

Size 7 (4.5 mm) knitting needles

Yarn needle

Scissors

Ruler

Size F/5 (3.75 mm) or smaller crochet hook

Cast on 121 stitches, using yarn A and the size 7 (4.5 mm) needles.

Cuffed edge:
Work in k1, p1 ribbing for 2 inches (5 cm).

Hat body:
1. Row 1: Still using yarn A, knit (right side).

2. Row 2: Purl (wrong side).

3. Continue to knit the odd rows and purl the even ones. This is stockinette stitch. Use only yarn A until the piece measures 3 inches (7.5 cm) long (including ribbing), ending with a purl row, which forms the first row of the charted pattern.

4. K49, then begin the second row of the 23-square-wide cat pattern with yarn B, still in stockinette stitch, starting from the lower right-hand side. Carry the unused yarn on the wrong side, looped around the working yarn every two or three stitches. Finish the row with K49 in yarn A.

5. Continue in stockinette stitch, following the chart. Switch to yarn C for the eyes, if your background color A is unsuitable for cat eyes.

6. When the cat pattern is done, continue in stockinette stitch, using yarn A only, until the piece measures 8 ½ inches (21.6 cm) from where you cast on, ending with a purl row.

Decreasing:
1. Dec Row 1: K2tog across.

2. Dec Row 2: Purl across.

3. Repeat Dec Rows 1 and 2 until only 8 stitches remain on the needle. P2tog across (4 stitches), k2tog across (2 stitches), then cast off the remaining 2 stitches in purl. Weave in all loose ends with a yarn needle.

Finishing:

1. Cut the yarn 12 inches (30.5 cm) from the hat and, using the yarn needle, sew the hat together along the wrong side until you reach the cuff.

2. Turn the hat right side out and sew the cuff portion along the right side, so that when the cuff is folded, you won't see the seam.

3. Use the crochet hook to weave any loose ends of yarn into the wrong side of the hat.

See Day 319 for a colorpointed variation of the chart.

 Yarn A ■ Yarn B

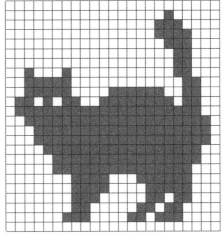

Chart for knitted hat and matching scarf.

Singapura

ALTHOUGH SOME CONTEND that the breed really comes from Houston, Texas, the Singapura is believed to have originated in Singapore as a feral street cat.

Characteristics: The Singapura has a distinctive coloring to its very short fur: The ground color is ivory, but the cat's flanks, back, and head have deep brown (sepia) ticking, with the deepest sepia on the tail. The eyes are large and either gold, green, or hazel.

The cat's chunky build makes its joints seem to connect at almost right angles. The ears are large and the chin small; the bone structure and large eyes of this cat give it an exceedingly pretty face. As a breed, it is believed to be the most petite of domestic cats, with adults weighing as little as 4 pounds (1.8 kg).

It has a playful personality and a sweet voice. Because of its delicacy, it should be kept indoors.

History: A fairly new breed, all Singapuras in the United States stem from a single cat family reared by Americans Hal and Tommy Meadows.

The Singapura was granted championship status in the United States in 1988, and by the end of just their second competitive season had won twenty-two championship titles for their beauty.

Singapura

Story: My Little Naiads

ALTHOUGH MOST CATS dislike getting wet, no one ever told that to mine, who, with the exception of one, are downright water sprites.

They stand at my elbow while I wash dishes or rinse vegetables . . . leap into the tub to splash in whatever water remains from a shower . . . rush to play on newly washed floors. More than once, Sophie has skidded clear off a countertop that has just been sponged, after eagerly jumping onto it at full gallop, drawn by its appearance of dampness.

When she was a kitten, my all-black Maine Coon, Clara, would wash her toys in the girls' communal bowl—sometimes forgetting them there, to the others' dismay. Batting a toy mouse around was one thing, but coming across one drowned in their dish was a definite turnoff!

Clara was also responsible for the worst water-related escapade. Never having accepted the adage "Look before you leap," she threw herself into a basin of clothing soaking in bleach. I immediately held her underneath cold running water (which, typically, she loved), before hurriedly calling Poison Control. The man who answered told me to keep washing her, so that's what I did—all afternoon. Every time she began to dry off, I held her under the tap once again. For me,

that was an important lesson to never allow her access to the bathroom while laundering clothing. But to Clara, being repeatedly doused for hours must have been one of the happiest experiences of her life. (And no, she didn't turn white from the bleach!)

It was Clara, again, who launched a summertime treat for all during a heat wave. She is very sensitive to heat, between her black coat and its length, and began panting from the high temperature in my apartment. My solution: to wet her down with cold water. She cheerfully ran about the house dripping wet, the need to pant instantly resolved. But my other cats were hot, too. So I introduced the idea to them, and they, too, appreciated the cold bath. All except Baby, who considered water fit for drinking only.

That is, until one really hot summer. I wetted down Clara, then the others. Baby sat off to the side, and—truly, this was her expression—crooked an eyebrow at me. "Do you want to try it?" I asked her. She visibly braced herself, expecting the worst. And then a new expression entered her face as the coolness of the water took positive effect: "Ooh! I like that!" So now, when the other girls are "watered," Baby is, too . . . provided I do all of them first, so she can see they survived it!

Territorialism

YOUR CAT JUST CHASED THE new kitten from a chair, though he doesn't even wish to sit there himself; or he goes ballistic at the sight of a neighbor's cat through the window. He sprays a foul scent around the house or, when you have moved to a new place, turns into a fraidy cat for the next month. What's going on? In a word, territorialism.

Cats are instinctively territorial. They like having intimate familiarity with their usual surroundings, resent intrusion and changes, and mark various areas as their turf. In fact, every time your cat brushes your leg, he is leaving behind not just some fur but a special excretion of his oil glands, marking you as his special property.

Studies show that a cat's sense of territory breaks into two parts: his home and usual visiting ground if permitted outside, and a more extensive distance used exclusively for hunting. Male cats, born hunters, may regularly cover as much as ten times more ground outdoors than do females. Because of their innate territoriality, "lost" cats, such as those accidentally shut out of their home, may often be found within just a few miles from home.

Outside, male cats will spray pungently scented urine and rub the scent glands of their head and tail against plants and other materials to stake their claim. They will take on any rival cats who enter or approach their turf.

If numerous cats live in the same area, they will divvy up the property along invisible borders and sometimes even times of day, and kowtow to whichever cats have aggressively declared themselves to be top (alpha) cat as well as to the cat equivalent of his aides or deputies.

Indoor cats still retain the instinct for territoriality, which can result in your cat's marking areas of the house as his (particularly a problem with intact male cats). He may regularly patrol the house to detect any changes and reclaim "his" property with his oils. Anything new or shifted will be investigated, and anything unsettling may result in even the toughest tom's disappearing under the bed.

Your cat probably has favorite places, often governed by time of day, as he follows the sun or other subtle factors around his home turf. He prefers privacy while eating or using his litter box, and may resent any other animal's sitting on a piece of furniture he considers his exclusively. He also learns your routines as they relate to him and expects you to keep to them, disliking, for example, erratic feeding times. A cat unaccustomed to your presence during the day may even seem resentful of your company if you take time off from work to stay home!

The Cat in Asian Art

THE LITHE AND COLORFUL CAT was an attractive subject for Asian artists dating back centuries. It is believed that cats lived in China as long as four millennia ago, and they began to feature cats in Chinese art in the year 1000 (during the Sung Dynasty), just about the time the cat first came to Japan from India. Silk paintings often depicted cats as household pets, in the company of children. The early scenes are outdoors, with lavishly illustrated flora and rock formations, and other animals such as dogs. The Metropolitan Museum owns numerous examples of this technique, such as the scroll *Spring Play in a T'ang Garden*, which depicts a variety of colored and patterned cats in typical feline poses amid greenery.

Japanese art developed with a different tone. Cats were depicted in paintings with beautifully garbed women, almost a part of the scenery. But during the 1700s and 1800s, Japanese artists began to appreciate cats, positioning them as a centerpiece in their works. A famous triptych by Kuniyoshi (1798–1861), called *Cats for the Fifty-Three Stations of the Tokkaido Road*, from 1848, shows a variety of Japanese Bobtails (see Day 180) engaged in every imaginable feline activity, including with kittens and mice.

Another Japanese artist of that period, the aptly named Katsushika Hokusai (1760–1849), perhaps most famous for *The Great Wave*, painted many images of cats. Unlike Kuniyoshi, he secretly studied Western art, which is evident in his works. Perhaps most famous, and current, is *Cat and Butterfly*, which has evolved into a sort of logo found on T-shirts, posters, and more.

Other eighteenth- and nineteenth-century Japanese masters who did justice to our feline friend include:

Suzuki Harunobu (1724–1770), *Girl and Cat*

Torii Kiyomitsu (1735–1785), *Woman, Man, and Cat*

Isoda Koryusai (1735–1790), *Cat and Goldfish*, from his series Kingyo Zukushi

Ando Hiroshige Utagawa (1797–1858), *Cat in a Window* from the series *One Hundred Views of Edo*

Toko (1868–1911), *Cat and Spider*

Toraji Ishikawa (1875–1964), *Leisure Hours*, showing a nude reading with a sleeping cat

Treating Cat Bites

A CAT THAT GETS TOO FRISKY during play or is annoyed—at you, or life in general—may bite you by accident or as a signal to "back off." Most of the time, these bites are little nips and do not puncture the skin. Providing a variety of stimulating toys to prevent boredom and restlessness can help. But even with a well-stocked toy basket, cats can and will bite, so prepare to treat the wound properly to stave off infection.

Clean and sterilize the wound with soap and water, rubbing alcohol, or hydrogen peroxide.

Add pressure to the wound to stop bleeding.

Dress the wound with a clean bandage.

Identify infection as redness or swelling, red streaking, warmth in the wound area, or fever.

Get a tetanus shot if more than five years have passed since your last shot.

CAT BITE RISKS

If your cat has not completed his series of rabies vaccinations, you are at risk. Make sure your cat's vaccinations are up-to-date (see Day 17), and seek a medical professional's opinion if you suspect your cat's vaccinations are not current.

Another risk of a cat bite is cat scratch disease, which is an infection caused by the bacteria in a cat's scratch or bite. Cats contract the bacteria from fleas and pass it to people through saliva. You can get cat scratch disease if a feline licks your open wound. The cat is a carrier—the disease is harmless to him. But you may experience swelling in the lymph nodes, sore throat, fever, headache, loss of appetite, or fatigue. See a doctor if you suspect that you've been infected. The disease will subside on its own, but a doctor may prescribe antibiotics to treat severe cases.

Cat-Faced Brownies

You'll need an 8-inch (20.3 cm) square straight-sided baking pan. Before you mix ingredients, measure the pan's base carefully and divide by three, to learn the exact dimension of each (nine) brownie square.

Make the cat-face pattern. Cut a square of thin cardboard to the exact dimensions of one brownie square. Fold it in half, and then open it with the crease vertical. Sketch onto the entire square, using a pencil: (a) a curved-bottomed wedge at the center top to become the cat's forehead and ear area and (b) a slightly curved triangle at each lower corner to give the cat a wedge-shaped face with a square chin. Fold the card in half down the middle and cut through both layers, so the two sides will match exactly. This is your pattern for each brownie.

If you are not fond of mint, use another flavor extract, such as orange or vanilla.

INGREDIENTS
Brownies
5 ⅓ tablespoons (⅓ cup [75 g]) butter, at room temperature

2 (1-ounce [28 g]) squares unsweetened baking chocolate

⅓ cup (66 g) granulated sugar

2 large eggs

1 teaspoon (5 ml) vanilla extract

½ cup (63 g) flour

½ teaspoon (3 g) salt

½ teaspoon (2.3 g) baking powder

½ cup (60 g) chopped walnuts or (75 g) raisins

Mint Frosting
1 cup (120 g) confectioners' sugar

2 tablespoons (28 g) very soft butter

1 tablespoon (15 ml) milk

½ teaspoon (2.5 ml) peppermint extract

All-natural food coloring of choice, if you wish to make the faces colors other than white

18 large golden raisins or similarly sized bits of dried apricots, papaya, or mango

9 dark raisins or dried cranberries

1. To make the brownies: Preheat the oven to 350°F (180°C, or gas mark 4) and grease an 8-inch (20.3 cm) square pan.

2. In a medium-size saucepan over low heat, melt the butter and chocolate. Turn off the heat and beat in granulated sugar, eggs, and vanilla.

3. Stir the flour, salt, and baking powder together in a small bowl, then add the mixture to the pot and stir until fully incorporated. Stir in the nuts.

4. Bake for about 25 minutes, until the edges of the cake begin to pull away from the sides of the pan and the center tests cleanly with a toothpick. Cool in the pan on a rack.

5. To make the frosting: Stir together all the ingredients, coloring it or leaving it white (divide among small bowls if you wish to color the cats' faces in different colors).

6. Slice the cooled brownie slab into nine square brownies. Working one at a time, place the face pattern on top, pencil side up, and use a sharp knife—hold it vertically and work slowly—to trim away the excess from the cheeks and between the ears.

7. When all the cats are trimmed into faces, frost their faces and add the fruit eyes and noses.

Snowshoe

THE SNOWSHOE, WITH ITS trademark white feet, is also known as Silver Laces, for its extended white stockings up the rear legs.

Characteristics: The standard eye color is bright blue, a holdover from its Siamese ancestry. Although other colors exist, only blue point and seal point are accepted for competitions at this time.

Another inherited trait from its Siamese past is a tendency toward vocalization. This breed is a bit emotionally needy, and should have a companion cat if you cannot devote enough attention to it.

History: Only about forty years old, this pretty breed developed in the United States from the crossing of Siamese with bicolor American Shorthairs, focusing on developing colorpoints everywhere but on the feet (the legs do have darker mottlings).

The result is sort of a shorthaired Birman (see Day 75). The Snowshoe was registered in the U.S.-based Cat Fanciers' Association in 1974, but other groups and countries have yet to adopt it as a separate breed.

Snowshoe

Journal Prompts, Part III

FILL UP THE JOURNAL YOU CREATED on Day 25 with more memories. Here are some writing prompts to stoke your creativity:

- Does your cat have any unusual habits?
- Where are Kitty's favorite places to take a nap—or hide?
- What scares your cat? How do you know he is scared?

- Describe a holiday memory with your cat.
- What are your favorite books, movies, poems, and plays that feature cats? Do you have a favorite famous cat character?
- How does your cat interact with other animals, such as the family dog? Share an anecdote.

Preparing a Safe Room

SETTING UP A SAFE ROOM IS ESSENTIAL when you are introducing a new cat to your home. A safe room gives your new cat a place to feel secure while he is getting used to his new home and family.

Choose a room that can be closed off from the rest of the house. This room should not be empty, but contain some furniture so your new cat has his pick of places to hide. If the room is bare, he will feel exposed and unsafe. If a room with furniture is not an option, set up a few cardboard boxes on their sides to create hiding spaces. Take a look around and make sure it is cat-proofed (see Day 85).

Set up a litter box in one corner of the room and food and water dishes in the opposite corner. Cats do not like to eat in the same area where they eliminate. Later, once the cat is used to his new home, you can gradually move his litter box and dishes to their permanent places.

Prepare a bed with a basket or box lined with several old, worn but unwashed T-shirts or sweatshirts of yours, so he can get used to your scent. He may not sleep there, but at least there will be something in the room that smells of you.

Leave space in the room for the carrier your cat will use to come home with you. This will give him a place to retreat that is already some-what familiar.

Illustrating a Devotion to Cats

WE CAN CREDIT THE FIRST organized cat show, the founding of the UK's first National Cat Club, and a collection of some of the most well-known cat illustrations to two devoted Englishmen, Harrison Weir and Louis Wain.

Sussex-born Harrison Weir (1824–1906) was apprenticed to an engraver at the age of thirteen and forged a respectable career as an illustrator of natural histories. In addition to his beautiful illustrations of such animals as dogs and poultry, he made a detailed study of cats. Weir was a champion of the domestic cat and wanted the cats to be champions, too. In 1871, he introduced the world's first organized cat show (see Day 12) at London's Crystal Palace, for which he designed his own poster. His goal was as follows:

> It would be well to hold Cat Shows so that the different breeds, colours, markings and so on, might be more carefully attended to and the domestic cat, sitting in front of the fire, would then possess a beauty and an attractiveness to its owner unobserved and unknown because uncultivated heretofore.

In 1889, Weir wrote a now-classic manual called *Our Cats and All About Them: Their Varieties, Habits and Management; and for Show, the Standard of Excellence and Beauty*, to help other cat fanciers set up their own shows. This was the very first book about pedigreed cats, illustrated by Weir.

Weir founded the UK's National Cat Club and served as its president. He was referred to as "the father of the cat fancy."

London-born Louis Wain (1860–1939) was always eccentric. He taught briefly at West London School of Art, but then his love of cats—he enjoyed sketching his cat Peter and teaching him tricks—became profitable, beginning with his 1886 illustration of a feline Christmas party in the *Illustrated London News*. The same year, he was hired to illustrate a children's book called *Madame Tabby's Establishment*. In 1890, he became president of the National Cat Club when Harrison Weir retired from the post, and he began to produce the kind of comical cat illustrations that would rocket him to fame as the artist of an imaginary world dubbed "Catland," in which wide-eyed cats, either in the altogether or sporting various clothing and accessories, indulged with curious intensity in a variety of human pursuits.

Two years later, the first Catland book appeared, titled *Pa Cats, Ma Cats, and Their Kittens*. Wain illustrated about one hundred books in all, plus periodicals and picture post-cards, which helped circulate his work to millions of homes. Wain also produced his own periodical, *Louis Wain Annual*, rife with distinctive pictures of mischievous cats. Until the time of World War I, Wain rode on a wave of almost fanatical interest in his illustrations.

Wain's whimsical Catland creatures live on, still prolifically available in replica as greeting cards and postcards and in books.

Ticks

TICKS ARE SMALL PARASITIC ARACHNIDS that feed on animal and human blood. There are several types of ticks, including the deer tick and the dermacentor tick, which live in different areas around the world. Ticks carry a number of diseases, including Lyme disease and Rocky Mountain spotted fever, which are potentially disabling or even fatal. As with fleas, prevention is the best cure, so work with your vet to develop a plan to repel these insects before they have a chance to bite.

If you find a tick on your cat, you need to remove it right away. Follow these steps:

1. Enlist another person to hold your cat still.

2. Light a match, blow it out, and apply the match heat to the tick. The tick will release its head so you can quickly pull it out with tweezers, head and all. If you only remove the body and not the head, your cat may get an infection.

3. Deposit the tick in a small dish and burn it with a smoldering match until you are sure it is dead. Ticks are extremely difficult to kill. If you are uncertain as to whether you removed the entire tick, see your vet.

4. If your cat is bitten by a tick, she may start to lick herself, which can lead to painful hot spots that burn and hurt her. You can apply tea tree oil to a hot spot to help it heal or use an over-the-counter product. If the spot isn't healing, see your vet to prevent its turning into other skin conditions.

Cat on a Mat

ANY FRAMED IMAGE CAN CELEBRATE the cat, when placed against a mat or background of cat- or paw-print fabric or paper.

Choose a frame one standard size up or larger than the image. Open the frame to remove the backing, and cut a piece of fabric or paper (such as gift wrap) to the size of the backing. Position your picture on the fabric/paper, centered or very slightly above true center (what artists call *optical center*), and reassemble the frame. Your picture will appear to be matted. This is a great solution for "matting" a picture whose image you don't want to cover with the edges of a mat.

Or you can cut a true mat, again by selecting a larger frame and first cutting your fabric or paper to the size of the backing. Position your picture on the wrong side of the fabric/paper, and lightly trace around it. Then remove your picture and, marking lightly again, increase the margins of the mat to overlap the picture area slightly, say, ¼ inch (6 mm) from each true edge of the art. Or you might wish to create an oval or other shape. When you are satisfied with the shape, remove the art, then use a sharp craft knife to cut out the center of the mat. Place your picture on the backing and put the mat, right side out, over it, then reassemble the frame. (You may need to use tiny bits of tape or a dab of craft glue to keep your picture from shifting.)

Depending on the depth of the frame, there may be space for you to add other embellishments, such as ribbons or lace, appliqués, stickers, or even buttons or collar tags beneath the glass of the frame.

Somali

THE SOMALI IS A LONGHAIRED ABYSSINIAN, resulting from matings that brought together recessive longhair genes natural to Abys (conversely, Somali matings may produce shorthaired Abys).

Characteristics: Although it is hard to tell under that shaggy coat, the Somali has a foreign body type with long legs. The lavishly ticked fur has as many as three colored bands, producing a beautifully shaded coat that is darkest along the top of the head, spine, tail, and upper limbs. The tail is deeply plumed and the ears have horizontal tufts of fur. The usual color range for a Somali is blue, silver, red (also known as sorrel), ruddy (or simply Somali), or fawn, with gold, hazel, or green eyes. Above each eye is a vertical dark stripe toward the bridge of the nose. Kittens are born dark and lighten with time.

Like Abys, the Somali may carry genes for PK deficiency, which causes anemia.

Although sometimes initially standoffish with humans, this cat is playful and tends to want to go outside. Like the Maine Coon, it tends to chirrup rather than meow.

History: The Somali was first shown in competition in Australia, in 1965, followed by Canada; U.S. cat associations began to recognize the breed in 1978, and European organizations followed.

feline fun fact > The breed name Somali wasn't assigned until 1969, when U.S. breeder Evelyn Mague selected it as being a country adjacent to ancient Abyssinia.

Somali

Story: Sophie, the World's Fastest "Slow" Cat

WHEN SOPHIE WAS A KITTEN—clearly the runt of her litter—I thought that she had trouble with her eyesight. She would hurl herself into the oddest places, jump 7 feet (21.1 m) in one bound, and stuff her head into openings just the right size to get stuck. But one day, I watched as she stalked a small insect and realized she could see very well. She just didn't *think* about where she was going!

I began to notice other things—her slow development of speech, her teething on remarkable objects even for a cat (such as her consuming nearly an entire bamboo chopstick), plus a tendency to "lose" me if I was even just in the next room (when she did begin to vocalize, forgetting where I was would launch her into blood-curdling shrieks). And even her body was a bit odd, very angular, flexible, and seemingly double-jointed. Sometimes she had the attention of a flea: It became a party trick for me to reverse her a full 180 degrees as she walked by—and she would head back where she'd come from, without noticing anything had changed!

Based on these observations, I concluded that she was congenitally mildly challenged. And *challenged* is certainly the word for it. Sophie is nearly fearless—fear requires not just awareness of the immediate, but also the ability to think ahead.

She races over trustingly to strangers, such as cuddling up to workmen as they try to do repairs, and happily gallops full tilt into mirrors and windows. And let's not forget the stove incident, when only the scent of singed fur alerted me to her decision to curl up serenely next to a lit burner.

Despite her bringing obliviousness to a high art, she has an extraordinary skill for opening things; she can use her front paws with the articulation of human fingers. It's like living with a monkey! Between one thing and another, all manner of extra cat-proofing has been done throughout the house, to protect her as well as my belongings.

Yet Sophie is a darling to live with. Taking life "slow" seems to have its benefits. At seventeen, she still looks and acts like a perpetual kitten—lack of anxiety has seemingly kept her young. She still leaps six feet (1.8 m) at a bound, tears around the house at breakneck speed, and prises open cabinets with the skill of a safecracker. Every day continues to hold exciting new places to try to stuff herself into. She has no idea that, in human terms, she is about eighty years old!

Introducing Kitty to Her New Siblings

IF YOU ALREADY OWN A CAT (or several) and plan to introduce a new feline family member to the bunch, take steps to integrate the new cat and assure the veterans that they are equally important. Cats are territorial and sometimes feel threatened by an unfamiliar animal in their space. The good news is that most cats are able to move past their initial distrust and at least tolerate, if not adore, other cats in the home.

Before bringing the new cat home, make sure she has been to the vet and has a clean bill of health. Prepare a safe room for her (see Day 302). Then, begin a gradual and controlled introduction. Let the new cat get used to her safe room and you. Your other pets may be curious about what is going on behind that safe room door, but don't let them meet the new girl just yet.

Once the new cat is comfortable with the safe room and with you, you can start introducing the pets to each other's scents. Rub a scrap of cloth or T-shirt on the new cat's fur, especially around the scent glands by her face. Do the same with a separate cloth for each of your other pets. Place your new cat's cloth in the established pet's space, and the established pet's cloth in the new cat's safe room. When they show interest in the new scent, give them affection or a treat. Repeat this for several days.

After they are used to each other's scents, introduce them face-to-face. Leave the door to the safe room open halfway, and let the animals find each other. Keep a close eye on them. Hissing and posturing are natural reactions, but separate them if it gets physical. Keep the new cat's safe room set up so they can sleep in separate quarters. The personalities involved will determine how long they will take to tolerate each other; sometimes, the process can take weeks, but your patience will pay off in the end.

You may have visions of your two cats cuddling together, but some cats will just never get along well with other cats. If your cats don't like each other much, be sure to maintain separate litter boxes and place food and water bowls in different locations. Each cat will likely stake out his or her own territory, and as long as they each have a space to call their own, you should have a mostly peaceful household.

Cats in Dance

THROUGHOUT HISTORY, dancers have been inspired by the cat's fluid, agile, and sometimes unexpected moves. In fact, a ballet step called *pas de chat* mimics the pounce of a cat.

For instance, wearing a fantastical mask that initially she refused to don, Margot Fonteyn starred as the cat-woman Agathe in Roland Petit's 1948 *Les Demoiselles de la Nuit*, in which Petit danced the role of a musician who falls in love with her, with fatal results. The story was by playwright Anouilh, and the music by Jean Français.

Other works that gave humans "cat moves" include:

- *The Sleeping Beauty* (1890), choreographed by Marius Petipa to a score by Tchaikovsky, which contains a variation for *Puss in Boots and the White Cat* (see Day 331), whose cat-like music is enhanced by the dancers' feline movements

- *Krazy Kat: A Jazz Pantomime*, choreographed by Adolph Bohm to a score by John Alden Carpenter (1922)

- *La Chatte*, choreographed by George Balanchine to music by Henri Sauguet, based on Aesop's fable "The Cat and Aphrodite" (1927)

- *Le Chat Botté (Puss in Boots)*, choreographed in 1986 by Roland Petit to music by Tchaikovsky

feline fun fact > While married to choreographer George Balanchine, ballerina Tanaquil Le Clercq wrote *Mourka: The Autobiography of a Cat* (1964), now something of a cult classic for its beautiful photo illustrations by dance photographer Martha Swope.

When Your Male Cat Can't or Won't Go

IF YOU DETECT NICKEL-SIZE urine spots in your male cat's litter box, or notice that he is straining during urination, the cause may be urethral obstruction. This condition occurs when your cat's urethra becomes partly or totally blocked. Total obstruction is a medical emergency; you should visit your vet immediately.

Neutered and male cats are at a higher risk for obstruction simply because of anatomy. A male's urethra is longer and narrower, and therefore more prone to plugging up with minerals, cells, and mucuslike protein. Factors that can produce uroliths and urethral plugs (the causes of the blockage) include bacteria, viruses, a diet high in magnesium, decreased water consumption, physical inactivity, urine retention, stress, and urine pH.

Here are some everyday scenarios that may trigger acidic urine, which can trigger mineral growth and cause urethral obstruction:

- Acidic urine can form mineral deposits, and cats that eat several small meals per day are more likely to produce acidic urine than cats that eat a couple of larger meals.

- If your cat is avoiding a dirty litter box or has difficulty using the litter box because of its height or design, he may hold urine in his bladder. This causes urine pH to become more acidic, and more likely to form a mineral deposit that can block the urethra.

Depending on the severity of the blockage, your vet may recommend catheterization to relieve the blockage, which generally requires sedation or anesthesia. Intravenous fluid therapy will restore electrolyte balance and rehydrate the cat. Also, antimicrobial medications will combat bacteria; drugs that restore bladder function are also helpful in some cases. If your cat experiences several blockage episodes, your vet may suggest surgery called perineal urethrostomy. This is a last resort because of its potential to cause bladder disease and its post-surgery side effects (incontinence, bleeding).

At home, take these steps to stabilize your cat's urine pH:

- Talk to your veterinarian about the food your cat eats, and discuss whether urinary acidifiers are necessary. If your cat eats commercial food, its contents likely provide necessary nutrients to balance urine. Acidic urine is a pH of 6.4 or less.

- Provide clean, fresh water at all times.

- Clean your cat's litter box daily.

A Salad Bar for Cats

MEAT IS THE CORNERSTONE of a cat's diet, but many occasionally enjoy a little bit of greens, too. Greens add fiber to her diet, which aids in digestion. A cat grass garden is a simple way to provide your cat with a salad bar she can nibble at when the mood strikes her.

MATERIALS

Wheatgrass, rye, barley, and/or oat seeds (often available at pet stores as "cat grass" mixture), approximately 1 tablespoon (6 g) for a 6-inch (15.2 cm) container

Small container for soaking seed

Heavy, shallow planter with drainage holes and a saucer to catch any water overflow

Small piece of screening

Growing medium or peat moss

1. Soak the seeds for 6 to 8 hours in a container in 1 to 2 inches (2.5 to 5.1 cm) of water.

2. Place the planter in the saucer. Cut the piece of screening to fit the bottom of the planter and place it there (this will prevent the growing medium from leaking out through the drainage holes). Fill the planter with the growing medium up to ¾ inch (1.9 cm) from the top.

3. Add water to the growing medium until it is uniformly damp.

4. Drain the seeds and sprinkle them evenly over the surface of the growing medium. Sprinkle ⅛ to ¼ inch (3 to 6 mm) of additional growing medium over the seeds. Water lightly and place in indirect sunlight where it won't be disturbed by curious cats.

5. Keep the growing medium moist (not wet), and the seeds should sprout in about a week. When the grass reaches 4 inches (10.2 cm) high, put it in a sunny spot where your cat can graze on it at will. Keep it watered, but avoid overwatering. After a few weeks, the grasses will usually start to die off; at that point, it's time to clean out the container and start again.

If your cat really enjoys her greens and seems lost without them while you're replenishing the planter, consider starting an additional planter as soon as you set this one out. Just about the time the current planter is depleted and starts to fade, the new one will be ready to go.

Sphynx

THEY'RE CALLED HAIRLESS CATS and they're notoriously naked, or at least not as equipped in the fur department as other breeds. However, run your palm across the back of a Sphynx and you will feel the barest layer of fuzz, much like the downy hair on your arms.

Characteristics: The Sphynx has a suedelike feel, and sometimes has neither eyelashes nor even whiskers. There may be a tiny tuft of hair at the end of the tail. The ears, muzzle, and feet feel furrier than the rest of the body, relatively speaking. Their ears seem enormous, their face is a long triangle, and their torso is surprisingly rounded and sturdy compared with the scrawny appearance of their long legs.

The Sphynx comes in many colors, and they are often bicolor. The color can often be seen as well in the skin directly beneath the fuzz. Because this cat can sweat all over its body, not just on its paws, it needs to be wiped down periodically to keep its skin from looking oily.

The Sphynx has a surprisingly large appetite, because it burns more energy to keep warm. Obviously, unless you live in a very warm climate, it is unwise to let your Sphynx outside.

History: The modern Sphynx is a spontaneous mutation that occurred in Ontario, Canada, in 1966, born to black and white shorthaired house cat whose secret rendezvous with an unknown sire adds a bit of extra mystery to the furlessness. But Aztec art shows that a similar breed once existed in Mexico, which in the winter grew only the barest covering of fur along its body and tail. A breed dubbed the New Mexican Hairless appeared briefly in cat shows around 1900.

It is possible that the genetics for this migrated northward to Ontario (even though it would make more sense for the cat to prefer to head south!).

To date, only one North American or British organization has recognized the Sphynx, although it does appear at cat shows as a novelty. Current American Sphynxes may be related to the results of French experimentation with black or brown and white varieties of this cat in the early 1980s.

feline fun fact > Many Sphynxes share the habit of sitting erect on their haunches with one forepaw raised.

Sphynx

Cat Commands: Body Parts

HERE IS A REALLY FUN LESSON for you and your cat—even better if you have several pets that you can seat together while you lead a language class.

Throughout the lesson, you will use your chosen name for yourself, such as Mama, and your cat's name, such as Mao, paired with a noun.

1. Begin with your respective face and neck area. Touch your own chin and say, "Mama chin." Touch your cat's chin and say, "Mao chin." Repeat several times.

2. Working one at a time, do the same with the words *ear* (touch each separately), *nose, neck, head*, and *mouth*. Stick out your tongue and point to it: "Mama tongue." Make a licking motion with your tongue and say, "Mama lick." Each time you introduce a term, repeat it several times before moving on to another term.

3. Once your cat has heard the basic terms, repeat them out of order, always pointing to and touching the relevant place.

4. Do the "scratch" motion and then proceed to give a little scratch to each relevant place, as you say, "Scratch Mama nose," "Scratch Mao chin," and so on, covering each body part.

5. Give the lesson a rest, but then return to it periodically. If your cat is paying attention, he will begin to respond physically, such as by raising his chin or head to be scratched before you actually touch him, when you announce the intended action.

6. Add additional terms in time, such as *fingers/ toes, hand, foot, tail*, and *tummy*, always touching the relevant area on your and your pet's body as you introduce the word.

Be creative, pairing the parts of your cat's body with known commands (e.g., "No hand!" if Mao reaches for something you are eating) as well as with new words that will gain meaning. For example, teach the term *happy* like this: If Mao seems to be enjoying listening to music, observe, "Happy ears." When he is eating something he likes, say, "Happy tongue!"

If you are working with more than one pet at a time, do the above with everyone together, so they can see one another as you name their body parts. At some point they will realize that everyone has a face with named places.

Think Twice before Declawing

WHEN YOUR CAT FIRST DIGS her claws into your expensive sofa, it can be tempting to haul her off to the vet to have her declawed. Before you do that, you should understand what declawing is, what the possible consequences are, and what the alternatives are so you can make an informed decision.

It is a common belief that declawing removes only the claw, but in fact, the entire end section of the toe is removed. In humans, it would be the equivalent of having your fingers amputated to the first joint. The procedure is done under general anesthesia and requires several weeks of recovery time. Even with painkillers, the recovery period is uncomfortable for your cat.

While many cats are fine after the recovery period, potential side effects include infections, severe pain, loss of feeling, and balance problems.

Cats that are declawed—even if only their front claws are removed—are nearly defenseless and thus must kept indoors for their own safety. You will still need to provide a scratching box or post so they can groom their back claws.

Many veterinarians these days consider declawing to be a last resort. Before contemplating declawing, try training your cat to claw only on approved surfaces, such as a scratching box or post, using deterrents (see Day 64) on surfaces you don't want them to scratch, and keeping your cat's claws trimmed (see Day 323).

T.S. Eliot's Cats

ACCORDING TO T.S. ELIOT (1888–1965), cats have three names—an ordinary one, used by family members; a fancier, unique name, for society at large; and a secret name known only to itself, which the cat meditates upon. For his collection *Old Possum's Book of Practical Cats*, composed for his godchildren in 1939, Eliot came up with fantastical names for his feline characters, clearly with the second point in mind.

In "Growltiger's Last Stand," for instance, Eliot names characters Growltiger, Grumbuskin, Tumblebrutus, and Lady Griddlebone.
He wrote a slew of other inventive cat names into the book—if you're brainstorming creative cat names, you could certainly borrow from this interesting list: Jennyanydots, Rum Tum Tugger, the Jellicle Cats, Mungojerrie and Rumpelteaser, Old Deuteronomy, Mr. Mistoffelees, Macavity, Gus, Bustopher Jones, and Skimbleshanks.

Surely, Eliot never dreamed the book of verse would become a musical forty-two years later: *Cats*, composed by Andrew Lloyd Webber.

Eliot's book concludes with instructions on how to "address" a cat, noting the animals' difference from dogs and cautioning that one must call a cat by name only once one has earned its respect. Presumably, Eliot reached that comfortable level of trust with his own imaginatively named cat—Jellylorum. (See Days 34 and 35 for suggestions on how to name your own cat.)

Understanding General Anesthesia

WE HUMANS TEND TO THINK OF being rendered unconscious as being necessary only for major surgical procedures. But in the case of your cat, something as simple as a teeth cleaning may require a general anesthetic, to keep Kitty from moving.

The chemicals and how they are given vary. The vet may use an injection, a vapor administered via a tube or mask, or some combination of the two, such as a sedative first to keep your pet still long enough to fit a trachea tube correctly. All general anesthesia carries some risk, even in a healthy cat. Make sure your vet checks your cat's vital signs and reviews with you any potential hazards, which include your pet's being elderly, having a cardiac condition, or having reduced liver or kidney function that could make it harder for the drug(s) to pass out of Kitty's system in a timely manner. If you decide to go ahead, make sure that your vet is prepared to give your cat extra intravenous fluids so the drugs do not linger in her body any longer than necessary to do their job.

An area of her fur, often on a foreleg, will be clipped or shaved, for the clean insertion of injections or monitoring equipment. Once the medical procedure is finished, your pet will be taken to a confined area for observation while and after she wakes. Just as when a person comes to after a general anesthetic, different parts of your cat's body will resume their normal function at different speeds. Don't be in a hurry to take Kitty home, because she may initially be disoriented, incontinent, or otherwise unprepared for her usual surroundings.

Once she is home, keep her in a quiet, safe place until she is back to feeling like herself. She may simply wish to sleep or hide, or she may want to stay on your lap. Stay home with her to monitor how she is feeling and make sure she is not worrying the procedure site. Avoid feeding her a lot at first, because her digestive system may still be recovering, but make sure she has plenty of drinking water available to continue to flush the anesthetic(s) from her system.

Knit a Cat-Motif Scarf

THIS STOCKINETTE STITCH SCARF is a companion piece to the hat on Day 291. The cat is worked right into the background in Fair Isle stitch.

This pattern depicts one cat per scarf end, using the chart shown in Day 291. Alternatively, you might wish to use other cat charts in this book to make a border of cat faces, paw prints, or seated cats, in a single color or in different colors, markings, and/or breeds, or to walk paw prints up one side of the scarf and down the other.

Adjust the length of the pattern to your preference; a 45-inch (1.1 m) length is good for simple overlapping across your chest, or work it 60 inches (1.5 m) long to also wrap cozily around your neck.

You might wish to choose a background color that will also serve for the cat's eyes, such as yellow or gold for black cats, or blue for Siamese.

MATERIALS

2 (6-ounce [170 g]) skeins worsted-weight yarn in a solid color (A)

1 small ball worsted-weight, angora, or mohair-blend yarn (B)

Small amount worsted-weight yarn, in a suitable color for eyes (optional) (C)

Size 7 (4.5 mm) knitting needles

Scissors

Ruler

Yarn needle

Size F/5 (3.75 mm) crochet hook

Cast on 39 stitches, using yarn A and the size 7 (4.5 mm) needles.

Row 1: Knit (right side).

Row 2: Purl.

Continue in this pattern (stockinette stitch) for 2 inches (5 cm), ending with a purl row, which forms the first (background color) row at the bottom of the chart.

Begin the first cat:

Cat row 1: K1, p1, k6, then begin the second row of the 23-square-wide cat pattern with yarn B, still in stockinette stitch, starting from the lower right-hand side. Carry the unused yarn on the wrong side, looped around the working yarn every two or three stitches. Finish the row, working the last two stitches with p1, k1, using yarn A.

Cat rows 2–24: Continue in stockinette stitch, following the chart—always working the first two stitches k1, p1 and the last p1, k1 on the right side and p1, k1 and k1, p1 on the wrong side—until the cat is completed. Measure how long the scarf has become and make a note of it (let's call this "end length"). Continue with yarn A only until the scarf measures your desired scarf length minus the "end length."

Begin the second cat:

To knit a cat that will walk in the same direction as the first when the scarf is worn, turn the chart upside down so that the tail is on the left and, starting with a knit row, work the pattern in the chart again, beginning right to left. You will be working an upside down cat whose tail is on the left when you view the scarf from the right side.

To knit a cat that will face the first cat when the scarf is worn, turn the chart upside down so that the tail is on the left, but start the cat picture, beginning from right to left, with a purl row, so that you will be working an upside-down cat whose tail is on the right when you view the scarf from the right side.

When the cat motif is completed, work 2 inches (5.1 m) with yarn A alone, then cast off.

Weave in the loose ends with a yarn needle.

To make a fringe:
1. Cut 78 pieces of yarn A, each the width of the scarf.

2. Take one piece of fringe yarn, fold it in half, and, using the crochet hook, draw the doubled end through the first cast-on stitch until you have a ½-inch (1.3 cm) loop. Pass the two ends through the loop, even up their length with a gentle tug, and then pull them through firmly.

3. Continue across every cast-on stitch, always pulling the loop through from the same side of the scarf.

4. When the fringe is complete, do the same along the cast-off edge.

5. Trim each fringe by aligning it along a straight edge and then snipping off any uneven tips.

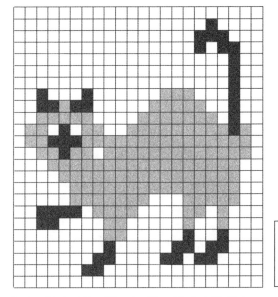

Yarn A
Yarn B
Yarn C

A colorpointed variation of the cat motif used for the knitted hat (Day 291) and scarf

Tonkinese

CROSS A SEAL-POINT SIAMESE with a sable Burmese, and you get a Tonkinese, originally referred to as a Golden Siamese.

Characteristics: The Tonkinese resembles early Siamese and Burmese cats with their muscular bodies. The hair is very short and colorpointed, with a range of colors, including several tones of "mink," a warm tan. Only five colors are permitted for showing in the United States. The colorpointing is softer than in the Siamese, and the body color is lighter.

A special trait that sets the Tonkinese apart from either Oriental ancestor: turquoise blue eyes, the result of mixing the Siamese's cooler blue with the Burmese's gold, an unusual instance of the eye colors actually merging in hue.

History: This is the first breed to be produced in Canada, courtesy of breeder Margaret Conroy, in the 1960s. Similarly crossed cats originating in New York a decade earlier were less well documented or perpetuated. Current pedigreed Tonkinese come from the Canadian strain. Tonkinese were registered in Canada in 1965; the United States followed suit seven years later.

feline fun fact > The Tonkinese is very mischievous and active, and is especially adept at breaking loose from confinement, be it from a carrier or a house. Be forewarned if you wish to keep one as an indoor-only cat!

Tonkinese

Story: Mischa, the Cat Who Loved Opera

ALTHOUGH THE OTHER CATS I have lived with could take or leave opera, Mischa was definitely a connoisseur!

He clearly recognized the voices of at least four singers I played often. It became something of a party gag for me to put on a recording of a tenor he didn't like, so my guests could see Mischa's tail shoot straight up in protest as he stalked out of the room. But one day I played his nemesis in a Donizetti opera—and Mischa seemed to think, "Hey, if he can sing *that*, he's okay." Afterward, he accepted this singer, even in recordings he'd previously spurned, and also became alert if other artists with a similar voice were played.

Luciano Pavarotti and Samuel Ramey were his heroes. Even if he was asleep, the sound of either gentleman would jolt Mischa awake, to run over to the stereo. A particular hit with him was a pirated cassette of Ramey in Boito's *Mefistofele*. The end of this opera is deeply thrilling as the demon is sent back to hell, which in the live recording was enhanced by the audience's own audible excitement. As it played, Mischa would be as rapt as they were, his jaw literally dropped, his eyes like saucers.

Which leads me to repertoire. He had specific tastes, thankfully parallel with much of my own: Rossini, Donizetti, and early Verdi, and, curiously, Rimsky-Korsakov and Prokofiev. (I had only to say, "Prokofiev!" and he'd wriggle on the floor as if inhaling catnip!)

His love for Prokofiev, in fact, led to my discovery of what became a personal favorite of mine: One day, when I hadn't been attending to what was on the radio, I noticed Mischa listening blissfully, head raised and eyes closed. What was playing? A quirky piece that I sat down to listen to also, quickly as enchanted as he—Prokofiev's Sonata for Flute and Piano. Excellent taste, that cat.

He also understood how my stereo worked, that speakers were only messengers and that LPs (in those dinosaur days) were the source of much of my music. One day when I played a parody of classical pieces, he recognized something was strange about the music and stood up on the turntable lid to peer through it, worried something was wrong with the record! However, his pièce de résistance was when he figured out which was the "off" button. While a record played, I exited the room, and then . . . silence. This happened several times until I tiptoed back in to find Mischa pressing the correct switch. He seemed to have done it as a practical joke and was content to stop once he had been found out.

Mischa's musical source switched to a celestial choir in 1990. Many operas later, there are still works, such as *Mefistofele*, that for me seem inextricably tied to him. But perhaps these days, he can happily tune into Pavarotti whenever he wishes, now that his idol has gone over as well.

Trimming Claws

IF THE THOUGHT OF GIVING KITTY a manicure makes you shudder, relax. The key is to start slowly and get Kitty used to having her paws handled before coming anywhere near her with the clippers. It's best to start trimming when she's a kitten, but adult cats can be trained to tolerate this kind of grooming, too.

Start the process when she is relaxed. Gently rub her paws and give her praise. If she starts to swipe or hiss at you, back off and try again in ten minutes. When she tolerates gentle rubbing (this may occur right away or take several weeks), move on to applying enough gentle pressure to the tops and bottoms of individual toes with your thumb and forefinger to make the claw come out. If she tolerates that, then try holding her in your arms, using the thumb and forefinger of your supporting arm to reveal her claws. At that stage, she's ready for the trimmers.

There are two main types of trimmers: guillotine and scissors. Which one you choose is a matter of personal preference.

You will also need styptic powder to stop the bleeding if you accidentally cut the claw's quick. Hold your cat against your body and use the thumb and forefinger of your supporting arm to reveal a claw. If your cat has light claws, you should be able to see the quick (the pink area), which is the living part of the nail. You want to be sure not to cut the quick, which will hurt your cat and elicit a yowl. If you do accidentally cut it, hang on to her and apply some styptic powder to stop any bleeding. If your cat has darker claws, it's a little tougher to know where the quick is, so cut only the sharp tips.

Many cats will not stay still to have their claws trimmed all at the same time. Hold her firmly and do as many as you can at a time. If she starts wriggling so much that it makes it difficult to cut, stop for the time being and try to get the rest another time. Your chances of hurting her when she's wriggling outweigh the benefits of trimming her claws.

Getting the Royal Treatment

Unlike many humans in the same position, he never wrote his memoirs of the White House and never discussed them for quotation, though he was privy to many official secrets.

—Obituary for Tom Cat, *Alexandria (Va.) Gazette*, August 22, 1962

NOT ONLY MAY A CAT LOOK AT A KING, but he may even sit on the king's lap! Presidents and emperors alike deal with the same cat issues (and experience the same cat joys) as the rest of us.

Here are some famous associations that felines have forged with religious leaders and heads of state:

- Popes Gregory the Great and Gregory III are said to have owned no worldly goods apart from a cat.

- The prophet Muhammad owned a cat named Muezza. Legend has it that when Muhammad needed to go to prayer but Muezza had fallen asleep on the sleeve of his prayer robe, the prophet cut off the sleeve rather than disturb the cat.

- French cardinal Richelieu left his last fourteen cats a pension but, after his death, the cats were rounded up and cooked into a stew by his opponents!

- Russia's empress Catherine the Great received a cat as a gift from her lover, Potemkin.

- In 1885, Britain's Queen Victoria commissioned painter Charles Burton Barber to do a group portrait of four animals, titled *Cat and Dogs Belonging to the Queen*. She owned two Persians, Flypie and White Heather. When the queen died in 1901, the Prince of Wales, Edward, and his wife, Alexandra, adopted the Persians.

- U.S. president Rutherford B. Hayes was the recipient of the first Siamese cat ever brought to the United States, a gift of the American consul in Bangkok, thus the cat's moniker, Siam; Hayes also lived with four American-born kittens during his administration.

- The polydactyl Slippers and a second cat, Tom Quartz, shared the White House with U.S. president Theodore Roosevelt. According to Fernand Méry, in *The Life, History, and Magic of the Cat*, Slippers's desire to roll on a carpet once caused a procession of international visitors to be rerouted, to avoid asking the cat to remove himself! Former Rough Rider Roosevelt also owned snakes, a lion, and a wildcat.

- U.S. president Calvin Coolidge, infamous for being a man of few words, evidently communicated well with cats, as he lived with Blackie, Smokey (a bobcat), Tiger, and Tommy, plus numerous dogs and other animals. Coolidge used to stroll around with Tiger draped across his shoulders.

- British prime minister Winston Churchill had a red tabby named Jock who slept with him. His black cat Nelson attended cabinet meetings. His other cats included Blackie, Bob (a bicolor), Tango (a.k.a. Mr. Cat, a red tabby), and Margate (black).

- When U.S. president Bill Clinton's infamous black-and-white cat, Socks, was introduced to the family's new Labrador retriever, he was not impressed . . . but Socks did befriend a stray cat while at the White House!

Healthy Giving

IF YOU DON'T HAVE THE TIME to volunteer at an animal shelter or be a foster caregiver for cats (see Days 83 and 84 and 167 and 168), there are other ways you can extend a hand to stroke the paws of many kitties—and cat lovers—who need help.

COMFY BEDDING

Shelters and animal clinics go through a lot of bedding for their temporary guests. Wash and donate "retired" towels, sheets, blankets, nonrubberized bath mats, or washable sweaters that could use a second home.

CAT FOOD

Every so often, there is a pet food drive by one organization or another—but this is a year-round need, both at animal shelters and at people shelters where cats are allowed to accompany their humans, especially in an emergency situation such as a storm or flood when many pets may be displaced. Your contributions of fresh wet or dry food could literally be a lifesaver.

THERAPY CATS

Do you have a super-affectionate, placid cat who enjoys meeting people? Contact pet therapy programs at your local hospital, rehabilitation center, nursing home, assisted-living residence, or hospice and ask how your cat might qualify. Qualification for such programs usually involves making sure all your cat's vaccines are up-to-date, as well as an interview with your pet to determine whether he can truly deal calmly with new faces and new surroundings.

BECOME A BUDDY

Do you have an elderly or a disabled neighbor with a cat? Is a friend or relative ill or otherwise unable to get out, such as during periods of inclement weather? Ask whether he or she needs help with shopping for pet supplies such as heavy bags of food or litter, taking the cat to the vet for checkups or other health care, or even such mundane matters as bending down to clean the litter box.

CAT RESPIRATORY MASKS

In a fire, cats, just like people, can be overwhelmed by smoke inhalation.

Help save lives by donating cat-size SurgiVet animal oxygen masks to your local firehouse. Ask the fire chief first whether the company already has them among its equipment. If you get the go-ahead to stock the engines with the device, ask how many fire trucks are in the company's fleet. On the other hand, if your local firehouse is already stocked or the fire chief declines your offer, ask around to learn whether neighboring firehouses could use an "angel" in this regard.

PetsAmerica.org, an organization that promotes first-responder relief for pets, sells the masks to anyone who wishes to purchase them; you don't have to be an emergency worker or a vet. You might want to chip in with a friend or two to buy enough masks to outfit a firehouse with one cat mask per fire truck, and perhaps a selection of large and small dog masks as well. (The organization also offers cat and dog "manikins" with working lungs, on which to practice CPR, splinting, and other first aid, if you are feeling extra generous.)

Create a Kitty Passport

IF YOU PLAN TO TRAVEL DOMESTICALLY or abroad with your cat, you'll want easy access to your pet's important documents: health certificate, vaccination record, and so on. One way to manage your cat's information en route is to create a "passport." You can use an envelope-size portfolio, a checkbook-size wallet, or a zipper vinyl case with dividers to hold papers. Choose a streamlined organizer so you can neatly tuck it into your carry-on bag. Make copies of the information you include in this travel pack so you have a set of documents at home, as well.

Include these documents in your kitty's passport:

- Updated health certificate

- Vaccination record

- Visas (if traveling abroad)

- An ID card with a photo, physical description, and your contact information; you can make this yourself

- Microchip ID number (see Day 358)

- Vet's name, address, and phone number, at home and at your destination

- A note card containing feeding and medication information, allergies, and behaviors

- Your emergency contact and next-of-kin information

Turkish Angora

THE ANKARA ZOO IN TURKEY preserves the original pedigree of pure white cats, including the Angora. The North American version of this breed traces back to this collection.

Characteristics: The U.S. Turkish Angora has a fine-boned body with a wedge-shaped face; the long, silky fur has no undercoat and is wavy on the cat's belly. The cat's heavy winter coat sheds heavily in the spring. The fur can be any color but colorpointed, and the eyes coordinated to the body color. Because odd eyes occur so infrequently in white cats of this breed, Angoras with this characteristic are considered very valuable.

History: The term "Turkish Angora" actually comprises two breeds. The North American version traces back to the Ankara zoo. Turkish Angoras began to be brought north to Europe in the 1600s.

Then, in 1962, an American breeder named Liesa Grant brought a pair of Angoras named Yildiz and Yildizcik (meaning "star" and "starlet") home from the Ankara zoo and, with another pair imported in 1966, began the U.S. Angora breed. This strain was recognized for competition by the U.S. Cat Fanciers' Association in 1973.

The British variety came about as recently as 1977, thanks to deliberate breeding of an Angora-like cat from Persians that omitted any actual ancestry from Turkey, and is now called the Oriental Longhair (see Day 236).

feline fun fact > Unusual for a cat, the Turkish Angora often carries its plumelike tail parallel to its back.

Turkish Angora

A Cat's Role in the Wedding

YOU WOULDN'T THINK OF LEAVING your best friend off the guest list for your "big day." Why should your cat be left at home during the nuptials? More cat owners are including their feline companions in wedding ceremonies than ever before, assigning them special jobs such as ring bearer or usher.

If you decide to create a role for your cat in the wedding, first consider these practical wedding planning tips:

- **Consider your guests.** You can't imagine celebrating "your day" without Kitty. But not all of your guests will share this sentiment—some may even be allergic to cats. Set boundaries. If you know your cat likes to jump on the table and help herself to the buffet, limit her appearance to the ceremony.

- **Choose an appropriate role for the cat.** Your cat won't saunter down the aisle like the bridesmaids. If you decide to involve your cat in the procession, consider a leash or assign a member of the wedding party to carry or cart the cat down the aisle.

- **Dedicate a "spotter" for your cat in case** she gets out of hand. The bride and groom should not wade into the crowd to correct their kitty's bad behavior. Ask a member of the wedding party to be on cat watch during the ceremony.

- **Primp your kitty for the big day.** Plan to have your cat bathed the day before the ceremony so her coat will be clean and shiny. Also, a just-groomed coat contains less dander.

- **Plan the wedding attire.** You can purchase cat-size tuxedos and dresses, tiaras, and special ring bearer pillows that strap to your kitty's back. If you order these items online, allow plenty of time for shipping (and for order mistakes—you never know).

- **Is this really a good idea?** You must feel confident that your cat's presence will enhance rather than add stress to your wedding day. The event is overstimulation central for humans. Imagine how cats will react. Deciding to include your cat means ensuring that she has the care she needs, is well monitored, and is escorted to a quiet place if she becomes scared or frightened. Although the wedding is "your day," pet ownership responsibilities are still in effect.

The Cat Palette: Eyes

LOOK INTO YOUR CAT'S SAUCER EYES—those peepers may change color over time or give other important clues about your cat's health.

Interestingly, all kittens are born with blue eyes. In some breeds, such as Siamese, the eyes typically remain blue; in others, another hue takes over with maturity: yellow, amber, orange, or green. Some cats have odd eyes, meaning their colors don't match, such as one orange eye and one green. Meanwhile, the blue-eyed gene in white cats is often paired with a deafness gene; if a white cat has odd-colored eyes and one is blue, that ear may be deaf.

Occasionally a true albino is born, with pink eyes, but it usually does not survive.

Perhaps the most interesting ocular trivia is a cat's third eyelid, the nictitating membrane. This is a thin cover that closes from the side and appears when the cat's eyelid opens. It helps adjust temperature, clear foreign matter from the eyes, and moisturize the eye. If you notice a partially closed membrane, your cat may be sick or the eye may be infected. Sleepy cats may also display the membrane. However, if the third eyelid is often visible, consult your veterinarian.

Puss in Boots and the White Cat

SOME MYTHS AND FOLKTALES evolved worldwide—"Puss in Boots" is a case in point.

It began as Giovanni Francesco Straparola's 1550 rags-to-riches tale of a peasant named Constantino whose poor mother dies and leaves him only a cat—actually a fairy—who introduces him to court and marries him to a princess.

Neapolitan writer Giambattista Basile's 1634 version featured a talking cat who, bequeathed to Gagliuso, advances his position only to abandon him for being ungrateful.

In 1697, Charles Perrault took up the story, adding the distinctive boots. Perrault's Puss kills an ogre by challenging him to turn himself into a mouse and then pouncing on him, guaranteeing his master the hand of a princess and her fortune.

British writer-illustrator George Cruikshank changed the story yet again in 1844, making Puss an enchanted gamekeeper who, turned into a cat, is restored to human form when he helps his master destroy an ogre. In Cruikshank's version, the cat wears clothing as well as boots.

Perrault's contemporary Marie-Catherine d'Aulnoy wrote "La Chatte Blanche" (The White Cat): Sent by his father on several quests, a prince discovers a castle populated by cats and is helped by their queen, the White Cat, to fulfill his trials. But only when he kills her, at her command, is a spell broken—and she becomes a princess. She is the White Cat in the ballet *The Sleeping Beauty* (see Day 310).

Chronic Renal Failure

CHRONIC RENAL FAILURE (CRF), also known as chronic kidney failure, is a potentially fatal condition that mostly affects elderly cats. The tragedy of this disease is that it is usually not detected until perhaps as much as 75 percent of your pet's kidneys are no longer functioning.

The kidneys are the organs that remove wastes from your cat's bloodstream, moving them along and out of your cat's body within urine. When the kidneys are functioning below par, these wastes build up in your cat's body, becoming toxins that can affect other organs. A cat with CRF may not die outright of this disease, but of another life-threatening complication, such as liver shutdown, caused by the buildup of toxins.

Although there is no surefire way to prevent CRF from developing, there are a few steps you can take to slow it down, even before Kitty shows any symptoms:

- Give your cat plenty of clean, filtered drinking water.

- If your cat prefers dry food, tempt him to drink more by giving him a bowl of all-natural chicken or turkey broth (made by simmering the meat and bones in water only, without salt or other flavorings, then straining and cooling).

- Offer the liquid from water-packed canned tuna, sardines, salmon, or other fish not packed in oil or sauces, or clam juice. Place in a bowl to drink, or mix it with your cat's wet food.

- Add water to your cat's wet food (as much as one can of water per can of food), beating it into a "soup." This is especially effective for cats that tend to lick away sauces but then leave the solids behind.

- Feed your cat a diet low in phosphorus.

- Have his teeth checked regularly. Oral bacteria from dental problems make the kidneys work harder.

Here are some of the symptoms of a toxin buildup from CRF:

- Foul mouth odor

- Turning away from favorite foods or pawing at the mouth while eating (CRF can cause nausea and painful ulcers in the mouth)

- Vomiting, especially a clear, white, or yellowish liquid or foam

- Increased drinking and urination

- Weakness and increased sleeping

- Joint pain (your cat avoids or has difficulty jumping or climbing up to or down from customary areas)

Your vet can perform blood tests to determine how well your cat's kidneys are functioning. If CRF has been diagnosed, the vet will probably place your cat on a regimen of regular hydration, either in-office dialysis to completely flush the kidneys or subcutaneous (under-the-skin) IV fluids.

Alas, CRF is irreversible. The best you can do is keep your cat as comfortable as possible and carefully follow your vet's recommendations for tending to symptoms that indicate a buildup of toxins.

Stamp That Cat!

MANY GREETING CARDS, note cards, notebooks, and other forms of stationery have attractive cat designs, but here is a way to design your own unique writing paper and journals—with rubber stamps. The creative options are endless, and you'll find that every holiday is an excuse for designing a fresh set of cards to "greet" friends and family with a bit of cat love.

Find inspiration by visiting stationers, art supply stores, craft stores, or online sites specializing in such products. You'll find various paw-print stamps, cat images, and additional designs that might be incorporated into a feline-centric theme, such as plants or furniture, mice or birds, or phrases.

Explore the effects of colorful stamp pads and inks, fine-tipped markers, and glitter pens. Some pads contain several coordinated or contrasting colors all on the same felt, or metallic inks. Consider pads using chalk inks rather than liquid inks—too glossy or smooth a paper, such as vellum, won't hold liquid ink well (it might bead up, run, or smear), so opt for a chalk ink for that kind of surface. As for paper, experiment with your inks on various textures and fiber contents until you get the look you desire.

Stamped cards, packaged as a stationery set, make great gifts for cat fanciers. Or give a cat lover a kit complete with paper, stamps, and inks to make his or her own feline-stamped creations.

The Turkish Van

AN ANCIENT ASIAN BREED with unique markings and unique predilections, the Turkish Van (originally called simply the Turkish Cat) became a European sensation in 1955, after Englishwomen Sonia Halliday and Laura Lushington, vacationing in Turkey, came across the unusual breed and brought home an unrelated male and female. The offspring of the feline couple had the same colors as the parents, and a cult was born.

Characterictics: The Turkish Van is a beautiful semi-longhair that is pure white except for coordinated tabby stripes on the top of its head and on its fluffy tail, a piebald color pattern that has come to be known as *van markings*. The hue of the markings may be golden to deep orange, cream, blue, or black. Some Vans have mottled markings in two colors that may appear in unusual combinations, such as cream and blue.

Occasionally, a Van will have a small spot of color on its torso, especially on one shoulder, which the Turkish people view as a special blessing of Allah. A rare color variation named Van Kedisi, pure white with odd-colored eyes, is the national cat of Turkey. Because they are considered national treasures, very few of these all-white cats are allowed to leave the country, thus their scarcity in the West.

As for their special personality—although cats, in general, notoriously avoid water, not so the Turkish Van. Indeed, they are perhaps most famous for being ardent swimmers, and willingly do daily laps in rivers or lakes when living freely in their homeland.

History: By 1969, the Van was accepted as a breed by the UK's Governing Council of the Cat Fancy, enabling it to enter British cat competitions; the breed arrived in the United States in 1970, where they were not registered with the council's U.S. equivalent, the International Cat Association, until 1985.

Despite such recent developments, the Van is centuries old, having developed in the Lake Van area of Turkey, where the climate is so extreme that the cats shed their main coat each summer to keep cool. Whatever the season, their fur is exceptionally soft and silky, comparable to cashmere.

Turkish Van

Story: I Say Orion, You Say Onion

I ADOPTED ONION FROM AN English professor in college, after his four-year-old daughter showed me a big scratch across her belly. Apparently, Onion was not a fan of little girls who wanted to chase and squeeze. The little girl had named her cat Odette—also my mom's name—and my professor asked me if I could provide the feisty furball a home. When I learned that this male cat shared a name with my mom, I figured it was meant to be. But clearly, the cat needed a name change. He couldn't share billing with the family matriarch.

I ruminated over possible names for the cat on my drive home. Really, the job of assigning a title to your soon-to-be housemate/best friend/ TV-watching companion is daunting. I decided to let his personality shine a bit before committing him to a moniker.

The cat didn't wait long to show his true colors. The first night home, he found a rodent and devoured all but the liver, which he left smack in the middle of the futon for my housemate and me to find the next morning. After some discussion, we rechristened the cat "Orion" the hunter. A perfect fit, we thought. This cat deserved to be named after a good, strong mythological figure.

What we didn't consider during the naming process is human error. *Orion* looks like *Onion* when scribbled quickly in longhand. Even typing Orion is awkward, actually. Onion is much more natural—easier to say and spell, or so we learned when a friend misread a note and began calling him Onion. He became Onion by default. And as he cozied himself into our lives, we realized that Onion is much more fitting. He is a cute bugger, after all. And still a hunter at heart.

Getting Kitty Used To the Carrier

TRAINING YOUR CAT TO BE used to her carrier before you have to go to the vet or on a trip will save you time, headaches, and scratches. You want your cat to have positive—or at least neutral—feelings about her carrier, not to automatically associate it with bad or uncomfortable things. Here are some tips to help you accomplish that:

1. Start by leaving the carrier in a corner of the room with the door open so she can get used to it being there. After a couple of days, place a treat a couple of feet (0.6 cm) in front of the carrier's opening and give Kitty praise when she takes it.

2. Every day, place a treat a little closer to the carrier's door, until you have reached the threshold. Then, place the treat just inside the carrier and work your way to the back of the carrier.

3. After Kitty has been happily receiving treats in the back of the carrier for a few days, start closing the door after she reaches her treat for just five or ten seconds to start, building up to thirty seconds or so over the course of a week or two. If at any time she seems stressed or rebels, backtrack a step or two until she feels comfortable again. Remember to give her praise and work at her pace.

4. Once she tolerates having the door closed, pick up the carrier with her in it and move it a few feet. Repeat this over the course of a couple of weeks, walking a little farther each time. When she emerges from the carrier, give her another treat or spend some playtime with her.

5. Encourage her to enjoy her time in the carrier during a car trip. Start with short trips around the block, and build up to longer trips. This will get her used to the motion and sounds of the car and teach her that not every foray into the carrier ends in a trip to the vet.

The Nonsense Cats of Lewis Carroll

"I didn't know that Cheshire-Cats always grinned; in fact, I didn't know that cats *could* grin."

"They all can," said the Duchess; "and most of 'em do."

—Lewis Carroll, *Alice's Adventures in Wonderland*

ONE OF THE MOST ENDURING feline characters in literature is the Cheshire-Cat, who makes his first appearance at the Duchess's home in *Alice's Adventures in Wonderland* (1865). But "enduring" is relative—he disappears and reappears at will, at times his grin alone hanging spookily in the air. He is a benevolent if cynical guiding force for Alice as she makes her way through the nonsense world that Lewis Carroll (1832–1898), lover of wordplay, created for her. Carroll clearly enjoyed and closely observed cats, as is evidenced by his fine details in writing about them.

Here are some highlights:

- Alice next spies the Cat sitting in a tree. He informs her, "We're all mad here"—including himself. His topsy-turvy logic runs as follows: "You see a dog growls when it's angry, and wags its tail when it's pleased. Now I growl when I'm pleased, and wag my tail when I'm angry. Therefore I'm mad." Alice objects, "I call it purring, not growling."

- In Through the Looking-Glass and What Alice Found There, the book starts and ends with Alice's three real cats. Wonderland already introduced one of them: On meeting a mouse in the pool of tears, Alice launched unthinkingly into a description of her cat Dinah back home: "She is such a dear quiet thing . . . and she sits purring by the fire, licking her paws and washing her face . . . and she's such a capital one for catching mice—oh, I beg your pardon!"

- In the start of Looking-Glass, Alice drifts into her favorite activity, "Let's pretend," and exclaims, "Let's pretend that you're the Red Queen, Kitty! Do you know, I think if you sat up and folded your arms, you'd look exactly like her." Still chattering, Alice holds Kitty up to the mirror over the mantel, pretending to put it through into the reflected version of the room . . . and this is what launches Alice's own passage through the mirror into the Looking-Glass world.

feline fun fact > Carroll delighted in word games, including one called Doublets, whereby one word would change into another of the same length, letter by letter. By such means he changed a *cat* into a *dog*: CAT, COT, DOT, DOG.

Out-of-Control Cat Population

OWNERS WHO FALL ON TOUGH TIMES may lose their homes and can't keep their animals, or they simply lose the resources to care for their pets. While many loyal pet owners would not think of turning their cats out onto the street, there are many who are desperate. Shelters and foster programs become packed with displaced pets, but others may end up on the streets.

Cats breed easily and often (see Day 143). In an uncontrolled environment, two cats will have an average of two litters per year, and 2.8 kittens per litter will survive. With continued breeding, the cat population multiplies.

> Year 1: 12 cats
> Year 2: 66 cats
> Year 3: 2,201 cats
> Year 4: 3,822 cats
> Year 5: 12,680 cats

If those two estranged-and-breeding cats have kittens for ten years, they will leave a whopping 80,399,780 cats to the animal kingdom.

That's a huge homeless problem to manage. Animal foster programs and shelters can only do so much.

There are other community initiatives that focus on "capturing" stray cats and spaying or neutering them before returning them to their natural habitat—sadly, the street. By clipping a tiny corner from the cat's ear, which is painless, volunteers know that the cat will not reproduce. The goal is to control an out-of-control population of cats that will not be cared for and loved, or properly immunized, therefore putting at risk the rest of the cat population (including house cats that go for night walks).

Investigate volunteer opportunities in your community to help control the cat population. Although you may feel that helping a cat or two isn't much, consider those two reproducing cats and the thousands that would end up on the street as a result. A little help does go a long way.

Staying Warm and Keeping Cool

WITH ALL THAT FUR, you wouldn't think cats would have trouble staying warm, but even long-haired felines can get the chills. Cats tend to become less tolerant of cold temperatures as they age. Help your older cat stay warm by providing a high-sided cat bed to help block drafts, and by leaving blankets so Kitty can snuggle up and stay warm while napping in his favorite spots.

Another important note: Wet fur doesn't insulate as well as dry fur does, so make sure your cat has shelter from wet conditions. Shelters for outdoor cats should be situated to protect your cat from the wind and rain. Line them with straw so your cat can burrow into it and make a protective "nest" for himself. (If he gets soaked, help him dry off by patting, not rubbing, him with dry towels.)

Cats are much more sensitive to heat than humans are. They don't sweat, but they cool themselves through respiration and by licking their fur.

As the temperature rises, cats breathe more heavily to dissipate the heat, and they may increase the frequency of self-grooming.

You can help your cat stay cool by making sure he has shady spots to retreat to in the heat of the summer and plenty of cool water to drink at all times. Never leave a cat unattended in a car, and avoid putting his carrier on the sunny side of the car when traveling. Brush him regularly to remove excess fur, and use a shedding tool on your longhaired cat as the temperature warms up to help him shed his winter coat.

Heatstroke is a dangerous condition. If you notice heavy panting, take your cat's temperature right away. If it is above 106°F (41.1°C), call your vet or animal hospital for advice on how to proceed.

York Chocolate

WITH A NAME THAT SOUNDS LIKE a candy bar, the York Chocolate doesn't disappoint in the sweet looks department.

Characteristics: As this new breed develops, color variations are creeping in, with some cats all brown, others all lilac, and still others a bicolor of one or the other and pure white. York Chocolates are big cats, yet underneath all that fur they have a Siamese-like body structure and a wedge-shaped face.

Every York Chocolate cat's lineage is carefully tracked to preserve its pedigree. The breed was recognized by several U.S. cat registries in 1990, and granted show status in Canada in 1995.

History: The name stems from New York State, where the first York Chocolate made its appearance as a spontaneous mutation in 1983. Owner Janet Chiefari had mixed-breed cats with a vague ancestry, apart from their having had Siamese relatives in some previous generation. One was a black longhair, the other a black and white longhair. And their offspring? Brownie was a deep, warm brown, with semi-long hair. When Brownie was mated with a longhaired black cat named Minky, several of their kittens, Teddy Bear and Cocoa, retained the chocolate coloring, leading Chiefari to carefully breed them—the mutation is apparently linked to the latent Siamese gene.

feline fun fact > Although their markings disappear with maturity, some York Chocolates are born with tabby spots or stripes.

York Chocolate

Story: Tree Hugger

SIMON IS AN UNABASHED LAP CAT. When I settle in to my favorite chair with a cup of tea, and a magazine or book, this is Simon's cue. He leaps up to join me, purring nonstop, and does not budge until I *nudge* him off. Simon is a softy, but he's not a scaredy cat, unless dogs are involved.

I witnessed his fear firsthand one afternoon. The neighbor's dog was off-leash and barking. In a panic about confronting this canine face-to-face, Simon raced straight up the trunk of an old, enormous maple tree, climbing almost higher than the third story. Simon is big-boned, nearly twenty pounds, so his tree scaling was quite a scene. He looked like a tiger shimmying its way up the century-old tree.

I felt sorry for him (and a bit anxious), but there was nothing I could do! I knew Simon eventually would ease himself down from the tree. I gave him a couple of hours. If he didn't make a safe landing, I'd call the fire department—or something. (Isn't that what they do in the movies?)

An hour later, I heard a crash, a yowl, and a little scuffle outside. I raced out to the yard to find him stretched out in the driveway, nonchalantly licking a front paw. He had made his descent . . . or crash landing. The look he gave me was one of part disdain, part adrenaline-soaked sheepishness. He saw me at the door, raced over, and slunk into the house, safely and soundly, and out of trouble—for now.

Bathing Your Cat

ALTHOUGH SOME BREEDS OF CATS require regular baths to maintain their coats, most cats will never need tub time. Still, it's a good idea to have the supplies on hand just in case she gets into a particularly nasty mess or gets really dirty.

Gather all of your supplies before starting:

- Rubber bath mat or towel for the bottom of the tub
- Shampoo specially formulated for cats
- Conditioner specially formulated for cats (if your cat has long hair)
- Handheld shower attachment or hose extension for the faucet
- Several large towels for drying off
- A quiet hair dryer with a low heat setting

Brush your cat's coat thoroughly before bathing to prevent tangles. Place the bath mat or a towel in the bottom of the bathtub to give your cat traction. Run the water to pre-warm it to near your cat's body temperature (keep the drain open), and open your shampoo and conditioner bottles. Bring your cat into the room, shut the door, and place her in the tub. You'll need to use one hand to hold her there; with the other, wet her from the neck down with the shower attachment. Avoid getting water near her face or ears.

Squirt a small amount of shampoo near the back of her neck and lather it into her fur, working back to her tail and down her legs. Rinse several times before applying conditioner (optional).

Wrap her in a towel and gently pat her dry. Avoid rubbing, which will tangle her fur.

The Eccentric Cats of Edward Gorey

Is there anything more heavenly than a silly little kitten?

—Edward Gorey, (1982 interview in *Publishers Weekly*)

WRITER-ARTIST-BALLETOMANE Edward Gorey (1925–2000) was a cat lover extraordinaire. As a small child, he only briefly owned one pet cat but, as an adult, he first held back to just a few at a time while living in small apartments and then, as space permitted, expanded to about a dozen. He had a soft spot for rescuing cats and preferred shorthaired pets. During media interviews, when asked to whom he was closest, meaning humans, he inevitably responded, "My cats." Felines served as models and inspiration for the artist.

Gorey had a unique, macabre style as both an author and an illustrator, perhaps best known to the general public as the artist behind the title art for the *Mystery* television series. Rendered in fine line in pen and ink, usually in black and white or with just a touch of color, his cat illustrations are unsettlingly humanlike, often ornamented with a striped T-shirt or pullover, scarf, or human accessory. They do not usually bear the cartoon bubbles of speech, but may be captioned with Gorey's elfin mix of gothic quaintness and understatement.

In addition to providing illustrations for a 1982 edition of **Old Possum's Book of Practical Cats** by T.S. Eliot (see Day 317), Gorey's own cat-related titles are **Gorey Cats**, a 1982 book of paper dolls, and the 1980 **Dancing Cats and Neglected Murderesses**, the first section of which depicts cats in a variety of poses and occupations, from juggling to semaphoring to taking a ballet class.

A cat figures prominently on the covers of his anthologies **Amphigorey** and **Amphigorey Too**, in each case spelling out the title in illuminated letters and then scrambling up the word as a mysterious anagram on the back cover. (In the spelling of "Amphigorey" on these covers, Gorey suitably depicts himself in his trademark fur coat, as the letter I.) The cats appear inside, too, as a decorative ornament. His book *Category* (1974 and 2006) is a collection cat illustrations originally produced for a limited edition of **Amphigorey**.

Gorey owned several original illustrations from *archy and mehitabel* (see Day 282) and was also a fan of **Krazy Kat** comics (see Day 261). During the latter part of his career and especially following his death, Gorey's own cat illustrations have become iconic, commercially available on calendars and stationery, on tote bags and T-shirts, even cast as jewelry. Some of his books are now collectors' items, but many others remain in print internationally.

Edward Gorey House, now a museum in Yarmouth, Massachusetts, carries on Gorey's legacy by contributing profits to Tufts Veterinary College and the Animal Rescue League of Boston, as well as to the Bat Conservation International Foundation, another interest dear to the heart of this master of the macabre!

All about Dander

YOU LOVE WHEN YOUR CAT NUZZLES up next to you on the couch, purring and pawing, showing her love. But, then come the sniffles, the watery, itchy eyes. How can love be so miserable?

Dander is the culprit—those tiny particles released from a cat's skin and hair. Dander and saliva, which eventually dries up into airborne flakes, carry a feline protein called Fel d 1, which triggers most cat allergies. This substance infiltrates homes by getting trapped in upholstery and carpet, and circulating through heating systems without proper filters. (Try electrostatic high-efficiency particulate arresting cleaners, known as HEPA filters.) Depending on the severity of your allergies, adopting a fastidious cleaning regimen may quell allergic reactions to dander.

Meanwhile, there are new drugs on the horizon that may allow people with moderate cat allergies to live sniffle-free with shorthaired pet cats.

Monthly injections of anti-IgE has shown in studies to reduce the need for inhalants and decrease inflammation and other symptoms. Obviously, steer clear of longhaired cats. The good news: If your allergies are mild and you own a shorthaired cat, these extra dander-removal steps may be the good medicine you need to prevent a flare-up.

Clear the air: Purchase HEPA filters, a high-efficiency air filter that removes most airborne pollutants.

Bathe Kitty: A twice-monthly cat bath will prevent dander buildup (see Day 344).

Be a neat freak: Vacuum regularly, and use an attachment to suck dust and dander particles from upholstery and drapes.

Keep Kitty out: Close your bedroom door to keep bedding dander-free.

Keeping Your Cat Off Your Computer

To your cat, the computer is a nice warm spot, a keyboard that beeps when pounded, a screen with moving pictures, cables to chew—and let's not even get into that mouse!

Cats can wreak havoc with electronics, and the more delicate and costly the equipment, the more important it is that you keep your pet and your computer's components apart.

Cute as it is for a cat to sleep atop your computer or printer, it is vital that the ventilation areas be kept unblocked and free of fur. Overheating can damage electronics. Even if the equipment is turned off, remember that fur tends to cling by static to the outside of machinery, and it will cling to wiring if it gets inside your computer. And if your cat chews on live wires, she may get electrocuted or burn her mouth.

Here are some of the simplest ways to protect both your electronics and your cats:

• Use a computer desk with slide-out elements that can be stowed when not in use.

• Buy or sew snug fabric or plastic covers for your screen, printer, and keyboard for when not in use (or use overturned baskets, attractive boxes, or closet-ware grids to cover components).

• Conceal wires and cables by blocking access to them or by enclosing them in tubing specially made for them (look for these at a computer or hardware store).

• Train your cat to sit in a designated safe area well away from the machinery while you are using it, for example, on a catnip-filled blanket on the floor by your feet (see Day 60 for how to make one).

• Provide cat toys to keep your pet's attention away from cords and switches.

• If necessary, make your computer area a cat-free zone behind a closed door.

Unusual and Rare Breeds

SOME BREEDS ARE SO RARE AND NEW that they are barely known. Here are a few examples; for more, visit www.pictures-of-cats.org/rare-cat-breeds.html.

KHAO MANEE

This rare breed, believed to be the original royal cat of Thailand, is solid white with one golden eye and one blue eye, or both eyes blue (which can cause deafness); it was sent to the United States in 1999 to Colleen Freymuth for breeding in the West.

OJOS AZULES

This cat, whose Spanish name derives from its blue eyes, traces to New Mexico, where a tortie American Shorthair had eyes of such a spectacular deep blue that it was deemed a spontaneous mutation. (Normally that kind of blue is only found in white or colorpointed cats.) Luckily, mating to other cats even without this color eyes produced kittens with the blue eye gene; care is being taken to keep the trait going.

Some Ojos Azules have heterochromatic eyes, meaning there is an extra color, such as amber, immediately surrounding the pupil. The fur comes in many color combinations, with a tendency toward white spotting on paws or the tip of the tail. There are both short- and longhaired versions.

Mating two Ojos Azules may perpetuate a genetic defect tied to the eye color: cranial and other deformities, and possibly stillbirth. A marker for carrying the abnormal gene is a tail with a flattened tip; still, it is advised to crossbreed Ojos Azules with non-blue-eyed cats.

PEKE FACE

The Peke Face, which originated as a mutation of the Red Persian, is a Persian with an exceptionally flattened face. It also has unusually long legs, and usually red or red tabby fur.

The jaw and nose of the Peke Face are so truncated that it is difficult for such cats to breathe and eat. Even the tear ducts are compressed, leading to a tendency to have teary eyes.

Some breeders have attempted to continue the line, but British cat associations refuse to recognize the deformed cats as a show breed.

SAFARI CAT

The Safari Cat is the result of matings between domestic cats and the wild Geoffroy's Cat (see Day 362). Virtually no cat association acknowledges it as a show breed. It is large with spotted fur, tabby markings on the face, and a fairly wild appearance. The color varies, depending on that of its parents.

SELKIRK REX

This Rex variation cropped up as a genetic mutation in Wyoming in 1987: A curly-furred kitten named Miss Pesto was mated with a Persian and some of her kittens had long, curly fur. Breeding one of the males with his mother perpetuated the trait. It is a longhaired, heavy-bodied Rex, with curly, wooly fur (some call it a "sheepcat") and a stocky build.

The Selkirk has a mixed ancestry: British/American Shorthair, plus Exotic Shorthair and Persian. The Selkirk gene is dominant, which helps distinguish this breed from the other Rexes. Selkirks may come in any color, including shaded and colorpointed.

Traveling by Plane and Train

IF YOU PLAN TO TRAVEL by plane or train with Kitty, prepare for your adventures with these pointers.

Plane: Before you book your ticket, research the airline's pet travel policies and determine whether a cat (crated, of course) is an acceptable carry-on item or whether cargo hold is the only option. If your cat is vocal (i.e., yowls incessantly while in the crate), then cargo is your only option. Always transport your cat in a crate, not a box that can be easily damaged en route.

Check pet regulations at your destination. Find out whether there are quarantine rules or special vaccinations required. For instance, Hawaii is considered rabies-free and requires incoming pets to be quarantined for six months. Regardless of your destination, you must keep a health certificate on hand. Make a passport for your cat to organize essential documents (see Day 326).

Train: Similar to traveling by plane, you should find out whether your cat is allowed to travel with you. Some rail lines allow only service pets to travel. In Europe, pets can travel on most trains. Check with the train operator in advance to learn whether the company is pet-friendly.

Introducing Your New Cat to Children

THE DAY YOU BRING YOUR NEW CAT home is an exciting one for the whole family. Your children will be eager to pet and play with the new kitty, but she will likely be feeling overwhelmed and not quite ready for all the attention. Although it may disappoint the kids, you need to limit their interaction with her until she is fully adjusted to her new home.

Before you bring Kitty home, let the children know that she may be feeling scared and uncertain at first, and that they must be patient and wait for her to get used to her new home before they can play with her. When you bring her home, allow the children a few minutes to see her before leaving her in her safe room (see Day 302). Instruct them that they are not to bother her in her safe room.

Once the kitty begins to feel comfortable with you, and you are sure she's ready for company, allow one child at a time to hold or pet her under your supervision for a few minutes. To avoid jealousy, the children can draw straws or numbers to see who can go first, then rotate each time thereafter. Warn young children to be gentle and let them know that cats can sometimes scratch or bite if they feel threatened. Show them how to pet her along the direction of fur growth. If Kitty starts squirming or hissing or lays her ears back, let her be alone in her safe room for a while and try another day.

Once Kitty starts exploring the rest of the house, let the children know that they must not chase her; let Kitty come to them. Show them how to play with her and teach them to watch for the signs that she's had enough (scratching, biting, hissing, ears drawn back). Praise both the children and the cat for playing well together. Soon your new cat will feel like part of the family.

Cats in Western Fine Art and Illustration

Even the smallest feline is a work of art.

—Leonardo da Vinci (1452–1519)

FINE ART BOASTS MANY BEAUTIFUL cat images, often integrated into a portrait or other scene. And if you fall in love with a painting or a sculpture, you might even be able to buy a reproduction to enjoy right in your own home. Because they don't always have the word cat in their title, it can take some sleuthing to find these works and their artists, so here are some especially fine, fine art examples:

- **Jean-Antoine Watteau's** *Le Chat Malade* (*Sick Cat* [ca. 1712]) shows a doctor treating said cat as it is clutched in the arms of its sobbing young owner. Watteau also produced lovely sketches of cats.

- Swiss-born **Gottfried Mind** (1768–1814), an autistic savant who adored and painted cats, was dubbed the "Raphael of Cats."

- The works of French artist **Louis Lambert** (1825–1900), who studied with Delacroix, specialized in paintings of dogs and cats; in fact, the success of his *Cat and Parakeet* (1857) was what launched his popularity. Several medals followed, including for his *L'Horloge Qui Avance* (1866) and *Les Chats du Cardinal* (1874). He, too, was dubbed the "Raphael of Cats."

- **Éduoard Manet's** work included *Olympia* (1863) depicting a nude who has a black kitten by her feet, and his engraving *Le Chat et les Fleurs* (Cat and Flowers [1870]).

- **Francisco Goya** painted *Don Mañuel Osorio Manrique de Zuñiga* (1787), in which two cats appear among other animals at the feet of little red-suited Don Mañuel.

- **John Singer Sargent** (1856–1925) produced numerous sketches of cats.

- **Marc Chagall's** *Paris though the Window* (1913) portrays a windowsill with a cat.

- **Leonardo da Vinci's** sketch *Virgin and Child with a Cat* (ca. 1480) depicts the Infant Jesus cradling a cat.

- **Henriette Ronner** (1821–1909) was a famous cat artist whose studio in Belgium included a glass miniature set in which she placed her subjects while she painted them. Many of her sentimental works depict families of fuzzy mother cat and kittens.

- British artist **Charles Burton Barber** (1845–1894) created numerous paintings of cats and gods, perhaps the most famous being *Suspense*, in which a little girl saying grace before eating is flanked by an eager terrier and tabby kitten.

- **Théophile-Alexandre Steinlen** (1859–1923), one of the most well-known illustrators of cats, produced the lithograph *L'Hiver, Chat sur un Coussin* (*Winter, Cat on a Cushion*) and many advertising posters, replicated in modern-day prints, posters, cards, and books.

In 1870, Champfleury (pen name of French journalist Jules Fleury-Husson) published a book, ***Les Chats***, illustrated by contemporary artists Manet, Tissot, and Delacroix. It was the first significant study of this species.

Tummy Trouble: Symptoms and Solutions

INTESTINAL DISEASES ARE QUITE COMMON, and they are generally triggered by a combination of diet, genetics, immune system, and intestinal bacteria. A perfectly healthy cat can develop an intestinal disease—tummy trouble that won't go away unless properly diagnosed and treated by a veterinarian. A poor diet is often the cause of intestinal disease, and problems often clear up once a nutritious, high-protein diet is established.

Depending on the severity of your cat's symptoms, a vet may recommend an elimination diet, supplements, medication, or steroids. Symptoms of intestinal disease are often confused with other health problems, including kidney disease, urinary tract obstruction, diabetes, and hyperthyroidism. With lab work and a urinalysis, your vet will identify whether your cat's symptoms point to tummy trouble or something else.

SYMPTOMS

The following behaviors are typical in cats with intestinal disease:

- Weight loss despite normal/increased appetite
- Loss of fat over the spine
- Vomiting food, fluid, and/or hair balls
- Diarrhea or constipation
- Reduction in normal appetite
- Lethargy or hiding
- Licking the lips (signaling nausea)

SOLUTIONS

Your vet will suggest a natural diet for your cat that is high in protein and contains no more than 7 percent carbohydrates. Common food triggers include grains such as corn, rice, and wheat; derivatives of those grains, such as gluten, flour, and starch; and vegetables and fruit, which are not "normal" foods for carnivorous cats. Poultry and rabbit are the best protein options. Beef, fish, pork, and lamb may cause allergic reactions in sensitive cats. A canned diet may be appropriate, at least as you learn what triggers your cat's tummy problems.

Medications can clear up intestinal diseases. Vitamin B12 injections may be administered weekly for a duration of time specified by the veterinarian. Folic acid supplements can also alleviate intestinal problems, as can probiotics and omega fatty acids (see Day 255). Your vet will make the best recommendation for your cat.

Steroids and immune-suppressing drugs can alleviate symptoms if the immune system is responsible for intestinal upset. These can cause side effects, such as palpitations, twitching, and trembling. Drugs such as cyclosporine and budesonide are also administered for some cases of intestinal disease.

Your best bet for preventing tummy troubles is to feed your cat a healthy diet that is low-carb, high-protein, and void of common allergens. If you're serving up canned food, choose poultry or rabbit for sensitive stomachs, and always provide fresh filtered water for your cat. Feed your cat only fresh food, left out no longer than four hours.

Homemade Cat Repellent

How do you cope when your cat's love for your guest bed or favorite chair is driving you crazy? Try this homemade cat repellent spray, which will discourage him from perching or pawing on surfaces that are off-limits to Kitty. This spray works because cats have a very sensitive sense of smell, and they will generally avoid areas that smell unpleasant to them. Keep in mind that some cats react more to some scents than to others, so you may have to experiment a little to find the right repellent for your cat.

MATERIALS

Clean spray bottle (from the drugstore)

Essential oils (from the health food store), your choice of cinnamon, citronella, lemon, lemongrass, lavender, orange, rosemary, ginger, eucalyptus, tea tree

1. Put 8 ounces (235 ml) of warm water in the spray bottle. Add ten drops of essential oil (all one type or a combination). Shake vigorously.

2. Test the spray in an inconspicuous spot on the item you want to protect. If, after it dries, there is no damage, proceed to spray the solution on the item you want to protect, shaking between sprays to mix the solution.

3. Store in the refrigerator. Reapply the spray daily to maintain effectiveness.

The Greater Family of Cats, Part I

DOMESTIC CATS ARE BUT ONE BRANCH of a feline family tree that extends to almost fifty other kinds in the wild, living all over the world.

All cats trace back to the Miacid, a small and furry descendant of the dinosaur, which lived in the Cainozoic Era roughly fifty million years ago.

Most are carnivores and share characteristics of house cats, from their whiskers and the shape of their paws to their long tail. Most of the big cats have flexible cartilage in their throat that amplifies their voice into a roar. Below are the better-known large wildcats; see Day 362 to learn about the many smaller, often rarer varieties. Asterisked names are endangered species.

Bobcat (North and Central America): A.k.a. Bay Lynx, reddish or gray with spots, short-legged with a short tail, white fur under its tail and on the back of its black-tufted ears

Canadian Lynx (Alaska, Canada): Reddish brown, sometimes spotted, with a short tail, black-tufted ears, and very furry feet

Caracal (Middle East, Central Asia, Eastern Europe): Fawn-colored with long legs and narrow ears

*Cheetah (Africa, Middle East): The world's fastest land mammal, achieving speeds up to 70 mph (110 kph). Males like to hunt together, in daylight. Born with a gray coat, grows up to have golden fur with black polka dots, with long legs, a long tail, and black-tufted ears.

Eurasian Lynx (nearly worldwide, except the Americas): Large, with dark spots and black-tufted ears

*Jaguar (Central and South America): Needs and loves water; a robust swimmer; also climbs trees. Massive build and large head; can have spots, in the form of rosettes on a golden to deep orange base coat, or may be black

*Leopard (Middle East and tiger regions): Males and females alike range across long distances and can survive without water if they have fresh kill. Smaller head than the tiger; has small black spots on a grayish or brownish ground, or can be solid black

*Lion (India, Africa): Lives in community with a leader; males hunt together and share the kill, females care for other cubs as well as their own. Males have a unique long mane; body coat is short and tawny.

*Ocelot (Southern Texas, Central and South America): Nocturnal and solitary, although does like to live in pairs. Golden fur with rosettes or spots often linked into horizontal bars; tail is barred or ringed with black. Ears have a white spot on the back

Puma (All the Americas): A.k.a. cougar, mountain lion, American lion, and catamount; appears in the art of pre-Columbian cultures. Can cover 25 miles (40 km) in a single day. Usually, strikes its prey rather than biting it. Evenly gold/red/brown (warmer regions) to gray (cooler ones); cubs are born spotted. Has a long, muscular body and a long tail

*Snow leopard (Asia, the Middle East, Eastern Europe): Very rarely seen; lives at high altitudes on snow and glaciers. Long, pale gray fur with dark spots and rosettes, and gray-green eyes. The coat is heavier in winter.

*Spanish Lynx (Western Spain and Portugal): Deeply spotted with a midsize tail

*Tiger (India through southern Asia, Eastern Europe): Hunts alone and can set up ambushes for prey. Only wildcat with stripes, which run vertically around its body. Base coat ranges from creamy gold to deep orange.

(See Day 362, Part II)

Journal Prompts, Part IV

FILL UP THE JOURNAL YOU CREATED on Day 25 with more memories. Here are some writing prompts to stoke your creativity:

- Describe your volunteer experience at the animal shelter.

- How would you describe your cat to a stranger? Explain her appearance, personality traits, and interesting characteristics. Tuck this description into your cat binder (see Day 81) in case your pet is ever lost and you need a description in a hurry.

- Has your cat ever "convinced" you to try something new (climb a tree to rescue her, visit a museum exhibit devoted to cats, etc.)?

- Describe a time when your cat comforted you when you were blue. What did your cat do to make you feel better?

- Does your cat know any tricks? Explain them.

- How do you spoil your cat?

Microchipping

IDENTIFICATION IS CRUCIAL to your being able to get your cat back should he wander off and get lost. ID tags are important, of course, but what if his tags get lost, too? New microchip technology provides a permanent way to identify your cat to strangers so he can be returned to you.

Microchipping is offered just about everywhere, and it is relatively inexpensive. If your cat is picked up and brought to a shelter, volunteers can read the chip with a scanner, call in the ID number, and contact you to let you know they have your cat. You must keep your contact information up-to-date with the database administrator, however.

The microchip is the size of a small grain of rice and is encoded with a number that can be read by a handheld scanner. The vet uses a special injector to place it under the cat's skin. This may be momentarily uncomfortable for him, so be sure to use a lot of rewards and praise while the process is taking place.

There is one potential problem with microchipping: Competing microchip technologies have recently come to the marketplace, and not all scanners can read all the microchips. Find out which scanners your local shelters have before choosing which type of microchip to implant.

Feline Fairy Tales and Folklore

IN ADDITION TO PUSS IN BOOTS and the White Cat (see Day 331), cats appear in worldwide literature and oral legends dating back centuries. The Brothers Grimm—Jacob and Wilhelm—collected cat stories from servants, friends, and neighbors.

- In "The Companionship of the Cat and Mouse," the cat tricks the mouse into believing he periodically must attend the christening of a new kitten, when actually he has been stealing away to lick fat from a jar they have been keeping to get them through the next winter. The cat's invented names for the supposed kittens ultimately gives the game away.

- A cat joins an interspecies journey in "The Bremen Town Musicians," in which various neglected animals team up to make their fortune. They come to a robber's den and so frighten the men with their raucous serenade that the thieves run away, leaving the donkey, dog, rooster, and cat to enjoy their spoils.

- A talking, enchanted, spotted cat helps a simple young man named Hans in "The Poor Miller's Apprentice and the Cat." She brings Hans to a castle staffed by feline servants and gives him various tasks to perform, and ultimately rewards him by turning into a princess and marrying him.

Story: A Royal Exit

SOMETHING WAS WRONG WITH REGINA—she was losing weight, barely eating, and breathing through her mouth.

My regular vet wanted to euthanize her on the spot, without even investigating the problem. In tears, I brought Reggie home, vowing to never use that clinic again.

Instead, I brought her to a large animal hospital an hour's drive away, where tests revealed dismal news: esophageal cancer. A tumor was wrapped like a doughnut around her gullet.

At that time, I was struggling to care for my elderly parents who both had Alzheimer's. They were in irreversable decline, but I wanted to give Reggie a chance. I told the vet to operate.

Surgery could not reach the entire growth but did gain us time. Regina began to eat with gusto. I gave her extra lap time, and she continued to sleep in her customary place, against my shoulder.

Periodically, fluids accumulating in her throat needed to be drained—a two-hour round-trip each time. But she somehow understood that the hospital made her better—her former history of wailing in cars changed to excitedly looking out the window all the way. And she absolutely adored her new vet, Heidi. On good days, Reggie was positively radiant; on bad, she trusted we'd make her feel better.

Heidi broached our trying a still-experimental procedure: radiation, to shrink what was left of the tumor. I decided that even if it didn't help Reggie, other cats might benefit from the staff's gained experience. I coached Reggie beforehand, saying her chest would feel "like a radiator." Afterward, when I visited her at the hospital, she ecstatically head-bumped me and one of the assistants. She had a small, ashy mark on her chest, but felt great. We all kept our fingers crossed.

Alas, while I was at work one day, Reggie's chest again flooded with fluid. She greeted me at the door, breathing laboriously. Off we went to the hospital, but she didn't make it, expiring on the way as her airways clogged, wetting herself in a release of urine. The last moments were, frankly, horrible, the taxi driver unable to go any faster in the rush-hour traffic.

Yet what tears me up is Heidi's reaction: She lifted Reggie from the carrier and cradled her in her arms, regardless of her soaked, smelly fur. We agreed that I had done the right thing to give Reggie those two extra months. My parents had died in that interim, and of the three, she had been the only "good" patient—appreciative of all who tried to help her, deeply embracing every pleasure of the moment—a testament to accepting a fatal illness with calm and dignity.

Assuming you have the time and financial means to treat a mortally ill pet palliatively, you'll learn a valuable lesson about viewing ebbing life as a glass half full. Put your squeamishness and pity aside, and listen to your pet. As long as she clearly wishes to live, please enable her to do so.

Make a Sisal Scratching Board

CATS LOVE TO SCRATCH ON SISAL. This easy-to-make scratching board will give your cat room to stretch out on an incline when he scratches. Sisal mats are inexpensive and often found in the doormat or rug sections of home improvement or general merchandise stores.

MATERIALS

2 pieces medium-density fiberboard (MDF), ¾ inch (1.9 cm) thick: one cut to the size of the mat; another one the same width, but ⅓ to ½ the length of the first

Construction adhesive

Small, thin sisal rope rug or mat, approximately 24 inches x 36 inches (61 x 91.4 cm)

Ruler

Pencil

Three 3-inch (7.6 cm) L braces

Drill with a bit slightly smaller than the diameter of your wood screws

Screwdriver

Twelve ⅝-inch (1.6 cm) wood screws

1. Place the mat-size fiberboard flat on your work surface. Using a generous amount of construction adhesive, glue the sisal mat to the board. (If your mat has a backing, make sure you glue it sisal side up.) Wipe up any excess adhesive around the edges of the mat. Place heavy objects across the surface of the mat and allow the adhesive to dry according to the manufacturer's instructions.

2. When the adhesive is dry, flip the board mat side down. Hold the smaller board upright on top of the larger board, approximately 1 inch (2.5 cm) from the end, to form an L shape. Draw a guideline with a ruler and a pencil along the edge of the short board to make it easier to place later.

3. Place an L brace approximately 2 inches (5.1 cm) in from the edge of the boards where the two boards meet, facing the long side of the large board. Mark the locations of the holes on both boards with the pencil. Repeat this on the other end and again in the center. Set the smaller board down.

4. Drill pilot holes at the locations marked on both boards, being careful to drill down only about ½ inch (1.3 cm).

5. Screw the L braces to the smaller board using two screws for each, with the unused part of each L brace aligned with the end of the board.

6. Apply construction adhesive to the end of the smaller board, then place it on the larger board, aligning the board with the guideline you drew in step 2 and the holes in the L braces with the pilot holes you drilled in step 4.

7. Screw the L braces to the larger board using two screws for each. Wipe up any excess construction adhesive that may have oozed out from between the boards. Allow the construction adhesive to dry.

8. Flip the finished scratching board over so it looks like a tent with the sisal surface on top. Apply some dried catnip to the mat and let your cats enjoy their new scratching board.

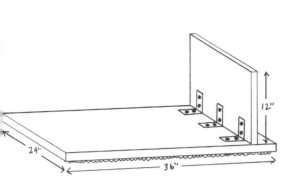

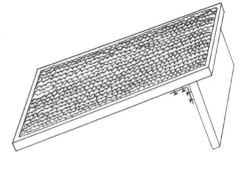

Assembling the scratchy board—L brace detail

Finished scratching board

The Greater Family of Cats, Part II

SOME OF THE FOLLOWING SMALL CATS may look almost like your kitty, but they are definitely on the wild side. Asterisked names are endangered species.

African Golden Cat (Africa): Relative of Temminck's Cat. Deep gold, auburn, or tan with spots and a deeper color along the spine

Bay Cat/Bornean Red Cat (Borneo): Deep, rich brown or blue

Biet's Cat/Chinese Desert Cat (China): Pale gold, with spots and a long tail

Black-Footed Cat (Africa): Smallest wildcat, weighs only about 5 pounds (2.3 kg), but has a loud roar. Large, spotted, with black-soled paws

Caffre Cat/African Wildcat/Gloved Cat (Africa): Smaller, more delicate European wildcat, with a narrow face and large ears

*Clouded Leopard of Asia (Southeast Asia): Arboreal; has large spots and rosettes that darken toward the rear, long barred tail

Colocolo/Pampas Cat/Gato Pajero (South America): Size of a house cat but very wild; longhaired, with a striped coat

European Wildcat (Europe): Resembles a heavy, cobby-bodied house cat; thick, tawny hair with low-contrast stripes and spots

Fishing Cat (India, Sri Lanka, China): Catches fish, shellfish, and snakes with its paws. Large, gray with spots; cobby body; resembles a civet

Flat-Headed Cat/Marten Cat (India, Southeast Asia, Pacific islands): Lives largely on fish and fruit. Long, flat head; longish white-tipped reddish fur

Geoffroy's Cat (South America): A good climber and swimmer. Usually spotted gray; can be other colors

Indian Desert Cat (India, Asia): Resembles a house cat; has golden or pale tan spotted fur, with a long tail

Iriomote Cat (Asia): Discovered on eponymous island near Taiwan, in 1967. Spotted and small, house cat size

*Jaguarundi (Texas, Central and South America): Weasel-like face; a good swimmer and hunter. Can be tamed; used to keep barns rodent-free. Solid-colored or striped reddish-tan or gray coat, long tail, short legs, very short ears

Jungle Cat (India, China, Southeast Asia): Large, with a short tail and tufted ears; usually taupe-colored with a striped tail

Kodkod (South America): Very rare; size of small house cat, deeply spotted or black on tan or gray coat, ringed midsize tail

*Leopard Cat (Southeast Asia): Swims well. In tropical regions, house cat size with black spots and striped head; in cooler areas, larger and pale gray with rosette markings

Marbled Cat/Bay Cat of Borneo (Southeast Asia): Has irregular rosettes with tweedlike filler on a yellowish ground; deeply spotted bushy tail

*Margay/Long-tailed Spotted Cat (Central and South America): Arboreal and solitary; its extra-wide rear toes let it hang off trees. Like a petite, childlike ocelot in appearance, with a round head and large eyes, black or brown rosettes or bars of rosettes, and a long tail

*Margueritte's Cat/Sand Cat (Middle East): Unusual side-set ears; broad furry paws enable it to walk on sand. Sandy coloring

Mountain Cat/Andean Highland Cat (South America): Can tolerate severe cold. Has a unique double-thick skull and thick, silvery fur spotted and striped with deep orange

Oncilla/"Tiger Cat" (Central and South America): Solitary, arboreal, and nocturnal; somewhat resembles the margay but not as agile. Size of small house cat; tawny with brown or black rosettes and a ringed tail

Pallas's Cat/Manul (Middle East, Asia, Eastern Europe): Once believed to be a primitive Persian or Angora. Has a cobby body with thick legs, a broad head, and small ears. Long gray or reddish fur with white tipping, and black markings on head only; fur is longer on the belly

Pantanal Cat (South America): Very rare; similar to the Colocolo

Rusty-Spotted Cat (India, Sri Lanka): Similar to the leopard cat; small build; high-contrast brownish fur with dark spots

Serval (Africa, Middle East): High-voiced, servals can purr; can be tamed. Has round spots; long neck, small head, large ears

*Temminck's Golden Cat/Asian Golden Cat (Asia): Named for its discoverer; often hunts in pairs; the males help raise their cubs. Same coloring as African golden

(See Day 355, Part I)

A Swimmingly Fun Pet for Kitty

IF YOUR CAT SEEMS BORED and needs stimulation, why not get her a pet? Instead of committing your time, space, and resources to another cat, consider a fish tank.

A fish tank full of swimmers will entertain your cat, like a television permanently tuned into the wild animal channel. In many ways, a fish tank provides a visual "hunt" for your cat. Just be sure to purchase a tank with a tight lid, and place it on a sturdy, elevated surface.

Cats and Critters

CATS ARE HUNTERS BY NATURE. In fact, cats first became prized as domesticated animals because of their hunting skills and their value in keeping rodents away from stored grain. For cats, hunting is more than merely a way to catch food; they seem to take pleasure in the hunt, too. Most cats like hunt-type play, even when a live animal is not involved (see Day 211 for ways to play that make use of the hunting instinct).

If your cat spends any time outdoors, chances are he will eventually catch a bird, mouse, or even a larger critter, such as a rabbit. Even house cats will occasionally catch a mouse, should one be unlucky enough to venture inside. Many times, cats will bring you their "prize." One theory holds that cats bring their owners prey as a caretaking gesture; another theory is that cats are trying to teach us to hunt. Either way, it can be a bit disconcerting to be faced with a dead chipmunk at breakfast.

Because it is their instinct to hunt, attempting to train a cat not to hunt is a lesson in futility, but controlling your reaction when he brings a caught animal into the house will avoid encouraging the behavior.

Don't scold your cat for merely following his instinct, but don't praise him, either. Don your rubber gloves and deal with the situation as calmly as possible. If the animal is dead, dispose of it quickly and without fuss. If the animal is still alive, try trapping it under an overturned trash can, then slide a piece of cardboard underneath. Pick the whole thing up and relocate the animal outside, keeping Kitty inside. Be careful—injured animals are more likely to bite. If the animal is badly injured or seems to be diseased, call your local animal control office for advice.

Outdoor cats should always be up-to-date on their vaccines and preventive treatments for rabies, fleas, and parasites. If it looks like your cat was bitten, scratched, or injured in his tussle with the critter, get him to the vet to be checked. Many wild animals carry diseases, some of which are transmissible to cats and/or humans.

To give wild critters a fighting chance against your brave hunter, put a bell on his collar, which will warn other animals that he is around. Keep him inside around dawn and dusk, when rodents and birds are most active. If you have bird feeders in your yard, place them so that Kitty can't get to them—the birds will thank you.

Index

Resources

ORGANIZATIONS

American Association of Feline Practitioners
www.catvets.com; 800-874-0498

American Cat Fanciers' Association
www.acfacats.com; 417-725-1530

American Society for the Prevention of Cruelty
to Animals (ASPCA)
www.aspca.org; 212-876-7700

Canadian Cat Association/Association Féline
Canadienne
www.cca-afc.com; 905-459-1481

The Cat Fanciers' Association
www.cfa.org; 732-528-7391

Doctors Foster and Smith
www.drsfostersmith.com; 800-381-7179

Fédération Internationale Féline (EU)
www.fifeweb.org

Governing Council of the Cat Fancy (UK)
www.gccfcats.org; +44 (0)1278 427575

The Humane Society of the United States
www.hsus.org; 301-258-8267

Human Society International
www.hsus.org/hsi

The International Cat Association
www.tica.org; 956-428-8046

Royal Society for the Prevention of Cruelty for
Animals (Australia)
www.rspca.org.au

Royal Society for the Prevention of Cruelty for
Animals (UK)
www.rspca.org.uk

Royal New Zealand Society for the Prevention
of Cruelty to Animals
http://rnzspca.org.nz

MAGAZINES

Cat Fancy magazine
www.catchannel.com

Your Cat Magazine
www.yourcat.co.uk

BOOKS

Health, History, and Breed Information

Arora, Sandy. *Whole Health for Happy Cats: A Guide to Keeping Your Cat Naturally Healthy, Happy, and Well-Fed*. Beverly, MA: Quarry, 2006.

Christensen, Wendy. *The Humane Society of the United States Complete Guide to Cat Care*. New York: St. Martin's Griffin, 2004.

Fireman, Judy, ed. *The Cat Catalog: The Ultimate Cat Book*. New York: Workman Publishing, 1976.

Frith-Macdonald, Candida. *Encyclopedia of Cats*. Bath, UK: Parragon, 2008.

Green, Martin I. *The Home Pet Vet Guide*. New York: Ballantine Books: 1980.

Johnson-Bennett, Pam. *Think Like a Cat: How to Raise a Well-Adjusted Cat—Not a Sour Puss*. New York: Penguin, 2000.

Janik, Carolyn and Ruth Rejnis. *The Pocket Idiot's Guide to Living with a Cat*. New York: Alpha Books, 1999.

Méry, Fernand. *The Life, History and Magic of the Cat*. Trans. by Emma Street. New York: Grosset & Dunlap, 1973.

Morris, Desmond. *Catlore*. New York, Crown, 1987. A sequel to *Catwatching* (1986).

Reader's Digest. *The Reader's Digest Illustrated Book of Cats*. Pleasantville, NY: Reader's Digest, 1995.

Repplier, Agnes. *The Fireside Sphinx*. Boston and New York: Houghton Mifflin Company, 1939.

Winslow, Helen M. *Concerning Cats*. Ann Arbor, MI: Lowe & B. Hould, 1996.

Yarnall, Celeste and Hofve, Jean. *The Complete Guide to Holistic Cat Care*. Beverly, MA: Quarry, 2009.

Cats in Literature and Art

Bast, Felicity. *The Poetical Cat: An Anthology*. New York: Farrar Straus and Giroux, 1995.

Boylan, Clare. *The Literary Companion to Cats*. London: Sinclair Stevenson, 1994.

Dale, Rodney. *Cats in Books: A Celebration of Cat Illustration through the Ages*. London: British Library, 1997.

Muncaster, Alice L., Chuck Wood and Ellen Yanow. *The Cat Made Me Buy It!* New York: Crown Publishers, 1984. Also, *The Cat Sold It!* (1986) and *The Black Cat Made Me Buy It!* (1990).

Suarès, J. C. and Seymour Chwast, eds. *The Literary Cat*. New York: Push Pin Press: 1977.

Wilson, Michael, ed. *V & A Cats*. London: V & A Publications, 1989.

Charted Cat Patterns

Box, Richard. *Cross Stitch Cats*. London: Batsford: 1998.

Cartwright-Jones, Catherine. *The Tap-Dancing Lizard*. Interweave Press, 1993.

Davidson, Amanda. *Tapestry Cats and Dogs*. Devon, England: David & Charles, 1995.

Mayhew, Jayne Netley, and Nicki Wheeler. *Cats of the World in Cross Stitch*. Devon, England: David & Charles, 2000.

Photographer Credits

Acknowledgments

A standing ovation to Team Cat for producing a book that will delight everyone who is loved (and owned) by their cats. Rochelle Bourgault, it has been such a pleasure to work with you on this book and others. You're a voice of reason and a sounding board ... and a friend. Thank you. (And Onion, thank you, too.)

Iris Bass, you are passionate about all things cat and detail-oriented in your pursuit to deliver interesting material. Is there a Jeopardy! for cat lovers? (If so, I'm signing you up.) Your deep commitment to this project is imprinted on every page. Your "kids" will be extremely proud.

Lori Paximadis, first dog, now cat ... and we're due for those margaritas by now, don't you think? Thank you for providing such practical insight, including projects. You've got plenty of "good material" roaming your home (but not surfing the countertops, thanks to those sticky boards).

Betsy Gammons, can we do this again? It's always a joy to work with you.

Karen Conant, for your design expertise. The book is a beauty!

Anita, Jill, Melissa, and Meredith, thank you for sharing your heart-warming, hilarious, and antic-laden stories. Anita, I will never think of your front porch in the same way again. Jill, the insight shared from your experience volunteering with Public Animal Welfare Society provided great value while penning sections concerning cat rescue, adoption, and mothering a houseful. Melis, I appreciate your thorough veterinarian expertise (A+!). You'll be a fantastic kitty doctor. Meredith, I think Ernie the cat could hold his own on reality television. And with nine lives worth of material ... no reruns.

Haven, meow. (Achoo!) This one's for you.

—Kristen Hampshire

Many thanks to the cats and cat lovers who have shared their lives with me.

—Iris Bass

Above all, deepest gratitude to John, my funny and cool (and sometimes silly) husband for always having patience with me, but especially during the writing process, and to our little family of cats—Spaz, Ciara, and Fiona—who keep us on our toes. Fond memories of Pete, Boo, and Neuman helped inspire some of my share of this content—I miss them all. Special thanks to Kristen, who made the first connection that led to one thing, then another, and now this book. Finally, thanks to my mom, who has always supported and encouraged me and swore that someday I would write a book. Here it is.

—Lori Paximadis